Public Policy and the Challenge of Chronic Noncommunicable Diseases

Public Policy and the Challenge of Chronic Noncommunicable Diseases

Olusoji Adeyi
Owen Smith
Sylvia Robles

THE WORLD BANK
Washington, D.C.

© 2007 The International Bank for Reconstruction and Development / The World Bank
1818 H Street, NW
Washington, DC 20433
Telephone: 202-473-1000
Internet: www.worldbank.org
E-mail: feedback@worldbank.org

This volume is a product of the staff of the International Bank for Reconstruction and Development / The World Bank. The findings, interpretations, and conclusions expressed in this volume do not necessarily reflect the views of the Executive Directors of The World Bank or the governments they represent.

The World Bank does not guarantee the accuracy of the data included in this work. The boundaries, colors, denominations, and other information shown on any map in this work do not imply any judgement on the part of The World Bank concerning the legal status of any territory or the endorsement or acceptance of such boundaries.

Rights and Permissions

DOI: 10.1596/978-0-8213-7044-5

Cover design: Quantum Think.

Library of Congress Cataloging-in-Publication Data
Adeyi, Olusoji.
  Public policy & the challenge of chronic noncommunicable diseases / Olusoji Adeyi, Owen Smith, Sylvia Robles.
    p. ; cm.
Includes bibliographical references and index.
ISBN-13: 978-0-8213-7044-5 (alk. paper)
ISBN-10: 0-8213-7044-8 (alk. paper)
eISBN-13: 978-0-8213-7045-2
  1. Chronic diseases—Government policy. 2. World health. I. Smith, Owen, 1973—II. Robles, Sylvia, 1958—III. World Bank. IV. Title. V. Title: Public policy and the challenge of chronic noncommunicable diseases.
  [DNLM: 1. World Bank. 2. Chronic Disease—economics. 3. Primary Prevention—economics. 4. Health Policy. WT 500 A233p 2007]
  RA644.5

[.A337007]
362.196'98—dc22

2007001291

Contents

Tables

Foreword

Within a few decades, chronic noncommunicable diseases (NCDs) will dominate health care needs in most low- and middle-income countries as a result of the epidemiological transition and aging. Increasingly, policy makers and program managers are being challenged to formulate effective strategies for preventing NCDs, to address cost pressures arising from new technologies, and to mitigate the effects of disabilities on those affected by NCDs.

But how can policy makers control health costs even as new technologies become available? How might program managers deliver services as efficiently and equitably as possible? What are some broad guidelines for determining the roles of public policy in relation to preventing and controlling NCDs? What are the implications of the NCD burden for public policy? This report addresses these questions with the aim of equipping policy makers with a framework to address these issues in their own countries. The report examines trends in NCDs and prospects for improving NCD control and outcomes through the lens of public policy. Finally, it presents an agenda for action by the World Bank.

Projections are not predictions, but the report suggests a plausible scenario that could arise from the doubling of historical rates of NCD mortality reduction worldwide during 2005–15. Because of the difficulty of offsetting aging trends, the total number of NCD deaths would still increase, but by about 3 million instead of about 6 million. This would be important progress, but also shows that even extraordinary success with NCD interventions would slow down, but not reverse, the overall upward trend in NCD morbidity and mortality because of population aging.

Thus the report presents two key messages. One is the need for public policies to prevent NCDs to the greatest extent possible, and in doing so to promote healthy aging and avoid premature deaths. The other is a concurrent need to recognize that the burden of NCDs will increase because of population aging, and therefore public policy has a role to play in dealing with the pressures that this will impose on health services. These messages are complementary and present both a challenge to action and a look at reality in terms of expectations under plausible scenarios.

The report is a call to action by countries and partner institutions. For the World Bank, it charts a course to help countries improve their health systems and outcomes, with an emphasis on those aspects that fit the Bank's comparative advantage in health financing, development economics, and multisectoral actions. This report will serve as a useful addition to the knowledge base to guide the Bank's work at the country, regional, and global levels.

Joy Phumaphi
Vice President
Human Development Network
The World Bank

Acknowledgments

This report was prepared with overall guidance from Jean-Louis Sarbib, former senior vice president, Human Development Network; Jacques Baudouy, former director, Health, Nutrition, and Population; and Kei Kawabata, sector manager, Health, Nutrition, and Population.

Olusoji Adeyi, coordinator, Public Health Programs, managed the work program and prepared the report together with Owen Smith, economist, Young Professionals Program; and Sylvia Robles, senior health specialist on secondment to the World Bank from the Pan American Health Organization and the World Health Organization.

In the appendixes, the case study on Georgia was commissioned by the World Bank and prepared by Martin McKee, professor of European public health, London School of Hygiene and Tropical Medicine; Dina Balabanova, lecturer, London School of Hygiene and Tropical Medicine; and Natalia Koroleva, research fellow, London School of Hygiene and Tropical Medicine. The case study on India was prepared by Jishnu Das, economist, Development Research Group. The case study on Indonesia was prepared by Jed Friedman, economist, Development Research Group.

The following individuals participated as discussants during the study: Ramanan Laxminarayan, economist, Resources for the Future and consultant to the World Bank; Miyuki Parris, knowledge management analyst, the World Bank; Jumana Qamruddin, consultant to the World Bank; and Marc Suhrcke, economist, European Office for Investment for Health and Development, World Health Organization. The report also contains contributions from Eleonore Bachinger, consultant to the World Bank; Melinda Elias, junior professional associate, the World Bank; Sue Gao, summer intern, 2005, University of Washington; and Davidson Gwatkin, consultant to the World Bank. Yvette Atkins, senior program assistant, provided administrative support.

The internal peer reviewers were Logan Brenzel, Joy de Beyer, and George Schieber. The external peer reviewers were Robert Beaglehole, World Health Organization, Geneva; Dean Jamison, Institute of Medicine, Board on Global Health of the Institute of Medicine and University of California, San Francisco (concept note review only); Carlos Augusto Monteiro, School of Public Health, São Paulo, Brazil (concept note review only); Philip Musgrove, *Health Affairs Journal*, United States; Thomas Novotny, University of California, San Francisco; Pekka Puska, National Public Health Institute, Finland; Adedoyin Soyibo, Department of Economics, University of Ibadan, Nigeria; and Derek Yach, the Rockefeller Foundation, United States.

The team acknowledges observations, criticisms, assistance with data searches, work on regional reports, comments, and suggestions from the following individuals: Anabela Abreu, Florence Baingana, Enis Baris, Peter Berman, Anthony Bliss, Eduard Bos, Mariam Claeson, Laura Coronel, Isabella Ana Danel, David Evans, Armin Fidler, Jean-Jacques Frere, Paul Gertler, Jeffrey Gilbert, Joana Godinho, Pablo Gottret, Keith Hansen, Eva Jarawan, Anne Johansen, Lucia Kossarova, Kees Kostermans, Preeti Kudesia, Rama Lakshminarayanan, Elizabeth Lule, Akiko Maeda, Patricio Marquez, Daniel Miller, Ok Pannenborg, Anne-Maryse Pierre-Louis, Tawhid Nawaz, David Peters, G. N. V. Ramana, Fadia Saadah, Andreas Seiter, Meera Shekar, Nicole Tapay, Cara Vileno, Erika Yanick, and Adam Wagstaff. They contributed during one or more of the following: prior work on noncommunicable diseases, an internal consultation (June 13, 2005), a concept note review meeting (September 19, 2005), a decision meeting (May 30, 2006), and subsequent stages of work. The authors alone are responsible for the content of this report.

The authors thank Mary Fisk, Paola Scalabrin, Alice Faintich, and their team for work that improved the quality of the manuscript.

Abbreviations

CEA	cost-effectiveness analysis
CVD	cardiovascular disease
DALY	disability-adjusted life year
g/dl	grams per deciliter
GDP	gross domestic product
HNP	health, nutrition, and population
HPV	human papillomavirus
NCD	noncommunicable disease
WHO	World Health Organization

Executive Summary

Since the early 1990s, the importance of chronic noncommunicable diseases (NCDs) to global health has gained increased recognition. This report contains an agenda for action in response to the growing economic, social, and health problems posed by NCDs. Its objective is to enable the World Bank and its clients to examine and, where appropriate, strategically shift their approaches to public policy as a tool to prevent and control NCDs.

Introduction

The report highlights two broad themes. First, public policies need to prevent NCDs to the greatest extent possible and, in doing so, promote healthy aging and avoid premature deaths. Second, at the same time, public policies need to recognize that the burden of NCDs will increase because of population aging, and therefore public policy has a role to play in dealing with the pressures that this will impose on health services. Thus the report has a dual purview: how to avoid the burden of NCDs as much as possible and how to prepare for the consequences of more NCDs associated with demographic change.

   NCD outcomes are typically measured in terms of mortality and morbidity, and the goal of policy is to improve both. Specifically, the main objective of addressing the NCD burden is both to postpone mortality and, for a given mortality profile, to postpone morbidity. The latter is referred to as healthy aging or the compression of morbidity.

NCDs are currently responsible for 56 percent of all deaths in low-and middle-income countries (Lopez and others 2006), and the World Health Organization projects that the burden of disease due to NCDs will increase rapidly in the years ahead. NCDs are by far the major cause of death in lower-middle, upper-middle, and high-income countries, and by 2015, they will also be the leading cause of death in low-income countries. The same is true for mortality among those of working age.

In part, the recent increase in NCDs reflects progress with respect to other international health priorities, such as infectious disease prevention and lower fertility. Deaths from NCDs are expected to rise over the next 25 years essentially because projected epidemiological trends, that is, declining death rates at any given age, will not be rapid enough to offset the effects of an older population structure.

By how much can current mortality trends in low- and middle-income countries be improved upon? The report presents the implications of doubling historical rates of NCD mortality reduction worldwide during 2005–15. Because of the difficulty of offsetting aging trends, the total number of NCD deaths would still increase, but by about 3 million instead of about 6 million. This would be important progress, but it also shows that even extraordinary success with NCD interventions would slow down, but not reverse, the overall upward trend in NCD mortality caused by population aging. This finding is the basis for the dual message to policy makers to both avoid and prepare for the future NCD burden.

An equally important measure of NCD outcomes is morbidity. NCDs account for 46 percent of the disease burden measured in disability-adjusted life years in low- and middle-income countries, and large increases in NCD-related disability-adjusted life years are projected for the future. (For an explanation of disability-adjusted life years and other terms used in this report, see the glossary at the end of the volume.) Prospects for achieving the objective of healthy aging and its implications for public policy will depend on two relationships: between life expectancy and health status and between health status and health care.

What is the relationship between longevity and health status? Different scenarios are possible. One is that longer lives reflect improved survival by sick people to such an extent that overall disability rates decline more slowly than mortality rates, resulting in an expansion of morbidity. Alternatively, the opposite could happen; namely, the successful control of risk factors and effective health care could mean that the health status of older cohorts improves more rapidly than longevity gains, leading to a compression of morbidity. Cross-country empirical evidence on these trends is inconclusive. Indeed, it suggests that patterns may evolve over time within the same country. In short, achieving healthy aging is possible, but by no means assured.

For public policy purposes, an equally important relationship is the one between health status and health care. If disability rates fall as morbidity is compressed (healthy aging), the need for medical care should, in theory, decline, but causation may also run in the opposite direction; that is, disability rates may decline precisely because of greater use of improved medical care. At present, many NCD interventions are not widely available in low- and middle-income countries, which spend far less on NCD care than the rich world. If healthy aging is achieved in this context, on balance it is more likely to be the result of more medical care rather than the cause of less medical care. This does not diminish the desirability of healthy aging, but rather underlines the need for policy preparedness for emerging challenges.

An improvement over past trends might be achieved through three broad channels. The first channel is achieving higher incomes through economic growth. The second channel is addressing NCD risk factors, such as tobacco use, obesity, high cholesterol, and high blood pressure, outside the clinical setting. The third channel is providing direct medical care for individuals in a clinical setting to screen for NCDs, to control risk factors clinically, or to provide treatment.

Indicators for certain NCD risk factors tend to grow worse as countries develop, and thus the challenge in many low- and middle-income countries will be to stay ahead of high-income countries in this regard. This highlights the importance of early action through population-based interventions to prevent an increase in exposure to the main NCD risk factors. At the same time, research into the successes of high-income countries in improving NCD outcomes has accorded a significant role to clinical interventions, and thus improved medical care in low- and middle-income countries will also be essential to reduce their NCD burden. Success in reducing the NCD burden will require action across many fronts.

Improving NCD Outcomes

Three distinct factors are likely to play an important role in determining the impact of public spending on NCD outcomes, and the overall chain that binds them together will be only as strong as its weakest link. These factors are (a) the net impact of the public sector, which depends on the extent of market failures; (b) the budget allocation decisions, which imply either more or less value for money, depending on the cost-effectiveness of interventions; and (c) the public sector's capacity to translate money into effective services on the ground. This trio of factors offers a useful framework for analyzing public policy related to NCDs.

NCDs impose a significant economic burden, not just on patients, but also on their households, communities, employers, and health care systems and on government budgets. Typical cost of illness studies often underestimate this burden.

The net impact of the public sector will be greatest when market failures are largest. If these are absent, government interventions may only serve to displace the private health sector without improving outcomes in either allocative (efficiency) or distributive (equity) terms. The economic rationale for interventions for primary prevention of NCDs rests primarily on taxes to address externalities related to tobacco, alcohol, and the environment, as well as the provision of information about various risk factors (tobacco, diet, exercise, and so on). The economic rationale with regard to treatment distinguishes between low-cost and high-cost NCD services, with equity concerns representing the main reason motivating a public role for the former, and efficiency issues related to insurance markets largely motivating the latter. For all services, governments can play a key regulatory and quality assurance role.

To what extent do NCDs affect the poor? The answer depends to some extent on the country and the indicator of the NCD burden that is considered. However, in all countries and by any metric, NCDs account for a large enough share of the disease burden of the poor to merit a serious policy response. While the potentially catastrophic costs of NCDs can be a cause of impoverishment, in most developing countries, infectious diseases remain a more important cause of the gap between rich and poor in relation to health outcomes, and NCDs are of relatively greater importance in middle-income countries than in low-income countries. This has implications for addressing inequality and for prospects for targeting the poor with NCD services.

What will an expanded NCD response mean for health budgets? A growing burden of NCDs will have potentially large budget implications, but the fiscal consequences of aging are likely to be much less important than the growth of age-specific expenditures (that is, spending at any given age), in particular because of the greater demand for both high-cost technologies and insurance coverage that NCDs may generate. Health technology assessments and the judicious expansion of benefits packages can help ensure that NCD costs remain sustainable over the long term. Nevertheless, a relatively larger burden of NCDs will mean that developing countries increasingly face the same challenges as high-income countries, where cost containment has become a constant theme in health sector reform.

Given a fixed budget, decisions about how funds are allocated (which interventions to "buy") will play a key role in determining the volume of services that can be delivered, and ultimately their impact on reducing morbidity and mortality. Budget allocation decisions are often based on political economy considerations (echoed in the common complaint that spending is biased toward expensive tertiary hospitals catering to an urban elite), and a more technical approach can potentially lead to better outcomes.

Cost-effectiveness analysis, despite its limitations and if all else is equal, can offer useful information for budget allocation decisions. Contrary to some beliefs, highly cost-effective interventions for the control of NCDs do exist. Among the most cost-effective are tobacco taxes and clinical interventions, including aspirin, beta-blockers, and statins, when appropriate, for primary and secondary prevention of cardiovascular disease. NCD services delivered at the tertiary level are generally not cost-effective. The report provides evidence on the cost-effectiveness of a wide range of interventions.

The third and final consideration affecting the extent to which a dollar of public spending on NCDs can lead to better outcomes is the public sector's capacity to translate its health budget into services of adequate quality. Service delivery in the health sector can be challenging, and often the ability of governments to achieve results on the ground has been weaker than hoped. The discretionary and transaction-intensive nature of many NCD services makes service delivery particularly challenging.

Service delivery issues will be central to achieving better NCD outcomes. Key characteristics of NCDs—including the need for long-term, sustained interaction with multiple levels of the health system; the importance of community engagement to improve access and patient self-care; and the intensive use of technology and drugs—can help inform policy decisions to improve service delivery. Many of the issues involved constitute what is often referred to as a health systems approach to improving outcomes.

How easily can the poor be reached through NCD clinical interventions? This will be an important challenge for policy makers to address. Achieving equity goals through NCD interventions will be a challenge in low-income countries for both conceptual and empirical reasons. While middle-income countries have a better track record in reaching the poor, in all settings, the challenge is to find innovative approaches to make interventions pro-poor.

The Agenda for the World Bank

The World Bank's approach to NCD control will be guided by the World Bank Strategy for Health, Nutrition, and Population Results (World Bank 2007). The preliminary recommendations underpinning the strategy underline the following: (a) renewing the emphasis on results (health, nutrition, and population outputs, outcomes, and system performance); (b) paying greater attention to the intersectoral linkages that contribute to better outcomes; (c) strengthening health system knowledge creation, policy, and technical advice in areas in which the Bank has a comparative advantage; (d) ensuring synergy between health system and single-priority disease control approaches in low-income countries; and (e) working with global partners selectively to complement the Bank's and global partners' comparative advantages at the country level. Each of these points is relevant to the prevention and control of NCDs.

The Bank will focus its policy discussions with countries on those areas in which it has a comparative advantage. It will emphasize the provision of technical assistance to countries to integrate NCD prevention and control into their health and development strategies and policies. Opportunities for engagement include the poverty reduction strategy papers of low-income countries, country assistance strategies, country economic memorandums, and informal consultations.

The Bank's focus with respect to analytical and advisory services will be on two mutually reinforcing approaches. The first approach emphasizes information generation and the sharing of knowledge that strengthens the basis for country decisions. Accordingly, the Bank will emphasize countries' capacity to develop results-based monitoring and evaluation systems for health policy and health systems. It will also actively promote the use of information for decision making with regard to public policies pertaining to NCDs and to health systems.

The second approach will involve coconvening with countries intersectoral forums to address tobacco control policies, alcohol abuse prevention, food and nutrition policies to prevent obesity and NCDs, and interventions to increase regular physical activity. The framework of the Multisectoral Bottlenecks Assessment for Health Outcomes (World Bank 2006b) will be adapted for this purpose as appropriate. This approach could build confidence among country officials, Bank staff, and partner agencies and could stimulate country demand for lending operations.

In addition, the World Bank can also play a key role in providing analytical and advisory services to help ensure the sustainability of health systems and financing through appropriate definition of benefits packages, supply- and demand-side reforms aimed at cost containment, health technology assessments, availability and affordability of pharmaceuticals, and other measures as needed.

Depending on country requests, the Bank will consider increasing its support for country-led efforts to prevent and control NCDs. This will be done within the context of both health sector and multisectoral programs that affect NCD outcomes. In this connection, the stepwise framework of interventions recommended by the World Health Organization provides a useful basis for action.[1] In terms of financing country-led programs, the Bank will support approaches that are consistent with the emerging consensus on the alignment and harmonization of aid with country operations and that are integrated into country strategies with predictable and sustainable financing.

The findings of this report can be reflected in World Bank lending operations through at least three approaches. The first is the inclusion of NCDs in multisectoral programs that include outcome and impact indicators of NCD prevention and control. The second consists of health system operations that help countries prepare for the pressures of a rising burden of NCDs associated with population aging. The third consists of NCD-specific projects, especially in countries where NCDs are most significant and governments request such an approach. The approaches will vary across countries.

What are the costs and benefits of treating NCDs? What are the market failures and how should they be addressed? Are public subsidies for treating NCDs through public health care systems more likely to benefit the rich or the poor? These are critical questions for efforts to tackle NCDs on a large scale, yet they are difficult to answer. Certain knowledge generation activities can be undertaken to help find some answers. Two particular priorities for the World Bank are (a) long-term monitoring of households and (b) monitoring and impact evaluation of large-scale programs for NCD prevention and control. In collaboration with partner agencies and financiers, the Bank will explore opportunities to commission such studies.

Overall, the appropriate policy response will entail avoiding the looming NCD burden to the extent possible, for example, through public health interventions and improved health care, while simultaneously preparing to deal with the health system and cost pressures arising from the increase in NCDs resulting from demographic forces. Policy makers should be made aware of both issues. An exclusive focus on prevention may lead to unrealistic expectations of a disease-free future, and thus a lack of readiness for emerging challenges. An overemphasis on aging, however, could result in a mistaken belief that policy cannot make a difference. The case for the World Bank and its clients to respond with action on both fronts is compelling.

Note

1. WHO 2005a.

CHAPTER 1

Introduction

The importance of chronic noncommunicable diseases (NCDs) for global health has gained increased recognition since the early 1990s and has been accompanied by calls for a stronger policy response (Feachem and others 1992; Ghaffar, Reddy, and Singhi 2004; Leeder and others 2004; WHO 2005a; World Bank 1993, 2004; Yach and others 2004; Yach and Stuckler 2006). Aging populations, rising incomes, and increased exposure to risk factors are contributing to patterns of illness, disability, and premature death due to NCDs that merit greater policy attention than they have received in the past. This report contains an agenda for action in response to the growing economic, social, and health problems posed by NCDs.

Objective

The objective of this report is to enable the World Bank and its clients to examine and, where appropriate, strategically shift their thinking about the role of public policy in the control of NCDs. The report addresses both NCD outcomes and systemic issues related to the control of NCDs. Its approach is consistent with the *World Bank Strategy for Health, Nutrition, and Population (HNP) Results*, which provides a framework for the Bank's analytical work and operations (World Bank 2007).

The report highlights two themes. First and foremost, public policies need to prevent NCDs to the greatest extent possible, and in doing so, promote healthy aging and avoid premature deaths. Second, at the same time, public policies need to recognize that the burden of NCDs will increase in line with demographic and epidemiological transitions, and thus they have a role to play in dealing with the pressures that this will impose on health services. Therefore, the objective will be addressed with a dual purview: how to avoid the burden of NCDs as much as possible and how to prepare for the consequences of the transitions.

The challenges policy makers face include how to address the links between NCDs and poverty, how to minimize the health and economic losses among the economically active population, and how to prepare for the pressures on health systems resulting from the growing numbers of people with NCDs associated with demographic change. Against this background, and based on the Bank's mission of poverty reduction, this report seeks to

- provide a framework for the World Bank's work with countries on NCDs, taking into account the emphasis on results in the *World Bank Strategy for HNP Results* (World Bank 2007).
- identify ways to integrate NCD prevention and control into the broader agenda of poverty reduction and economic development, with an emphasis on integration into each country's sectoral and multisectoral strategies and macroeconomic and budgetary context
- identify pathways through which to realize the control of NCDs in different operational settings
- define the short- to medium-term priorities for the World Bank's work on NCDs, bearing in mind its comparative advantages
- identify major gaps in knowledge and options for closing those gaps.

The report provides a framework, not a blueprint, for action in each country or region. Blueprints are more appropriately developed on the basis of analyses and consultations at the country and regional levels. Figure 1.1 shows the share of the disease burden attributable to NCDs in each World Bank region. Even though the report is global in outlook, the section at the end of this volume entitled "Selected Noncommunicable Disease Indicators" includes selected country-specific indicators.

Figure 1.1. Share of the Disease Burden Attributable to NCDs by World Bank Region, 2002

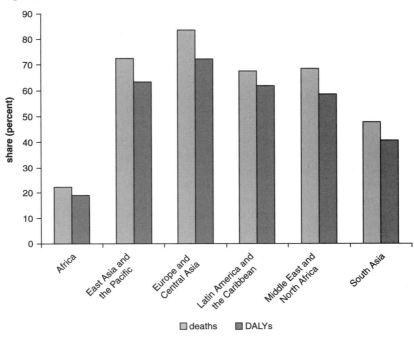

Source: WHO 2004, annex table 4.
Note: DALYs = disability-adjusted life years.

Scope and Audience

The term NCDs, as used in this report, refers to one of the three major categories of the disease burden as defined by the World Health Organization (WHO) (2004). The others are (a) communicable, maternal, perinatal, and nutritional conditions and (b) injuries. The WHO classification is an exhaustive classification system to which all causes of death and disability-adjusted life years (DALYs) in a population may be attributed. Note that neither NCDs nor chronic diseases are ideal terms, in that some NCDs have an infectious origin, for example, cervical cancer, whereas some infectious diseases are chronic in nature, for instance, HIV/ AIDS. Moreover, as a result of comorbidities, some people may suffer from both NCDs and communicable diseases at the same time. Readers should bear these caveats in mind as the term NCDs is used throughout this report.

The two most important NCDs in terms of mortality are cardiovascular disease (CVD) (heart disease and stroke) and malignant neoplasms (cancers). Others include respiratory and digestive diseases and diabetes. However, the report does not follow a disease-specific approach. Instead, it examines the policy and organizational responses that are appropriate in light of some of the key characteristics of NCDs. For example, many NCDs are preventable and some share the same risk factors. Many of the conditions are of relatively long gestation and include extended periods during which the patient may be asymptomatic. Once developed, they are chronic in nature, but some may have acute episodes. They tend to require multiple contacts with health systems over long periods of time, but exhibit fewer health externalities than communicable diseases. In short, these shared features of NCDs provide inputs for analysis. The report draws on examples that emphasize, but are not limited to, CVD, cancer, and diabetes. Beyond these examples, appendix 2 summarizes cost-effectiveness estimates for interventions against NCDs. A more comprehensive catalog of conditions and interventions is beyond the scope of this work, but is available elsewhere (see, for example, Jamison and others 2006b).

This report has three audiences. The first is internal, consisting of World Bank country directors, macroeconomists, sector directors, managers, and health specialists. They will find it useful in the course of policy dialogue within country teams and with country officials. The second is external, including country policy makers in ministries of finance, economic development, trade, agriculture, and health. This audience will find the report helpful in placing the prevention and control of NCDs within a broad public policy context. The third is also external, consisting of decision makers and technical specialists in partner agencies and foundations, for whom the report may be useful in discussions with the World Bank and with country officials.

The report is organized into three chapters, three technical appendixes, a glossary, and a data appendix. While the main section provides an integrated narrative, each appendix is prepared as a separate section for readers who wish to explore an aspect of the underlying subject matter in more detail.

Trends in NCD Outcomes and Possibilities for Improvement

NCD outcomes are typically measured in terms of mortality and morbidity, and the goal of policy should be to improve both. More specifically, the main objective in addressing the NCD burden is both to postpone mortality, and for a given mortality profile, to postpone morbidity. The latter is referred to as healthy aging or the compression of morbidity, whereby disability rates decline faster than mortality rates. This socially compelling ideal combines longer life spans with fewer years of disability at the end of life. The objective recognizes that while death is inevitable, it should ideally be neither premature nor preceded by years of poor health (Fries 1980). This section begins with a discussion of current mortality trends and prospects for improvement, and then shifts its focus to morbidity issues and the potential for achieving healthy aging.

What Are the Current Trends in NCD Mortality and What Explains Them?

NCDs are currently responsible for 56 percent of all deaths and 46 percent of the disease burden measured in DALYs in low- and middle-income countries (Lopez and others 2006). The burden of disease due to NCDs is projected to increase rapidly in the years ahead. Figure 1.2 shows projected deaths due to NCDs in low- and middle-income countries in 2005 and 2030. Currently, NCDs are by far the major cause of death in lower-middle, upper-middle, and high-income countries. By 2015, they

Figure 1.2. Projected Deaths due to NCDs by Country Income Level, 2005 and 2030

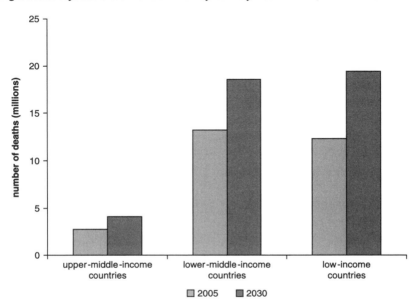

Source: Lopez and others 2006.

will also be the leading cause of death in low-income countries. The same is true for mortality among those of working age.

Several factors help explain the upward trend of NCDs in global burden of disease projections (Mathers and Loncar 2005; Murray and Lopez 1997). These include aging; the decline in communicable diseases and in conditions related to childbirth and nutrition; and changing lifestyles as they relate to smoking, drinking, diet, and exercise. As indicated by the first two reasons, in part the rise of NCDs reflects progress with respect to other international health priorities, such as infectious disease prevention and lower fertility. Observers often emphasize the role of demographics in NCD trends. The WHO Burden of Disease Project notes that "ageing of the population will result in significantly increasing total deaths due to [NCDs] over the next thirty years" (Mathers and Loncar 2005, p. 65). Marks and McQueen (2002, p. 119) note that "aging of the population in the first quarter of the twenty-first century will be the major force in the further tremendous increase in the burden of chronic diseases."

Figure 1.3 represents one way to depict the underlying factors behind the projected rise in NCDs. The forecasted increase in NCD deaths

Figure 1.3. Decomposing NCD Mortality Trends by Country Income Level, 2002–30

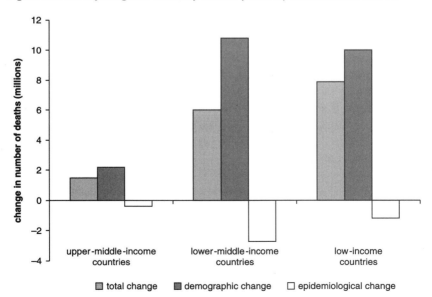

Source: Mathers and Loncar 2005.

between 2002 and 2030 is decomposed into two parts: demographic and epidemiological (Mathers and Loncar 2005). For each income group, the first bar indicates the total projected increase in NCD deaths between 2002 and 2030, the second bar shows the contribution of demographic change to this process, whereas the third bar reflects a measure of epidemiological change.[1] As the figure indicates, NCD deaths are expected to rise over the next 25 years essentially because projected epidemiological trends, that is, declining age-specific death rates, will not be rapid enough to offset the effects of an older population structure.

Two important policy messages emerge from this decomposition of trends. Specifically, the appropriate policy response to NCDs will entail avoiding the looming NCD burden of disease to the extent possible, for example, through public health interventions and improved medical care, and simultaneously preparing to deal with the health system and cost pressures associated with an aging population. Policy makers should be made aware of both issues. An exclusive focus on prevention may lead to unrealistic expectations of a disease-free future, and thus a lack of readiness for emerging challenges. An overemphasis on aging, however, could result in a mistaken belief that policy cannot make a difference. This report addresses issues underlying both messages.

By How Much Can These Mortality Trends Be Improved Upon?

While the demographic forecasts underlying the previous figures are fairly reliable, the epidemiological projections are subject to much greater uncertainty (Mathers and Loncar 2005), as they are based on historical trends that may or may not persist in the future. If a wide range of NCD interventions is successfully adopted in the years ahead, more rapid progress in reducing age-specific death rates may be achieved. This would provide a stronger counterweight to the upward pressure exerted on NCD morbidity and mortality by population aging.

What would be a feasible target for NCD mortality reduction? Historical experience, used as the basis for WHO's 2002–30 burden of disease projections, indicates that NCD mortality reduction in recent decades has typically been achieved at a rate slightly below 1 percent annually for the key age groups between 30 and 69 (Lopez and others 2006). A few countries, however, such as Australia, Canada, the United Kingdom, and the United States, have achieved CVD mortality reductions at a rate of close to 3 percent per year over the last three decades (WHO 2005a). A plausible scenario may therefore be constructed that improves significantly upon historical rates, but acknowledges that the experiences of high-income countries with excellent medical care are likely to be beyond the reach of most low- and middle-income countries in the immediate future. Specifically, figure 1.4 shows the implications of doubling historical rates of NCD mortality reduction worldwide during 2005–15.

Given the difficulties of offsetting aging trends noted earlier, the total number of NCD deaths would still increase, but by about 3 million, instead of about 6 million as in the baseline (which is based on historical trends). Among the population under 70, the doubling scenario would mean that the aging process could be almost fully offset to keep deaths constant between 2005 and 2015, instead of rising by 1.5 million as in the baseline scenario. In all, roughly 13 million deaths could be averted for all age groups cumulatively over 10 years. This would translate into a gain of nearly 30 million years of life in 2015, thereby holding years of life lost in that year to virtually the same level as in 2005. Additional details on these estimates are described in appendix 1. The methods are similar to those found in Strong and others (2005), and as in that study, the estimates here use deaths and years of life lost instead of DALYs as the unit of measurement. The focus on mortality is not intended to diminish the potential gains in morbidity reduction that can be achieved through improved NCD outcomes.

Figure 1.4. NCD Mortality Reduction Scenarios, 2005–15

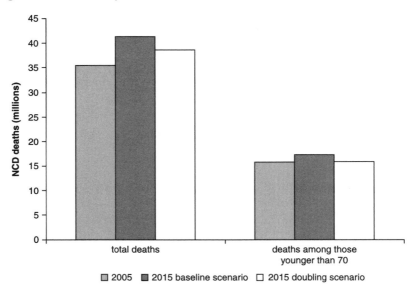

Source: Authors' calculations.

In sum, the results suggest that extraordinary success with NCD interventions will slow down, but not reverse, the overall upward trend in NCD mortality due to population aging. The same message can be conveyed based on the results of a cross-country study of CVD risk factors. The Asia Pacific Cohort Studies Collaboration (2006) found (a) that the risk of dying from coronary heart disease increases substantially with age; (b) that systolic blood pressure is the most important risk factor explaining the age-related excess risk of coronary heart disease; but (c) that in comparison with the effects of age itself, the effects of blood pressure and other cardiovascular risk factors are small. Thus, although highly desirable, the scope for risk factor reduction to fully offset the implications of an aging population is limited.

Can the Compression of Morbidity Be Achieved?

The focus thus far has been on mortality, but an equally important measure of NCD outcomes is the trend in morbidity. Policy makers are often justifiably more interested in the illnesses that precede death, because of the implications for treatment and costs. The two are closely related, of course, and WHO burden of disease projections also forecast large increases in NCD-related DALYs (Lopez and others 2006). In addition, because health expenditures are often concentrated at the end of life, a discussion of mortality trends offers a useful first approximation of potential health system pressures. However, as noted at the outset, our objective in addressing NCDs is not only to achieve reductions in both death and disability, but also to reduce morbidity for a given mortality profile, or healthy aging.

Achieving healthy aging and its implications for public policy depend crucially on two relationships: between life expectancy and health status and between health status and health care. First, what is the relationship between longevity and health status? Different scenarios are possible. One is that longer lives reflect the improved survival of sick people to such an extent that overall disability rates decline more slowly than mortality rates, resulting in an expansion of morbidity. Alternatively, the opposite could happen: improved behaviors and health care could mean that the health status of older cohorts improves more rapidly than longevity gains, leading to a compression of morbidity. This is healthy aging.

Cross-country empirical evidence on these trends is inconclusive. Some evidence suggests that compression of morbidity may be occurring over time in some low-mortality countries as death rates at older ages continue to decline (Crimmins, Saito, and Reynolds 1997; Manton, Stallard, and

Corder 1995). However, country context appears to matter a good deal, for example, Taiwan (China) appears to match the first scenario (overall disability rates are declining more slowly than mortality rates), whereas France, Switzerland, and the United States correspond more closely with the second (the health status of older cohorts is improving more rapidly than longevity gains). In the United Kingdom, there appears to be an equilibrium between falling mortality and increasing disability (Michel and Robine 2004). Across industrial countries, the evolution of disability rates varies considerably (Cutler and Sheiner 1998).

Indeed, investigators have suggested that patterns may evolve over time within the same country. Under this scenario the aging of the population follows a cyclical movement where, first, sicker people survive into old age and disability rises; then the number of years lived with disability decreases as new cohorts of healthier people enter old age; but, finally, the number of years lived with disability rises again when the average age at death rises so much that many people spend their last years at an advanced age burdened by multiple chronic illnesses and frailty (Michel and Robine 2004). If this is the case, then today's low- and middle-income countries face a future with periods of both expanding and compressing morbidity. Trends may also vary across income groups within the same country. In short, achieving healthy aging is possible, but by no means assured.

For public policy purposes, an equally important relationship is the one between health status and health care. If disability rates fall as morbidity is compressed (healthy aging), the need for medical care should, in theory, decline, but causation may also run in the opposite direction: disability rates may decline precisely because of greater use of improved medical care systems. Various studies in high-income countries suggest that the latter is indeed important. The evidence indicates that disability rates have declined to a significant extent because of medical interventions as well as more healthful behaviors (Cutler 2001; Cutler, Landrum, and Stewart 2006; Vita and others 1998). This relationship may help explain why studies on the link between health status and subsequent health care costs have yielded mixed results with regard to whether expenditures on the relatively healthy are lower, higher, or similar to spending on those who are relatively sick (Daviglus and others 1998, 2005; Lubitz and others 2003; Russell 1998). Over the long term, historical experience and projections for the future suggest that the upward pressure on costs resulting from the introduction of previously unavailable technologies far outweighs the downward effect of improvements in health status (Mortensen 2005).

The relatonship between health status and medical care over long time horizons is especially relevant in low- and middle-income countries, where many existing NCD interventions are underprovided. Thus, a large number of people do not receive the drugs or procedures from which they could greatly benefit. As a result, improving health status is unlikely to be cost saving relative to a status quo in which only a few dollars per person are spent annually on NCD care. In this setting, the immediately relevant question is not about potential cost savings within a high-income context, but rather how to improve outcomes by introducing the many services that are currently not available and how to accomplish this transition on a more affordable cost trajectory. In this sense, the compression of morbidity should not automatically be associated with a decreased use of medical interventions and the alleviation of health system pressures.

What can we conclude? First, note that a common theme in the literature is that much remains unknown about the two relationships, their underlying causes, and how they may evolve in the future. Second, the compression of morbidity is an important objective, and even though cross-country evidence is mixed, the experience of certain countries at certain points in time suggests that it is achievable. Lastly, improving health status in low- and middle-income countries is, on balance, more likely to be the result of more medical care rather than the cause of less medical care, and thus the imperative for public policy to both avoid and prepare for NCDs is a key message.

How Can Current Outcome Trends Be Improved?

An improvement over past trends might be achieved through three broad channels. The first channel is achieving higher incomes through economic growth.[2] This matters, because higher incomes can help households escape the vicious circle of poor health and poverty by reducing their vulnerabilities to falling ill and expanding their choices when they do become ill. The second channel is addressing NCD risk factors, for example, tobacco use, obesity, high cholesterol, and high blood pressure, outside the clinical setting. This may take the form of legislation, such as cigarette taxes or mandatory nutrition labeling, or it may entail the provision of information and behavior change interventions to address such factors as smoking, drinking, diet, and exercise in a range of settings, for instance, at the population, community, workplace, or school levels. The third channel is providing direct medical care for individuals in a clinical setting to screen for NCDs, control risk factors clinically, or provide treatment.

The broad stylized facts related to these three channels are instructive. As countries develop, incomes rise and medical care improves. At the same time, risk factors tend to worsen on average. Overall, NCD outcomes as measured by age-specific mortality and morbidity improve as development unfolds. Thus, on aggregate, the positive impact of higher incomes and better medical care is stronger than the negative influence of certain deteriorating risk factors over long time horizons. Better outcomes will require reinforcing the former while minimizing the latter. Despite variation around these trends and some exceptions, the patterns generally hold true.

Thus, with respect to addressing NCD risk factors in many low- and middle-income countries, the challenge will generally be to stay ahead of (or at least keep level with), as opposed to catch up with, similar indicators in high-income countries. Thailand, for example, scores better than France in terms of blood pressure, smoking, cholesterol, and obesity, and yet it has a higher NCD mortality rate. Appendix 1 shows the broadly consistent international evidence, which reflects both time lags and different lifestyles, for example, as related to smoking, urbanization, and dietary habits. This evidence justifies strong efforts to prevent an increase in exposure to the main risk factors for NCDs.

With respect to medical care, the challenge will be to catch up with high-income countries. Many NCD clinical interventions are not yet widely available in low- and middle-income settings. Because risk factors are often better in these countries whereas outcomes are worse, the importance of improved medical care (and economic growth) for reducing the outcome gap is clear. Moreover, research into high-income countries' success in improving CVD outcomes in recent decades has accorded a significant role to clinical interventions (Critchley and Capewell 2002; Cutler 2001; Cutler, Landrum, and Stewart 2006; Laatikainen and others 2005; Tunstall-Pedoe and others 2000). Finland and Poland are noteworthy examples of countries that have rapidly improved NCD outcomes based on a large role for nonclinical interventions; however, their initial conditions were characterized by high levels of risk factors. This, along with variations in both capacity and social contexts (including literacy rates), suggests a need for caution against generalizing the Finnish and Polish experiences to other countries.

In sum, success in reducing the NCD burden will require action across many fronts. A holistic approach that addresses the full continuum of population-based and clinical services is ideal, although given limited resource envelopes, prioritization is inevitable. A key message is that economic growth, nonclinical interventions to control risk factors, and direct medical care will all play important roles in improving future NCD outcomes and achieving the objective of healthy aging. None of the three in isolation is likely to be adequate to significantly improve upon current trends. The next chapter explores the challenge of improving outcomes in greater detail.

Key Messages

The key messages of this chapter are as follows:

- NCDs represent a large and growing share of the disease burden, and therefore cause for concern, in countries around the world. Their relevance to the World Bank arises from the known and potential linkages with poverty; the health and economic losses they impose on populations, including those of working age; and the demands they will place on resources because of the growing NCD burden associated with aging populations.
- The objective of addressing NCDs is both to reduce premature mortality and, for a given mortality profile, to reduce morbidity. The latter is referred to as the compression of morbidity or healthy aging.
- NCD deaths are expected to rise over the next 25 years essentially because projected epidemiological trends, namely, declining age-specific death rates, will not be rapid enough to offset the effects of an older population structure. Thus, NCDs pose a dual challenge for public policy: to avoid the burden of disease imposed by NCDs to the greatest extent possible, but also to prepare for the aging-related pressures that NCDs will impose on health systems.
- The compression of morbidity is an important objective, and even though cross-country evidence is mixed, the experiences of certain countries at certain points in time suggest that it is achievable. On balance, however, healthy aging is more likely to be the result of more medical care (given the large underprovision of many NCD interventions in low- and middle-income countries at present) rather than the cause of less medical care due to better health. This does not diminish its desirability, but rather underlines the need for policy preparedness.
- Economic growth, nonclinical interventions to control risk factors, and direct medical care will all play important roles in improving future NCD outcomes in low- and middle-income countries. None of the three in isolation is likely to be adequate to bring these countries' mortality rates down to the levels currently prevailing in high-income countries.

Notes

1. More specifically, the contribution of demographic change is approximated by calculating the difference between 2002 mortality and mortality in the hypothetical scenario in which 2002 age-specific death rates are applied to the projected 2030 population (that is, the demographics change, but the epidemiological structure does not). Similarly, the contribution of epidemiological change is approximated by calculating the difference between 2002 mortality and mortality in the hypothetical scenario in which projected 2030 age-specific death rates are applied to the 2002 population (that is, the epidemiological structure changes, but the demographic profile does not). See Mathers and Loncar (2005) for more details.

2. How to achieve higher growth is outside the scope of this report, so the focus here will be on the other two channels. It is also clear that income is not an all-determining factor in health outcomes, given the observed cross-country differences in those outcomes when controlling for gross domestic product per capita or health spending (see World Bank 2004).

CHAPTER 2

Improving NCD Outcomes: A Public Policy Perspective

Identifying the dual challenges that policy makers confront—to avoid noncommunicable diseases (NCDs) to the greatest extent possible while preparing for a likely higher burden in the future because of demographic forces—is only a first step toward laying out an agenda for addressing NCDs. The purpose of this chapter is to provide a more detailed framework for analyzing potential pathways toward improving NCD outcomes. Although the focus is on public policy, this is not intended to deny the important role of the private health sector, which will be addressed where appropriate. It is merely a recognition that the perspective of government, including its regulatory role, is foremost in the World Bank's dialogue with its clients. The approach set forth in this chapter is intended be useful in a wide variety of settings, as the NCD challenges World Bank clients face are highly varied and cannot all be addressed individually in this report.

The approach focuses on three broad factors to consider when formulating public policies aimed at improving NCD outcomes. Each of these will help determine the extent to which a dollar spent on NCDs is successful in achieving the objective of lowering morbidity and

Figure 2.1. How Strong Is the Chain That Links Public Spending on NCDs to Better Outcomes?

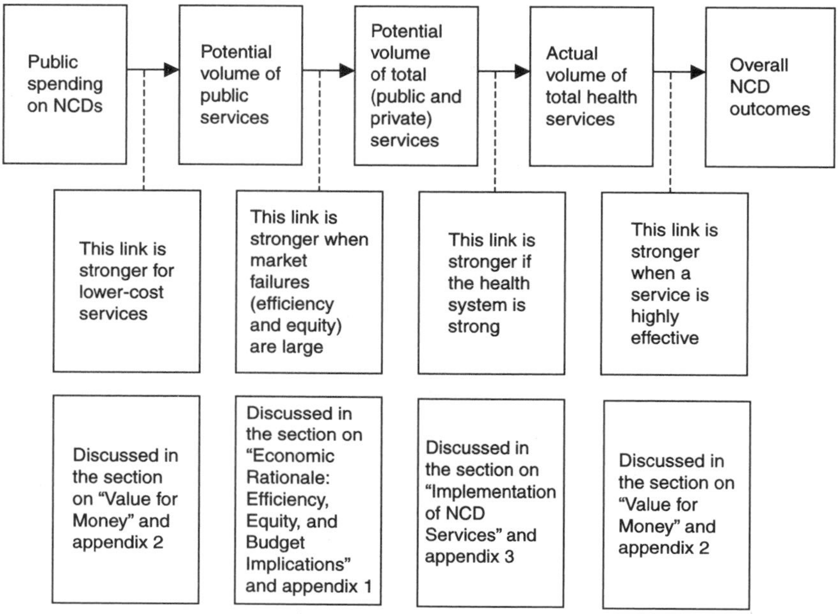

Public spending on NCDs	→	Potential volume of public services	→	Potential volume of total (public and private) services	→	Actual volume of total health services	→	Overall NCD outcomes
		This link is stronger for lower-cost services		This link is stronger when market failures (efficiency and equity) are large		This link is stronger if the health system is strong		This link is stronger when a service is highly effective
		Discussed in the section on "Value for Money" and appendix 2		Discussed in the section on "Economic Rationale: Efficiency, Equity, and Budget Implications" and appendix 1		Discussed in the section on "Implementation of NCD Services" and appendix 3		Discussed in the section on "Value for Money" and appendix 2

Source: Authors.

mortality. All three factors matter, as the chain from public spending to better health outcomes will only be as strong as its weakest link (this analogy and the overall framework are drawn from Filmer, Hammer, and Pritchett 2000 and Filmer and Pritchett 1999). The factors are as follows (figure 2.1):

- The net impact of public spending on health outcomes will be greater if it addresses needs that the private sector satisfies poorly or not at all. This embraces the standard approach of establishing the economic rationale for public intervention, including the goal of achieving more equitable outcomes for the poor. The private health sector represents an important player in nearly every country. If public spending merely displaces the private sector with the same allocative (efficiency) and distributive (equity) results, including the risk of impoverishment, then its net impact will be low.
- Not all interventions imply the same value for money in terms of health improvements per unit of expenditure. For example, a government

health budget of a given size translates into fewer health gains for the population if it is spent exclusively on bypass surgery instead of aspirin to reduce the probability of a heart attack. Thus, all else being equal, robust evidence on cost-effectiveness can be a useful input into budget allocation decisions.

- The impact of public spending will also be greater when the public sector's capacity to translate money into effective services on the ground is stronger. Among other things, this will tend to reflect the institutional capabilities, incentives, and accountability of the various actors within the public health system. If doctors do not show up for work, drugs are not available in clinics, and equipment is not maintained, then even the best budget plans will not result in better NCD outcomes.

The importance of all three issues bears repeating: the failure of just one factor means that the impact of public spending on NCD outcomes will be diminished. For example, a health service aimed at the poor may have a strong economic rationale, but if the health system cannot ensure its delivery on the ground, public funding will be to no avail. Or a low-cost curative intervention may be cost-effective, but if the private sector already provides it to the same clientele, public provision will not necessarily change the total volume of health services delivered (and thus outcomes achieved) in the country. Lastly, a public sector hospital may provide a surgical procedure of excellent quality, but better value for money in terms of health gain may be available through other interventions. The potential list of similar scenarios is long.

This framework also implies that an exclusive focus on inputs, for example, more money for NCDs, is not appropriate, as improved outcomes may be achievable within an existing budget by strengthening each of the three links. Indeed, doing so may be the best way to make credible claims for a larger budget in the future. In general, while governments can, and often do, serve as a force for good in addressing NCDs, their effect could be greatly enhanced if they gave these three issues careful consideration. Note also that even though the framework has a supply-side focus, the chapter will also address issues affecting the demand side, such as information, financing, and quality.

Economic Burden of NCDs

NCDs impose a significant economic burden, not just on patients, but on households, communities, employers, health care systems, and government budgets. The direct morbidity and mortality burden of NCDs on patients and their families is reflected in diminished productive activity and lower returns to investment in human capital. When aggregated across economies, these household costs have an important impact on the size and productivity of the labor force and on national incomes in general. Of course, good health is an important objective in its own right and need not be viewed only as a contributor to better economic outcomes. Nevertheless, the economic burden resulting from NCDs is an important subject to address in policy dialogue.

Empirical work frequently draws on microeconomic approaches to measure the economic burden of a disease condition at the household level. The most common method for computing the cost of illness is the human capital method, which involves an accounting of both the direct costs (private and public spending on disease prevention and treatment) and the indirect costs (productivity losses associated with the illness and forgone income of both the patient and the caregiver). Many studies have aggregated costs assessed at the individual or household level into national cost estimates.

Even though evidence from high-income countries is much more abundant than from low- and middle-income countries, a growing body of literature from the latter reveals a significant economic burden attributable to NCDs. In general, the direct costs of illness may be lower in poorer countries and among poorer populations, as they have less access to advanced, and therefore costly, health care services and to social support provided by the government. However, lower direct costs of illness because of a lack of medical options tend to be associated with a significant increase in indirect costs. Studies have found significant effects of NCDs on a wide range of labor market outcomes, including wages, earnings, workforce participation, hours worked, retirement, and job turnover. People with chronic diseases and risk factors are more likely to face barriers to employment arising from productivity limitations, costs of disability, and, in some cases, stigma.

Appendix 1 provides more details on these findings and the costs associated with specific diseases and countries. The following illustrative examples offer an indication of the economic burden:

- A few studies have estimated the large costs of risk factors for some NCDs, including tobacco and alcohol use, obesity, and hypertension. In 1995, the costs of tobacco-related disease accounted for 1.5 percent of gross domestic product (GDP) in China, whereas obesity-related costs were equivalent to 1.1 percent of GDP in China and 2.1 percent in India (Hu and Mao 2002; Popkin 2002). In 1996, the economic burden associated with hypertension was roughly US$20 per capita in Mexico (Villarreal-Rios and others 2000).

- The total costs of cardiovascular disease (CVD) are between 1 and 3 percent of GDP in most developed countries. The annual per capita burden of CVD is about US$4 to US$8 in China and India, US$15 to US$30 in Brazil and South Africa, and about US$70 to US$90 in Russia (Leeder and others 2004).
- The direct costs of diabetes range from 2.5 to 15.0 percent of annual health care budgets, depending on local prevalence and the sophistication of the treatments available (IDF 2003).[1] Among low- and middle-income countries, total diabetes-related costs were highest in Latin America and the Caribbean, where the economic burden of diabetes has been estimated at US$65 billion annually, or typically between 2 and 4 percent of GDP in most countries.

NCDs are not restricted to older populations who have already left the labor force. As indicated by table 2.1, a significant share of the burden of NCDs occurs in populations of working age. Although NCDs generally afflict people at older ages than communicable diseases, because a large share of communicable diseases is concentrated among children younger than five, NCDs are a more important cause of illness and death among working-age populations. Moreover, about three-quarters of the NCD disability burden in low- and middle-income countries occurs among those

Table 2.1. Share of Disease Burdens Falling on Those between the Ages of 15 and 69 in Low- and Middle-Income Countries, 2005

Disease category	Total deaths, all ages (millions)	Percentage of deaths accounted for by those aged 15–69	Percentage of DALYs accounted for by those aged 15–69
All causes	32.8	46	54
All NCDs	23.6	43	74
CVD	10.3	38	72
Cancers	5.4	62	81
All communicable diseases	5.5	35	32
Injuries	3.6	76	69

Source: Lopez and others 2006.
Note: CVD = cardiovascular disease; DALYs = disability-adjusted life years.

between the ages of 15 and 69. Achieving a goal of lower morbidity and mortality would help lower these shares, reduce indirect costs and the economic burden more generally, and contribute to healthy aging.

Furthermore, estimates of the costs of NCDs found in cost of illness studies tend to underestimate the true burden of NCDs, and are therefore conservative in their assessment of economic impact (Suhrcke and others 2006). Several issues can be identified in this connection. First, households do not react passively to chronic disease. To cope with the costs of a family member with a chronic illness, households in developing countries often mobilize and reallocate their productive resources in ways that may have long-term repercussions and risk perpetuating socioeconomic inequalities. The most frequently invoked coping strategy involves tapping savings and liquidating assets to cover the costs of care and lost productivity, which can in turn affect investment decisions. Another coping response is to engage other household members, often women and children, in caring for sick family members. Children are more likely to be removed from school during health crises to care for a sick older relative, compensate for production losses, or reallocate school expenditures to help cover medical costs. Although these effects of poor health are not unique to NCDs, the longer duration of chronic diseases makes the negative impacts larger than in the case of acute illnesses.

These various costs of NCDs can cause a household to fall below the poverty line. While little direct evidence attributes impoverishment to NCDs specifically (for some exceptions, see Bonu and others 2005; Suhrcke and others 2006), the general findings on catastrophic health expenditures, the relatively high costs and long durations of NCDs, and the evidence that the poor are less able to insure consumption against "severe" illnesses all suggest that the costs of NCDs can be impoverishing (see Gertler and Gruber 2002; Wagstaff 2005; Xu and others 2003). This would be a valuable direction for future research.

A second reason why cost of illness studies may underestimate the economic burden is that the behaviors associated with risk factors, as well as with chronic diseases themselves, play a role in poverty, as they can displace expenditures on food purchases and capital investments. For example, tobacco and alcohol use is costly (Esson and Leeder 2004), and the poor tend to spend a disproportionate share of their incomes on these products, potentially substituting for investment in human capital, such as health and education. Appendix 1 identifies several studies that have analyzed the impact of tobacco spending on other household expenditure decisions. Risk factors also have distal impacts, as the behavioral decisions of adults are reflected in the health outcomes of their children. Secondhand smoke is the most obvious example.

Finally, many of the cost of illness estimates do not adequately capture the effects of NCD on employers and their broader impact on investment. Employers may absorb a considerable portion of the economic burden of chronic disease through absenteeism, decreased on-the-job productivity, increased employee turnover, and health care costs (Berry, Mirabito, and Berwick 2004; Bleil, Kalamas, and Mathoda 2004).

The economic burden attributable to NCDs can also be approached in terms of their macroeconomic impact. Health—measured as life expectancy or adult mortality—is a robust and strong predictor of economic growth (Barro 1991, 1996; Barro and Lee 1994; Barro and Sala-i-Martin 1995; Sachs and Warner 1995, 1997). As mortality from chronic disease accounts for a significant portion of reduced life expectancy and adult mortality, it would be expected to have a negative impact on economic growth. Quantifying this impact is a difficult task, however. Although one recent study (Urban and Suhrcke 2005) looked at the impact of CVD mortality on growth, such estimates should be viewed as indicative only, as cross-country regressions for identifying the determinants of growth have numerous drawbacks (Pritchett 2006). In general, while there is good reason to believe that NCD mortality has a negative impact on growth, substantiating this relationship empirically is extremely difficult.

In sum, a wide range of pathways exists through which NCDs may impose an economic burden on individuals and societies. However, evidence of a significant economic burden does not alone imply an economic rationale for government intervention to address NCDs.

Economic Rationale: Efficiency, Equity, and Budget Implications

The introduction to this chapter identified the issue of an economic rationale for public intervention as one of three key considerations for improving the impact of spending on NCD outcomes. It noted that the net impact of the public sector will be greatest when market failures are largest. If these are absent, government interventions may only serve to displace the private health sector without improving outcomes in either allocative (efficiency) or distributive (equity) terms, including the risk of impoverishment. This section focuses on the economic rationale for a public role to address NCDs.

To improve efficiency and equity in health care, and following the framework set out in Musgrove (1996), we can identify three broad reasons for governments to intervene in health care instead of leaving it to the private sector. One is to achieve the optimal level of production and consumption of public goods and those goods that are partly public in character because of the presence of externalities. This can include the provision of health care services, of information that helps people improve their own health, or of other interventions. A second reason is to make insurance markets work more efficiently and equitably for services that are private goods, but for which risk sharing is required because of high costs or uncertainty about need (or both). The third reason is to help those who are too poor either to buy insurance or to buy services that the nonpoor can afford out-of-pocket (Musgrove 1996). These three reasons correspond, respectively, to public goods, high-cost private goods, and low-cost private goods. All three are relevant to the rationale for a public role in relation to NCDs.

A key difference between communicable and noncommunicable diseases is that because the former can be transmitted, one person's illness increases the probability that others will also be infected. To the extent that individuals do not factor the prospect of infecting others into their own behavior, the optimal level of health care consumption will not be achieved, and thus government intervention makes sense. While some exceptions exist, such as secondhand smoke, in general the same logic does not apply to NCDs; that is, the health impact of NCDs is largely internalized. Nevertheless, goods of a public nature do exist for NCDs as well, albeit less commonly than for communicable diseases. Public goods and externalities will be the focus of the discussion on prevention, whereas low- and high-cost private goods will be addressed under the section on treatment.

Prevention

The economic rationale for a public role in NCD prevention rests primarily on information and some externality issues arising from the public character of many health care goods. Information has many features of a public good that private markets will tend to undersupply, and the resulting lack of knowledge on the part of consumers can result in suboptimal outcomes. In the case of NCDs, incomplete information will typically take the form of a lack of awareness about the health risks associated with tobacco and alcohol use, dietary choices, and physical inactivity. For tobacco and alcohol, there is an added dimension of ignorance about the addictive nature of these commodities.

Whether consumers in a given country have been sufficiently informed about the health consequences of certain choices is an empirical question, and at least some will continue making unhealthy choices despite awareness of the attendant health risks. In general, a lack of information is more likely to prevail in cases where the health effects of a behavior are insufficiently understood, for example, because of the long time lag between behavior and outcome; in developing countries, for instance, strong evidence points to this effect in relation to smoking in China (Chinese Academy of Preventive Medicine 1997); among children and teenagers; and where industry marketing efforts have distorted information (Suhrcke and others 2006).

Externalities with regard to NCD risk factors arise for secondhand smoke and drunk driving. Evidence about the harmful effects of second-hand smoke is growing (Department of Health and Human Services 2006; WHO 2004), although the effects are smaller than the direct health impacts for smokers. While most health risks are internal, the financial repercussions (or monetary externalities) can be much larger. Some house-hold impacts were noted earlier. In industrial countries, the rest of society bears part of the additional medical bill for smokers, although a full accounting would also include factors working in the opposite direction, for example, old-age security, because smokers, on average, tend to die at a younger age than nonsmokers (Manning and others 1989; Viscusi 1995). In developing countries, by contrast, publicly funded treatment options are fewer and old-age security is less comprehensive. To be clear, these narrow financial calculations do not imply that the premature death of smokers is socially desirable.

Similarly, there is an economic rationale for alcohol taxes on the basis of health and monetary externalities. These are especially associated with drunk drivers who may cause injury and death on the roads and impose burdens on the government or on group medical services as a result of alcohol-induced illness. The greater risks of personal violence and public disorder associated with alcohol are also relevant here (Kenkel and Manning 1996; Manning and others 1989; Pogue and Sgontz 1989; Saffer and Chaloupka 1994).

A final potential externality relates to environmental health. Increased air pollution as countries develop is an important factor in the rise of asthma and chronic obstructive pulmonary disease. Pollution of water, land, and the food chain can also result in NCDs, including cancer; the case of arsenic poisoning in Bangladesh is an important example.[2] The multisec-toral nature of this problem lends itself to World Bank engagement.

Specific interventions to address both information and externality issues may take a variety of different forms, with the intent of the main government instruments being to inform, mandate, or regulate.[3] Examples include populationwide or targeted public information campaigns; product labeling; or restrictions on the marketing of unhealthy commodities, such as bans on tobacco and alcohol advertising. In some cases, direct government action works better than the provision of information. For example, measures could include lowering the fat composition of manufactured foods through regulation; limiting sodium intake by mandating lowered salt content in manufactured foods; or encouraging physical activity by designing appropriate fuel tax, transportation, and urban policies. In general, behavior change can be difficult to achieve. Appendix 2 addresses the evidence on the effectiveness of interventions.

Perhaps the most effective way to address market failures and discourage risky behavior is through taxation, especially for tobacco and alcohol. Taxation is possibly the most effective intervention for discouraging smoking initiation and encouraging smokers to quit. Another reason for tobacco and alcohol taxation is to raise revenues to pay for public spending, as both theoretical and empirical work suggest that optimal commodity taxes exceed levels warranted on externality grounds alone for commodities that are relative leisure complements (Nugent and Knaul 2006; Parry, Laxminarayan, and West 2006a, 2006b; Sandmo 1975).

Finally, with respect to tobacco (and on a more institutional level), as of May 2007, 147 countries are parties to an international health treaty, the Framework Convention for Tobacco Control (appendix 2). However, translation of the treaty into action at the country level is fraught with difficulties because of the political economy of implementing those provisions that run contrary to the interests of the tobacco industry, including farmers. This area should receive more attention from countries and the World Bank in order to implement the convention at the country level.

Treatment

If preventive interventions are successful, the need for treatment to address an NCD could be delayed until old age, after a healthy and productive life has been lived. At this stage of life the productivity-related costs of illness are also likely to be minimized. However, as the earlier discussion of demographic trends highlighted, rising demand for NCD treatment is highly probable in most countries. This has implications for deciding what combination of interventions may best achieve healthy aging.

The economic rationale for a public role in NCD treatment rests mainly on the second and third arguments in favor of government intervention presented earlier, namely, to address the insurance problem for high-cost private goods that require risk sharing and to subsidize access by the poor to low-cost private goods that they cannot readily afford out of pocket. Although the distinction is not absolute, the former stems largely from an efficiency argument, while the latter reflects equity concerns.

The relative expense of health care services is thus an important distinguishing factor between the two justifications. Of course, whether a particular service is expensive depends on the income of the patient in question. Empirical work can help determine households' ability to finance care out of pocket (Das and Hammer 2006). In general terms, the long list of possible medical interventions available to address NCDs covers the entire range from the cheap, for instance, aspirin to reduce the risk of heart attack or a so-called polypill to address multiple risk factors, to the expensive, such as coronary bypass surgery, with many others in between, for example, mammograms to detect breast cancer. In addition, the relative expense of different interventions is not immune to government action, for example, NCD drug prices vary widely around the world, and in their role as purchasers and market regulators, governments can help achieve lower drug prices (Gelders and others 2006).

The challenge of ensuring financial access to high-cost health services is particularly acute for NCDs, because in general, and despite important exceptions, interventions for NCD clinical care tend to be more expensive per unit of health gained than either nonclinical NCD or communicable disease interventions (Laxminarayan, Chow, and Shahid-Salles 2006). The resulting prospect of high and unpredictable out-of-pocket expenditures for NCD-related medical care underpins the case for providing financial protection against the cost of illness. If private insurance markets do not work, the result will be a welfare loss. Of course, these markets do tend to fail for reasons that are many and complex, arising largely from the familiar problems of moral hazard and adverse selection. Indeed, adverse selection is likely to be greater in the case of NCDs because of their chronic nature: many of those who will be sick tomorrow are already sick today, heightening the danger of risk selection leading to market inefficiencies. However, risk selection is only a problem for private insurers, who can refuse customers or charge them more.

Thus, a strong rationale exists for government intervention to address the failure of private insurance markets to help finance high-cost NCD care, but additional challenges may arise depending on the form that this intervention takes. A government's capabilities and resources are often as important as the economic rationale in determining policy prescriptions.

Correcting private insurance markets through regulation or, to a lesser extent, providing public insurance both require administrative capacities that are frequently inadequate in many low-income and some middle-income countries. In addition, relatively small formal sectors and limited tax handles often constrain revenue mobilization. This poses challenges to both social insurance mechanisms financed by payroll taxes and public provision of benefits packages financed by general tax revenues (noncontributory). Again, these issues are particularly acute in low-income countries and they are not specific to NCDs. Fiscal sustainability also becomes a key concern if, as is common, the response to insurance market failure is greater public financing of health care. For a more extensive treatment of health financing issues see World Bank (2006a).

In the case of low-cost NCD treatment services that the nonpoor are able to finance out of pocket, the justification for a public role reflects equity concerns to improve access for the poor. These interventions may be subsidized or, in countries where governments are deeply involved in the provision of health care, they may be included directly in packages of essential services. In either case, the health financing challenges will also apply.

NCDs and the Poor
Poverty reduction is the central mission of the World Bank, and looking at NCDs through that lens is essential. Poverty and ill health can be reinforcing, and this is likely to be at least as true for NCDs as for other health problems. Indeed, the long duration of chronic NCDs can make this a particularly vicious circle. The earlier discussion of economic burden identified potential pathways linking NCDs and poverty. The purpose of this section is to briefly address a commonly asked question, namely, how much do NCDs matter to the poor?

The extent to which NCDs matter to the poor has been the subject of some debate (Gwatkin, Guillot, and Heuveline 1999; WHO 2005a). Some advocates of increasing the focus on NCDs disagree with what they refer to as the myth that NCDs are not important for the poor. At the same time, some skeptics of expanded efforts to address NCDs believe that they are a problem that is more relevant to the nonpoor. The policy implications revolve around the relative importance that might be attached to two alternative agendas when health priorities are established: the emerging agenda of NCDs versus the unfinished agenda of communicable disease control. Why should the relative burden of NCDs among the rich and poor matter as long as we know that there are poor people who suffer from NCDs? One reason is that it helps to identify sources of inequality, which are relevant to the extent that we care about gaps in health outcomes across groups and not just their absolute levels. The relative burden also has important implications for the ability to target the poor.

In reality, the data on the NCD burden among the poor present a nuanced picture, and understanding these nuances can help generate a more productive debate than taking an either-or perspective (see appendix 1 and Smith 2006b for further details on the data presented). One reason for the nuanced picture is that the metric chosen to evaluate the importance of NCDs to the poor can affect interpretation. For example, when deaths are measured in absolute terms, NCDs are by far the leading cause of death worldwide, accounting for about 75 percent or more of the total in all World Bank country income groups except the poorest. Even in low-income countries, NCDs are projected to overtake communicable diseases as the leading cause of death by 2015. By this metric, NCDs are highly important to the poor.

An alternative yardstick is to analyze excess deaths, or in other words, what explains the gap between mortality in the world's richest countries and the rest of the world? The answer here is that NCDs account for a significantly smaller share of the disease burden—typically less than one-third in the world's two poorest quintiles—when we measure excess deaths rather than total deaths. The reason underlying the gap between total and excess deaths attributable to NCDs is that while the poor are twice as likely to die from NCDs as the rich (based on age-standardized mortality rates), they are 20 times more likely to die from communicable diseases.

Evidence on socioeconomic differences in NCD outcomes within countries is scant, but as average income in the country where a person lives explains about 70 percent of global income inequality between individuals, the cross-country data are strongly indicative (World Bank 2005f). If anything, this approach will overstate the importance of NCDs among the world's very poor. Nevertheless, by any metric, NCDs are more important (relative to communicable diseases) in middle-income countries than in low-income ones.

Analyzing some NCD risk factors according to country income levels is also informative. No correlation with per capita GDP is apparent for blood pressure. In the case of adult smoking prevalence, cross-sectional data reveal a slight, inverted, U-shaped relationship, with rates increasing at lower income levels before ultimately declining at higher levels (although the decline may reflect temporary lagged effects). Cholesterol levels and body mass index have a positive relationship with income: these risk factors increase as countries grow richer (Ezzati and others

2003; Mackay and Eriksen 2002). For still other risk factors, such as indoor air pollution, the risk factor diminishes as country income rises. These patterns do not apply in certain countries, and the level of a given risk factor may be more dangerous for a poor person than a rich one because of worse access to medical care, but in general, NCD risk factors tend to be better than the cross-country average in poor countries and worse in rich ones (this is shown graphically in appendix 1). Within countries, the relationship between risk factors and socioeconomic status appears to vary widely across different world regions (Blakely and others 2005). As with the NCD burden, NCD risk factors tend to be worse in middle-income countries than in low-income ones.

In sum, in all countries and by any metric, NCDs account for a share of the disease burden that is large enough to merit policy attention. The increasing importance of these illnesses over time reinforces this message: NCDs are the future. At the same time, we acknowledge that in most countries infectious diseases remain a more important cause of the rich-poor gap in health outcomes and that NCDs are of relatively greater importance in middle-income countries than in low-income ones. This is relevant to questions of inequality, targeting, and ultimately the relative emphasis that policy makers might place on combinations of interventions at the country level.

Budget Implications of NCD Interventions

As private insurance markets often work poorly (or not at all) and government regulation is a challenge even for countries with excellent administrative capacity, many countries opt for public financing or provision of high-cost NCD services that require risk sharing (or both). For equity reasons, they often do the same for low-cost services.

Important upstream and downstream linkages exist between a higher NCD burden and each of four major causes of health expenditure growth: aging, technology, insurance, and economic growth. Aging societies have more NCDs than younger ones, even where efforts to achieve healthy aging are successful. More NCDs, in turn, will tend to generate demand for both more technology for NCD diagnosis and treatment and more insurance coverage to provide financial protection against technology-driven costs. This process can be self-reinforcing. Finally, economic growth tends to be associated with behavioral changes that can increase some of the risk factors for NCDs, but it will also generate more demand for medical care to address them (see Smith 2006a for further discussion on the links between NCDs and expenditure growth).[4]

As the NCD burden rises, how are budgets likely to evolve? A useful distinction can be drawn between the spending pressures associated with aging societies (as older people, on average, require more health care) and those that result from higher age-specific expenditures (changes over time in health spending for people of a given age resulting from such factors as new technology or insurance expansion). This is relevant because the aging process is essentially beyond the reach of government action, while policy choices can affect changes in age-specific expenditures to a significant extent. A key message is that both historically and in projections undertaken for this report, the age-specific component of expenditure growth is likely to be substantially larger than the demographic (aging) component (see appendix 1 and Smith 2006a for more details). In brief, countries facing a higher burden of NCDs will also face growing demand for both complex medical technologies and financial risk protection through insurance. The former will tend to raise the cost per episode to the health system, whereas the latter will reduce the cost the patient faces at the point of service. This combination can potentially result in rapidly increasing age-specific expenditures with a magnitude much larger than can be accounted for by aging alone.

Thus, while aging is an important reason for the growing burden of NCDs, it will not necessarily be the major direct cause of higher health expenditures. The latter will instead be driven primarily by policy decisions that affect age-specific health expenditures, for example, how decisions pertain to technology adoption, more expensive pharmaceuticals, and insurance expansion. Careful health technology assessments, judicious expansion of benefits packages, and ultimately financing mechanisms that promote the sustainability of health spending over time will all play an important role in helping countries adjust to the financial implications of the epidemiological transition. In high-income countries where NCDs predominate, how to contain rapidly rising expenditures has been a recurrent theme in health policy reform, with major fiscal implications. The same challenges await many middle-income countries. Appendix 1 provides additional discussion on this topic. A case study of Indonesia in appendix 3 explores some of health system pressures of NCDs in a specific country context.

Value for Money

The second major determinant of the impact of public spending on NCD outcomes, as identified at the outset of this chapter, is the value for money attained through alternative interventions. Health-improving interventions vary greatly both in their cost of implementation as well as in health gained. Thus, given a fixed budget, decisions about how funds are allocated (which interventions to "buy") will play a key role in determining the volume of services that can be delivered and ultimately their impact on reducing morbidity and mortality. This section briefly discusses examples of interventions that offer value for money in addressing NCDs (the information presented here draws heavily on Laxminarayan and others 2006). Appendix 2 presents a more detailed discussion of the effectiveness of NCD interventions.

The previous sections indicated that an economic rationale exists for a range of different NCD interventions to correct market failures on either efficiency or equity grounds, and in many settings further prioritization within this range may be necessary. Having decided to intervene against NCDs, policy makers can use cost-effectiveness analysis (CEA) to redirect resources to achieve more health gains (see Jamison and others 2006a for more details). CEA is a tool for weighing the costs and health outcomes of different interventions and allows policy makers to ascertain the "price" of buying health through different interventions.

CEA has numerous drawbacks. The evidence it provides is often highly context specific (with respect to both time and place); depends on scale considerations, prevailing unit prices, and local epidemiology; and can vary according to service delivery models, for example, individual or bundled. It should also be placed in the context of this chapter's broader framework. The earlier discussion on economic rationale implies that if a publicly provided, "cost-effective" intervention offers services for which market failures are few and therefore displaces private health sector activity, then its net impact will be much lower than suggested by an analysis of the public sector alone. Furthermore, as the next section will discuss, cost-effectiveness evidence drawn from a study in a well-functioning health system has limited relevance in an environment where public sector and service delivery capacities are low.

These caveats are important, and thus CEA should be only one of many inputs into policy making. Nevertheless, its imperfections should not obscure an important point: that political economy considerations often guide decisions on health budget allocations (echoed in the common complaint that spending is biased toward expensive tertiary hospitals catering to an urban elite), and as a result such allocations do not yield improvements in health outcomes on the scale that could be achieved, all else being equal, through a more technical approach (see Birdsall and

James 1993 on the political economy implications of the epidemiological transition). When used appropriately, CEA can be helpful in identifying highly cost-effective opportunities to improve health that policy makers are currently neglecting as well as widely prevalent investments that are not cost-effective.

Whether a specific public information campaign to promote diet and exercise works or by how much a particular drug reduces the likelihood of heart disease matters greatly for public policy to improve NCD outcomes. Medical and public health research is constantly evolving, and robust evidence of effectiveness should precede large-scale implementation of an intervention. More broadly, monitoring and evaluation to provide evidence on the health production function should be viewed as a public good worthy of government and donor support.

What does the CEA evidence reveal? Contrary to some beliefs, many NCD interventions are cost-effective. Cigarette taxes are possibly the most effective intervention to curb smoking. Tobacco control through tax increases often has dual benefits of increasing tax revenues as well as discouraging smoking initiation and encouraging smokers to quit. The cost-effectiveness of a policy to increase cigarette prices by 33 percent ranges from US$13 to US$195 per disability-adjusted life years (DALY) averted globally, with a better cost-effectiveness ratio (US$3 to US$42 per DALY averted) in low-income countries (Laxminarayan and others 2006). Nonprice interventions, such as banning advertising, providing health education information, and forbidding smoking in public places, are relatively less cost-effective (US$54 to US$674 per DALY averted) in low-income countries, but are still important components of any tobacco control program.[5]

Cost-effective interventions also exist for other CVD risk factors. Population-based primary prevention interventions can effectively lower the risk of coronary heart disease and stroke at a relatively low cost and without expensive health infrastructure. For example, replacing dietary trans fat with polyunsaturated fat is likely to be effective in settings where intake of trans fat is high. If this occurs during manufacture rather than through changes in the behavior of individuals, the cost would be US$25 to US$73 per DALY averted. Replacement of saturated fat with monounsaturated fat in manufactured foods accompanied by a public education campaign is considerably more expensive: US$1,865 to US$4,012 per DALY averted.

Clinic-based prevention strategies targeted at individuals at high risk for CVD—measured as a combination of nonoptimal blood pressure, lifestyle, and genetic risk factors—can also be effective, especially when implemented in tandem with population-based measures. The cost-effectiveness of primary prevention of CVD may vary greatly depending on the underlying risk factors, the age of the patient, and the cost of medications. The cost of treating acute myocardial infarction with aspirin and beta-blockers is less than US$25 per DALY averted in all regions. In regions with poor access to hospitals, a combination of aspirin plus the beta-blocker atenolol is highly cost-effective in preventing the recurrence of a vascular event: US$386 to US$545 per DALY averted. Treatment of acute ischemic stroke with aspirin costs US$150 per DALY averted, and at US$70 per DALY averted is also the cheapest option for secondary prevention.

Single-pill (polypill) combinations of blood pressure–lowering medications, statins, and aspirin offer the potential dual benefit of being highly effective at lowering the risk of CVD and facilitating patient compliance with a drug regimen. A hypothetical multidrug regimen that includes generic aspirin, a beta-blocker, a thiazide diuretic, an angiotensin-converting enzyme inhibitor, and a statin may be implemented at a cost-effectiveness ratio of US$721 to US$1,065 per DALY averted (compared with no treatment in a population with an underlying 10-year CVD risk of 35 percent). The use of the multidrug regimen for prevention in patients with a lower underlying CVD risk improves health benefits, but costs increase more than proportionately.

Little evidence is available on the cost-effectiveness of programs to encourage exercise and other behavioral changes. For example, while strong evidence of the health benefits of regular physical activity is available, population policies to promote physical activity are scarce, and if present are rarely evaluated on their own. Research attempting to understand the factors that influence physical activity, including urban environment, use of leisure time, occupation, and transportation, is only just beginning to emerge. Also, few studies have established the effectiveness of policies to encourage higher consumption of fruits and vegetables. Issues for study include how to ensure the availability of fruits and vegetables in poor neighborhoods, how to reach populations who are often misinformed on the benefits of various nutrients and diets, and what the potential benefits of taxing energy-dense snacks might be.

In sum, highly cost-effective interventions for the control of NCDs do exist, and although not the only relevant criterion, evidence on best buys can be a valuable input into resource allocation decisions. Table 2.2 shows the cost-effectiveness ratios for selected interventions (including two that are not cost-effective) and associated DALYs averted per US$1 million spent. (For more examples see appendix 2 and for a more exhaustive list see Jamison and others 2006b.)

Implementation of NCD Services

The third and final consideration affecting the extent to which a dollar of public spending on NCDs can lead to better outcomes is the public sector's capacity to translate its health budget into services of adequate quality. Service delivery in the health sector can be challenging, and governments' ability to achieve results has often been weaker than hoped. The challenge of service delivery is receiving increased attention and is particularly relevant for health (see, in particular, World Bank 2003). Decades of anecdotal observations—absentee health workers, empty drug cabinets, facilities without power—and a growing body of literature have revealed that the quality of medical care is often woefully inadequate (Chaudhury and others 2006; Das and Hammer forthcoming;

Table 2.2. Selected Cost-Effectiveness Ratios for Interventions against NCDs

Service or intervention	Cost per DALY (US$)	DALYs averted per US$1 million spent
1. Taxation of tobacco products	3–50	20,000–330,000
2. Treatment of acute myocardial infarction or heart attack with an inexpensive set of drugs (aspirin and beta-blocker)	10–25	40,000–100,000
3. Treatment of acute myocardial infarction with inexpensive drugs plus streptokinase (costs and DALYs for this are in addition to what would have occurred with inexpensive drugs only)	600–750	1,300–1,600
4. Lifetime treatment of heart attack and stroke survivors with a daily polypill combining four or five off-patent preventive medications	700–1,000	1,000–1,400
5. Coronary artery bypass graft or bypass surgery in specific identifiable risk cases, such as disease of the left main coronary artery (incremental to 4)	>25,000	<40
6. Bypass surgery for less severe coronary heart disease and lifetime treatment (incremental to 4)	Very high	Very small

Source: Jamison and others 2006b.

Leonard and Masatu 2005). This section briefly considers how the public sector can achieve better results in the field. Many of the issues discussed constitute what is often referred to as a health systems approach to improving outcomes (for further discussion, see World Bank 2007). Appendix 3 presents three country case studies related to service delivery issues.

A first step is to conceptualize the nature of the problem. The range of NCD services may be characterized using the framework developed by the World Bank (2003). This categorizes services as discretionary, transaction intensive, or both. Discretionary services are those that require significant judgment on the part of the provider about what service to provide and how to deliver the service to the client, who has significantly less information. Transaction-intensive services require repeated, frequent interaction between provider and client.

In general, most nonclinical NCD preventive services, such as public information campaigns about risk factors or tax policies for tobacco and alcohol, are discretionary but are not transaction intensive (although tax collection may be transaction intensive). Their design requires a certain level of judgment by the policy maker, but once this step has been accomplished, it does not need to be repeated regularly. By contrast, most clinical NCD services are both discretionary and transaction intensive: the health worker needs to make judgments about the appropriate diagnostic technique, drug therapy, or other intervention and must do so on many separate occasions. This is the case for most curative health care, but is particularly so for chronic NCDs.

The discretionary and transaction-intensive nature of many NCD services is precisely what makes service delivery so challenging. This is because of the difficulties it poses for establishing accountability in the institutional relationships—among patients, providers, and policy makers—that are critical to service delivery success. On a conceptual level, measures to improve accountability will be important for strengthening public sector capacity to deliver services.

On a practical level, considering some of the characteristics of NCDs that are particularly relevant to service delivery issues is helpful. In other words, what is different about NCDs when compared with the more "traditional" priorities of acute communicable diseases and maternal and child health? The focus here will be on clinical services, where the challenges are likely to be greatest as they are both discretionary and transaction intensive. A nonexhaustive list of some of these characteristics follows, along with some of the necessary inputs and strategic directions that they suggest. Empirical research on this topic in low- and middle-income countries is sparse.

- NCD services are typically more complex than other health interventions. They require a greater number of interactions with the health system (that is, they are transaction intensive), at multiple levels of care (primary, specialized, laboratory, and so on), and often in the presence of comorbidities. The continuity, coordination, and comprehensiveness of care are critical in this setting. Strong information systems will be a key input for addressing all three challenges (Renders and others 2001; Wagner and Groves 2002), and can also serve to strengthen accountability. Another challenge in the face of complexity is the quality of care, underlining the need for clinical guidelines and a clear articulation of roles, responsibilities, and accountability relationships. Finally, the complexity of NCDs does not imply an emphasis only on higher levels of care; indeed, stronger primary care services have been associated with better chronic disease outcomes in industrial countries (Starfield and Shi 2002).
- NCDs' long-term nature implies greater responsibilities for self-care by the patient, highlighting the need for health systems to equip patients to take on that role. This is a recurring theme in the literature from industrial countries on chronic care service delivery (Renders and others 2001; Wagner and Groves 2002). Promoting patient education programs and engaging communities can help promote patient self-management. A more informed patient also has the potential to improve the accountability of providers and to participate more actively in decision making.
- NCDs are often characterized by long periods during which the patient may be asymptomatic, which underlines the importance of new approaches to access, especially by reaching beyond facility-based services to engage communities. Contracting with civil society organizations to, for example, disseminate information, promote awareness, and encourage screening if and when appropriate may be a promising approach in this regard.
- NCDs often entail extended use of pharmaceuticals, with important implications for drug access, quality, and affordability. This highlights the value of stewardship functions, such as a competitive generic drug policy to help reduce costs, and a consumer information agency to help inform and protect those paying for medications out of pocket.
- NCD treatment is often more technology intensive than other health services. In this context, health technology assessments will

become crucial inputs to the policy process, particularly in relation to cost containment.

- Numerous studies have stressed the role of skilled workers, midlevel cadres, and nonmedical personnel in chronic care provision (Renders and others 2001; Rothman and Wagner 2003; Singh 2005; WHO 2005a, 2006b). A shift in the mix of skills and human resources has implications for training, but does not necessarily imply an emphasis on higher-level skills.

Reflecting these characteristics, a number of models have been developed that recognize the complexity of the strategies that are required to manage chronic disease. Examples include the following:

- The chronic care model was developed in the United States and variations have been used in other high-income countries (Bodenheimer, Wagner, and Grumbach 2002a, 2002b; Wagner 1998). The model comprises four components: self-management support, delivery system design, decision support, and clinical information systems. The model implies strong linkages between the community and the health system and involves a range of multisectoral interventions (Wagner and others 1999). Some recent empirical studies have lent support to components of the chronic care model (Piat and others 2006; Tsai and others 2005).
- A systemic approach that includes risk factor surveillance, prevention, disease management, and monitoring underlies the development of conceptual models to target chronic disease developed by WHO (2002a).[6] These models focus primarily on low- and middle-income countries.
- The St. Vincent Declaration, adopted in 1989 under the aegis of the International Diabetes Federation (Europe), established a widely accepted set of goals and principles for the prevention, diagnosis, and management of diabetes and its complications.[7] This was followed by practical guidance on how to implement such a strategy (European Diabetes Policy Group 1999a, 1999b). The declaration emphasizes self-management of diabetes and a "therapeutic partnership" and introduces the idea of a treatment team rather than reliance on individual health professionals.

The characteristics of NCDs relevant to service delivery should also be viewed through the lens of prospects for reaching the poor with NCD services. NCDs are qualitatively different from communicable diseases in a number of respects that suggest additional challenges in reaching the poor. For example:

- *Higher nonclinical costs.* The potentially higher frequency of contacts with trained service providers required for chronic diseases implies greater transport and opportunity costs for the patient.
- *Poorer financial access.* NCDs are characterized by higher costs per episode of illness, heightening the importance of insurance mechanisms. However, the difficulties of providing insurance coverage to the informal sector, where the poor tend to be concentrated, are well known.
- *Economies of scale.* The hospital bias of certain NCD interventions, resulting in part from economies of scale for the deployment of technology, makes reaching rural areas more difficult than reaching urban areas.[8] Even if some follow-up services can be delivered through health centers, diagnosis may require an initial hospital contact, which can effectively exclude the poor.
- *Specialized labor.* Similarly, the complexity of some NCD interventions makes it more difficult to use less skilled human resources of the type available through health centers, outreach, and so on. Issues of access by the poor to specialized facilities and labor is particularly important for conditions requiring urgent care, such as heart attack or stroke.

Thus, reaching the poor with clinical NCD services is likely to pose some important challenges. Although studies have not looked at NCDs explicitly, general findings indicate strongly that this is indeed the case. Figure 2.2 shows the results of several expenditure incidence studies in different countries. In a wide range of settings, expenditure incidence for health services tends to be skewed in favor of the rich.[9] The contrast is even larger for hospital services than for primary care, highlighting the potential difficulties for NCD interventions. In addition, the studies indicate that progressivity tends to be better in middle-income countries than in low-income countries. Thus, the countries in which NCDs are relatively more important are also those that have a better chance of successfully tackling the issue.

The incidence studies suggest that if a country has a poor track record with respect to reaching the poor with services for communicable diseases, it should be cautious in terms of launching massive new efforts to provide NCD services in the clinical setting, as the latter will probably be even more difficult to do in a progressive manner. This should not be a reason for inaction, but rather a motivation to do a better job. In all

Figure 2.2. Expenditure Incidence for Primary and Hospital Care, Selected Countries, Various Years

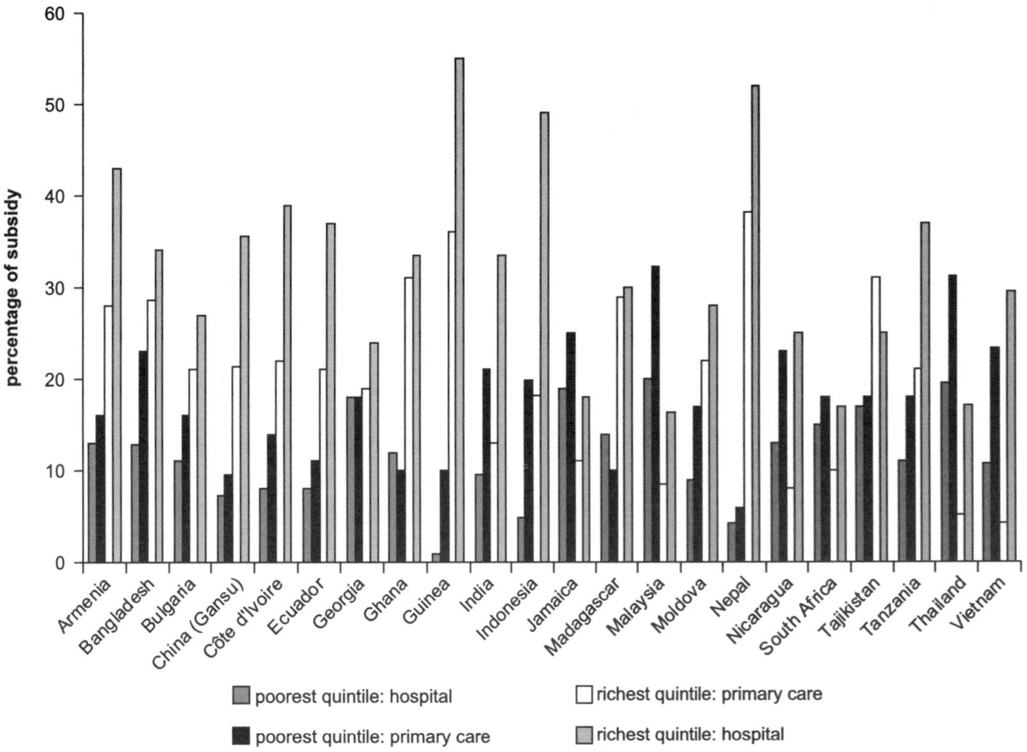

Sources: Filmer 2003; O'Donnell and others 2005.

countries, the challenge will be to find innovative solutions to reach the poor with NCD services.

A final note on targeting can help identify one other challenge for reaching the poor with NCD services. In many settings, NCDs represent a larger share of the overall disease burden than communicable diseases and more poor people have NCDs than communicable diseases. Even in this context, categorical targeting through a focus on communicable diseases can, in principle, be a more promising way to reach the poor than undertaking NCD interventions. This is because there tend to be fewer nonpoor people with communicable diseases, and thus less potential for leakage. In this scenario, even if everyone (nonpoor and poor) suffering from a condition has an equal probability of benefiting from public expenditures (and the incidence studies suggest this is often not the case), a dollar invested in NCD interventions will be less progressive than spending on communicable disease.[10]

NCDs and other health interventions share some commonalities. In particular, HIV/AIDS also entails chronic disease management and sustained contacts with health service providers, and the engagement of communities in detection and diagnosis plays a critical role. Tuberculosis and sexually transmitted diseases also offer potential parallels with NCDs with respect to case detection and management. The many lessons learned in recent years in relation to addressing HIV/AIDS and these other conditions may be highly applicable to NCDs and vice versa.

In sum, the ability of health systems to translate public spending on NCDs into better outcomes cannot be taken for granted. The difficulties of service delivery for interventions that are simpler than those for NCDs and the potential complexity of NCD service delivery emphasize the need to carefully consider NCDs' key characteristics and how systems can be adapted to produce results. This is particularly true for reaching the poor with NCD interventions. This note of caution should be balanced with optimism that innovative solutions exist: the challenge is to identify and incorporate them into policies. An awareness of the challenges is a critical first step toward developing those solutions.

Summary: A Matrix of the Economic Rationale for NCD Interventions

This chapter has presented a framework for analyzing public policy for improving NCD outcomes. It was built on three major considerations: economic rationale, value for money, and public sector capacity to deliver services. As emphasized throughout, all three are important determinants of the effect of public spending on NCD outcomes: the chain is only as strong as its weakest link.

Table 2.3 summarizes the economic rationale for public intervention in NCDs in the form of a matrix. The case for primary prevention rests primarily on taxes to address externalities related to tobacco and alcohol

Table 2.3. Illustrative Matrix on the Economic Rationale for Public Intervention in NCDs

Level of care	Low-income countries	Middle-income countries
Primary prevention (primarily nonclinical services)	Strong rationale on efficiency grounds for tobacco and alcohol taxes, advertising bans, and a ban on smoking in public places. The provision of information to improve knowledge about risk factors (for example, alcohol, tobacco, diet, exercise) is also justified, with a special effort to reach poor populations.	Strong rationale on efficiency grounds for tobacco and alcohol taxes, advertising bans, and a ban on smoking in public places. The provision of information to improve knowledge about risk factors (for example, alcohol, tobacco, diet, exercise) is also justified, with a special effort to reach poor populations. Regulation to address the content of manufactured foods.
Secondary prevention and treatment (primarily clinical services)	A limited set of simpler, possibly nonhospital, low-cost interventions for which there is a good probability of reaching the poor (and that will not strain the government budget) might be justified on equity grounds, for example, if included in a well-targeted basic package of services. There is a good efficiency rationale for high-cost interventions (for example, by addressing the insurance problem), but achieving this is difficult because of the likelihood that these will not be pro-poor if delivered via hospitals, limited administrative capacities, and resource constraints on the public purse. Other: Governments should commission monitoring and evaluation of interventions to determine what works. They may also be able to negotiate lower NCD drug prices.	Intervention in low-cost NCD services is justified on equity grounds (for example, they could be included in a well-targeted basic package), with special attention to reaching the poor. There is a strong efficiency rationale for high-cost interventions, intervening either via insurance markets or public financing (with or without public provision). However, special efforts should be made to make these pro-poor, and new services should be added to benefits packages only at a pace that can be sustained by the public purse. Other: Governments should commission monitoring and evaluation of interventions to determine what works. They may also be able to negotiate lower NCD drug prices.

Source: Authors.

and the provision of information about various risk factors. The section on treatment distinguishes between low- and high-cost NCD services, with equity concerns motivating a public role for the former and efficiency issues related to insurance markets largely motivating the latter. Any expansion of clinical services should be mindful of the challenges of reaching the poor and of resource constraints resulting from limited health budgets where public financing is pursued. For these reasons, a less ambitious set of interventions than in middle-income countries is advisable in low-income countries. The rollout of new interventions should also be accompanied by direct or indirect public support for monitoring and evaluation mechanisms to help determine what works.

How do cost-effectiveness and service delivery capacity affect this matrix? For the top row on primary prevention, the message does not change significantly. The services for which an economic rationale exists generally tend to be cost-effective, although robust evidence on how best to provide the public with information is often lacking. Also service delivery of these interventions in most settings will generally not be problematic, as they are not transaction intensive (with the possible exceptions of tax collection, as opposed to design, and the suppression of smuggling if it arises in response to taxation), and do not typically rely heavily on strong health systems. Thus, primary prevention activities are a logical first priority in low-income countries.

The picture is somewhat less clear for the second row on secondary prevention and treatment. Many low-cost clinical interventions against CVD are cost-effective, but unless they reach the poor who would otherwise not have access (thereby achieving equity goals), the economic rationale is weaker. Neither consideration will matter if service delivery in a widely scattered network of primary health clinics is weak, and this is often a concern in low-income countries. With respect to higher-cost hospital interventions, the economic rationale is stronger in middle-income countries, and service delivery capacity here tends to be better, although value for money is less than for lower-cost alternatives. Ultimately, the resolution of some of these tensions will rely on country-specific factors (see Filmer, Hammer, and Pritchett 2002 for further discussion).

Key Messages

The key messages of this chapter are as follows:

- Three distinct factors are likely to play an important role in determining the effect of public spending on NCD outcomes, with the overall chain that binds them together being only as strong as its weakest link. These factors are (a) the net impact of the public sector, which depends on the extent of market failures; (b) the budget allocation decisions, which imply either more or less value for money depending on cost-effectiveness; and (c) the public sector's capacity to translate money into effective services. This trio of factors offers a useful framework for analyzing public policy related to NCDs.

- NCDs impose a significant economic burden, not just on patients, but also on households, communities, employers, health care systems, and government budgets. Typical cost of illness studies often underestimate this burden.
- The economic rationale for NCD interventions for primary prevention rests primarily on taxes to address externalities related to tobacco and alcohol and on the provision of information about various risk factors. The economic rationale with regard to treatment distinguishes between low- and high-cost NCD services, with equity concerns motivating a public role for the former and efficiency issues related to insurance markets as the main motivation for the latter.
- In all countries and by any metric, NCDs account for a large enough share of the disease burden of the poor to merit serious policy attention. At the same time, in most countries infectious diseases remain a more important cause of the rich-poor gap in health outcomes and NCDs are of relatively greater importance in middle-income countries than in low-income ones.
- A growing burden of NCDs will have potentially large budget implications, but the fiscal consequences of aging are likely to be much less important than the growth of age-specific expenditures, particularly because of the greater demand for both high-cost technologies and public insurance coverage that NCDs may generate.
- Cost-effectiveness analysis, despite its limitations and if all else is equal, can offer useful information for input into budget allocation decisions. Highly cost-effective interventions for the control of NCDs do exist. Among the most cost-effective are tobacco taxes and clinical interventions for primary and secondary prevention of CVD.
- Service delivery issues will be central to achieving better NCD outcomes. Key characteristics of NCDs, including the need for long-term, sustained interaction with multiple levels of the health system, the importance of community engagement to improve access and patient self-care, and the intensive use of technology and drugs, can help inform policy decisions aimed at improving service delivery.

- Both conceptual and empirical reasons provide grounds for the belief that achieving equity goals through NCD interventions will be a challenge in low-income countries. Middle-income countries have a better track record of reaching the poor. In all settings, the challenge will be to find innovative approaches to make interventions pro-poor.

Notes

1. IDF (International Diabetes Federation). 2003. *Diabetes Atlas*. 2nd ed. Brussels: International Diabetes Foundation.
2. WHO. "Arsenic in Drinking Water." Fact Sheet 210. WHO. http://www.who.int/mediacentre/factsheets/fs210/en/index.html. Date consulted: October 31, 2006.
3. This terminology is from Musgrove (1996). Two other instruments, finance and provision, are somewhat less common for NCD prevention, but more so for treatment.
4. Note that technology can also be cost saving, but a growing body of literature points to technology as the most important driver of health expenditure growth, so the savings are outweighed.
5. The World Bank considers health interventions that cost less than US$100 per year of life saved as highly cost-effective for poor countries.
6. See also WHO 2005a.
7. St. Vincent Declaration. "Diabetes Care and Research in Europe: The St. Vincent Declaration." International Diabetes Federation. http://www.idf.org/webdata/docs/SVD%20and%20Istanbul%20Commitment.pdf. Date consulted: November 15, 2006.
8. Many NCD interventions are recommended for the hospital setting (Laxminarayan and others 2006).
9. The data presented in figure 2.2 show average incidence. A more relevant indicator, but one that is more difficult to determine, is marginal incidence, which may be more pro-poor (Lanjouw and Ravallion 1999).
10. In practice, some individuals may have comorbidities that include both communicable diseases and NCDs, and both will require treatment.

CHAPTER 3

The Agenda for the World Bank

The previous chapters addressed global noncommunicable disease (NCD) trends and offered a framework for improving outcomes in relation to the prevention and control of NCDs. Against that background, this chapter looks at the extent to which the Bank's portfolio of analytical and advisory services and lending operations addresses NCD issues. It then presents the Bank's agenda for action in support of the prevention and control of NCDs.

NCDs in the World Bank's Portfolio

To what extent has the Bank addressed NCDs in its portfolio? The following subsections summarize the findings of a background paper that addressed this question (World Bank 2006d).

Analytical and Advisory Services

The scope and application of the Bank's analytical work on NCDs has been limited. Tobacco control is one area in which the Bank has made a visible and substantial contribution to global efforts to control NCDs. The Bank has funded analytical work on the economics of tobacco control in a number of countries, building local analytical capacity. In addition, it published and disseminated *Curbing the Epidemic: Governments and the*

Economics of Tobacco Control (World Bank 1999). This landmark report examined the costs of tobacco control policies and set out an agenda for action by governments. It also identified roles for international agencies in reducing the avoidable toll of smoking-related premature death and disability. Other major Bank publications on tobacco include *Tobacco Control in Developing Countries* (Jha and Chaloupka 2000) and *Tobacco Control Policy: Strategies, Successes, and Setbacks* (de Beyer and Brigden 2003). An unpublished report on tobacco control and the World Bank's partnership with the U.S. Centers for Disease Control and Prevention describes a substantial program of work in many countries (World Bank 2005e).

In 2005, the Bank prepared two important reports on NCDs in Brazil (World Bank 2005a) and Russia (World Bank 2005b). Both these reports are contributing to country-led strategies and programs for the control of NCDs. Boxes 3.1 and 3.2 provide examples of analytical and advisory services at the regional and country levels.

Box 3.1

Regional Focus: Epidemiologic Surveillance Systems in the Europe and Central Asia Region

With funding from the government of the Netherlands, the World Bank's Europe and Central Asia Region commissioned a study of epidemiological surveillance systems in the region. The report contained important information on the systems' features and limitations and recommended improvements (Miller and Ryskulova 2004). Despite a shared legacy of central planning and standardization of processes and systems in the former Soviet Union and Eastern Europe, the completeness, timeliness, and quality of disease surveillance data widely vary across countries, and in many cases are weak. Data completeness and quality do not appear to be high priorities for the governments and agencies responsible for health and disease surveillance. The surveillance systems tend to be overly complex, with duplicate and parallel reporting, fragmented reporting, delinking of important data, and lack of integration among parts of the surveillance systems.

Birth and death registration systems in the region are better developed than other forms of epidemiological surveillance, but even these are in need of reform, rationalization, and modernization. Infectious disease surveillance systems have serious limitations, with potential implications for global health. The region's surveillance systems need to be brought up-to-date in relation to case definitions and national procedural manuals and adapted to meet the information needs of public health programs.

The reporting burden is overwhelming in many of the region's countries: too many data items are being collected for unclear purposes. For example, the collection of morbidity data consumes a large volume of resources, but the data are incomplete and of poor quality, leading to incorrect conclusions and actions or no action at all because the presumed end users discount the data. Behavioral risk factor surveillance for NCDs is rudimentary. This leaves governments, international organizations, and donors without the critical information required to prevent and control the leading causes of morbidity and mortality. The study could not verify that surveillance data were being used for a variety of health and public health uses.

The state of epidemiological surveillance in Europe and Central Asia has critical policy implications, including the limited nature of the basis on which to design, implement, and evaluate programs and policy interventions to prevent and control the leading causes of morbidity and mortality. Further research, evaluation, and significant investments are required to reform and improve the region's surveillance systems.

Source: Miller and Ryskulova 2004.

Box 3.2

Country Focus: Addressing the Challenges of NCDs in Brazil

A recent World Bank report (2005a) provides an overview of the changing burden of NCDs in Brazil and its causes. It examines the costs and effectiveness of alternative policy interventions to address this growing burden, the costs of disease, the potential returns from expanding NCD activities, and the policy implications of a stronger response to the challenge of NCDs.

What Were the Report's Main Findings?

Brazil's NCD mortality rate is higher than in developed countries and is high in all regions, including the poorer areas of the north and the northeast. The poor suffer a double burden, as they are also more affected by communicable diseases than the nonpoor.

(continued)

Box 3.2 (*continued*)

The report estimated that in 2003, the financial and economic costs related to diseases caused by three preventable risk factors—physical inactivity, smoking, and hypertension—were equivalent to 10 percent of gross domestic product. If no additional efforts were made, it estimated that during 2005–9, productivity losses would amount to US$72 billion and treatment costs to US$34 billion. Seventy-five percent of treatment costs would be for ischemic heart disease.

The study estimated the cost-effectiveness of a tax increase on cigarettes, a comprehensive physical activity campaign, and the provision of treatment for hypertension to 25 percent of those with the disease. The three interventions could potentially save US$3.1 billion over the 2005–9 period in treatment and productivity losses.

How Has the Government of Brazil Used the Report?

The Ministry of Health is developing a strategic action plan for health promotion, including the reduction of NCD risk factors. It is focusing its initial efforts on interventions to increase physical activity. Brazil has been fairly successful with its antismoking interventions: smoking prevalence decreased from 35 percent in 1989 to 18 percent in 2003. The government is studying increased taxation and other methods to reduce smoking rates further, particularly among the poor, where the prevalence of smoking is now the highest.

The Ministry of Health has taken action in the following areas that the report identified as gaps: (a) improving its NCD risk factor surveillance in urban areas (most state capital cities were to have a system providing continuous data by the end of 2006); (b) strengthening NCD surveillance, prevention, and control activities at the state level; and (c) developing research projects to assess the effectiveness of some of its health promotion interventions.

Source: Isabella Danel, personal communication, May 12, 2006.

During 1999–2004, the Bank undertook a work program on mental health that was supported by a mental health specialist with financing from the MacArthur Foundation, the U.S. government's National Institutes of Health and Center for Mental Health Services, and the Bank. The scope of work included generating and compiling knowledge on mental health through analytic work; disseminating this knowledge within the Bank and to the Bank's clients; providing policy and technical advice and preparing tools to facilitate the integration of mental health components into country assistance strategies and poverty reduction strategy papers; and undertaking partnership activities with the World Health Organization (WHO), the United Nations Development Fund for Women and other United Nations agencies, bilateral agencies, and global nongovernmental organizations working on mental health.[1]

Lending Operations

This section is based on a 20-year retrospective assessment of the World Bank's work on NCDs in the health, nutrition, and population (HNP) sector from 1985 to 2005. Figure 3.1 presents the five-phase approach the authors used to find documents.

The major types of Bank documents the authors collected and reviewed were project appraisal documents, staff appraisal reports, implementation completion reports in the case of closed projects, and project status reports. The types of document reviewed for each project depended on what was electronically cataloged. The authors identified 17 World Bank–financed projects for more detailed analysis.

Over the past 10 years, the Bank's lending (grants, credits, and loans) for HNP has remained at about US$1.4 billion per year. The largest thematic allocations for HNP projects approved in fiscal 2005 were concentrated under health system performance (US$462 million), followed by injuries and NCDs (US$331million) (World Bank 2005c). Of the 17 projects reviewed in preparing this report, 7 were already closed and the most recently approved projects were scheduled to close in 2010. The regional distribution of these 17 projects is as follows: 9 in the Europe and Central Asia Region, 3 in the Latin America and the Caribbean Region, 3 in the South Asia Region, and 2 in the East Asia and the Pacific Region. There were none in the Africa Region or the Middle East and North Africa Region.

Figure 3.1. Document Search Methodology

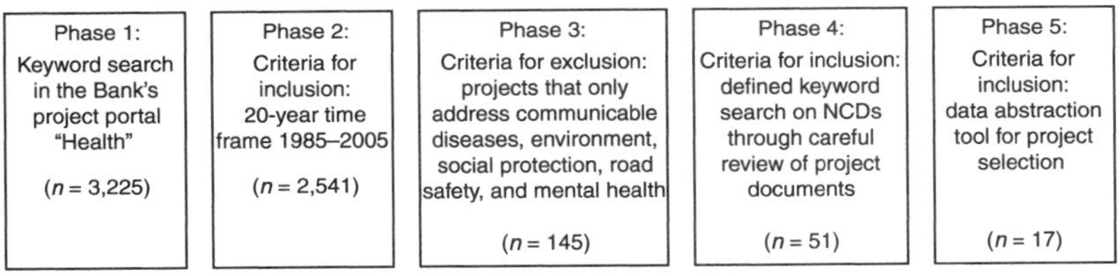

Phase 1: Keyword search in the Bank's project portal "Health" (*n* = 3,225)	Phase 2: Criteria for inclusion: 20-year time frame 1985–2005 (*n* = 2,541)	Phase 3: Criteria for exclusion: projects that only address communicable diseases, environment, social protection, road safety, and mental health (*n* = 145)	Phase 4: Criteria for inclusion: defined keyword search on NCDs through careful review of project documents (*n* = 51)	Phase 5: Criteria for inclusion: data abstraction tool for project selection (*n* = 17)

Source: Authors.
Note: n = number of projects.

Ascertaining how much money has been allocated to NCD control is difficult, as the documentation does not track expenditures by disease. The only conclusion on financing that can be made with confidence is based on free-standing components, which have a modest total cumulative commitment of US$18.8 million. In addition to these funds, expenditures on general strengthening of health services in some projects probably contribute indirectly to the prevention and control of NCDs.

Agenda for Action

Much of the Bank's future work on NCDs will focus on policy advice to governments. The potential scope of such work includes undertaking situation analyses; generating information and sharing it with policy makers; and supporting the design of appropriate responses, including multisectoral strategies, resource allocation, and progress monitoring. This approach is informed by two main considerations:

- Strong grounds exist for government intervention in the control of NCDs, as do effective public policy instruments and interventions through which governments can act.
- To be viable, the roles of the Bank must be few and of high impact. The Bank will concentrate on those aspects of NCD control that fit best with its comparative advantage, the most important of which is the combination of (a) expertise in development economics, (b) multisectoral perspectives that can be brought to bear on public policy dialogue and programs, (c) analytical and advisory services and demand-led investments in NCD prevention and control, and (d) capacity to be an informed consumer of the literature and to work in partnership with specialized technical agencies such as WHO without duplicating their work.

Guiding Principles from the World Bank's Strategy for HNP Results

The Bank's approach to the control of NCDs will be guided by its Strategy for HNP Results (World Bank 2007). The considerations underpinning the strategy are as follows:

- *Renewing emphasis on results (outputs, outcomes, and system performance).* This means paying greater attention to the pathways from policies and inputs to health outcomes and system performance. An important part of this effort will be to strengthen the link between advisory services,

HNP-related operations, outputs, outcomes, and the performance of specific elements of the health system as much as possible. In an environment of programmatic operations and efforts by multiple donors, the purpose is not to emphasize the attribution of health outcomes to specific Bank operations, but to bring more rigor to bear on such operations wherever doing so is feasible.

- *Paying greater attention to the intersectoral linkages that contribute to better outcomes.* This implies changes in the Bank's institutional incentives to influence behaviors. The relevance to NCDs lies in their integration into outcome-oriented strategies at the multisectoral level, regardless of the sectoral origin of a particular input or intervention. Some NCD interventions are multisectoral. In addition to central ministries of finance and planning, key sectors for highly effective interventions include health, agriculture, nutrition (World Bank 2006c), rural development, and trade.

- *Strengthening health system knowledge creation and policy and technical advice in areas in which the Bank has a comparative advantage.* This report has noted the pressures on health systems that may arise as a result of NCDs among aging populations and the potential financial consequences of NCD interventions. The Bank will concentrate on those aspects of NCD control for which it has a comparative advantage. These are health financing; fiduciary, logistical, and financial management of health systems; system governance; and household behavior in relation to health. Concurrently, the Bank will seek advice from local and international partners with comparative advantages in the following areas: stewardship (sector oversight); organization and management of service providers; technical aspects of disease control, training, human resources, and medical technologies; and clinical and field research on the effectiveness of health interventions and clinical protocols.

- *Ensuring synergy between health system and single-priority disease control approaches in low-income countries.* Here the need is to combine the development of health systems, which is crucial, with attention to context-specific priorities for disease control and systems for outcomes rather than systems versus outcomes.

- *Working selectively with global partners to complement Bank and global partners' comparative advantages at the country level.* In partnership with governments, the Bank will rely on local institutions, WHO, international research institutions, and other specialized technical agencies for up-to-date information on the evidence base for NCDs. It will work with appropriate nongovernmental organizations to improve the reach of service delivery at the country level. It will also work with other financiers and with foundations to address the financing needs of NCD prevention and control within countries' budget frameworks.

Approach to Analytical and Advisory Services

As noted earlier, the Bank will focus its policy discussions with countries on those areas in which it has a comparative advantage. The emphasis will be on quality and relevance to country needs and on technical support for countries to integrate affordable and highly effective interventions into their health and development policies, processes, and strategies. The channels include poverty reduction strategy papers in low-income countries as and when appropriate, informal consultations, country assistance strategies, and country economic memorandums. In both low-income and middle-income countries, the Bank will work more actively with WHO, foundations, research institutions, and nongovernmental organizations to convene informed discussions with country officials responsible for NCD control within the broader development agenda.

As strategies are country led, the Bank's services should include two mutually reinforcing approaches. The first is generating information and sharing knowledge that strengthens the basis for country decisions. The second is coconvening with countries selected intersectoral forums for policy analyses that have consequences for health in general, and for NCDs in particular, without any ties to a lending operation. For example, the Framework Convention for Tobacco Control is now in force and provides a clear basis whereby the World Bank can strengthen its support for tobacco control.

Under the first approach, the Bank will emphasize the improvement of country capacity to develop results-based monitoring and evaluation systems for health policy and health systems. Although this is not limited to NCDs and is best undertaken across the health sector, given the previous prominence of maternal and child health and infectious diseases, NCDs are notoriously absent from health monitoring systems and may require special attention. The Bank will work with countries to assess their capabilities and readiness to monitor and evaluate NCD interventions and to improve the quality and use of existing data sources, including the following:

- death registration
- disease-specific and health service data in health information systems
- incorporation of assessments of risk factors, morbidity, and anthropometric measures related to NCDs into living standards measurement studies by creating and testing special modules

• strengthening and modernization of local health information technology to monitor outputs and the performance of interventions.

Furthermore, the Bank will actively promote the use of information for decision making regarding NCDs in relation to public policies and health systems. Areas of work will include studies of costs, cost-effectiveness, and affordability of priority NCD interventions.

The second approach is relevant to both low- and middle-income countries, but is especially important for the latter. The Bank will make wider use of the approach of coconvening intersectoral policy forums to address tobacco control policy, alcohol abuse prevention, food and nutrition policies to prevent obesity and NCDs, and interventions to increase regular physical activity. The framework of the "Multisectoral Bottlenecks Assessment for Health Outcomes" (World Bank 2006b) will be adapted for this purpose as appropriate. This approach, which is not tied to any lending operation, could build confidence in relation to NCD control among country officials, Bank staff, and partner agencies and could stimulate country demand for pertinent lending operations.

As NCDs have implications for the private sector as well as the public sector, the Bank will also engage in this arena. In many low- and middle-income countries, the private sector plays a large role in the delivery of health services. At the same time, governments, particularly ministries of health, have modest capacity for undertaking the regulatory functions to ensure that the private sector conforms to appropriate standards of practice. The agenda for action will involve strengthening public institutions to perform these functions as part of the broader responsibility for stewardship, an endeavor that is both necessary and challenging.

The World Bank will also help countries prepare for the pressures NCDs will exert on the growth of costs. Countries should, in particular, place NCDs within the context of budgeting for multiple sectors, including health, and consider NCDs alongside discussions of mobilizing the fiscal resources (or finding the fiscal space) for financing the required spending on health (for more on this subject, see Heller 2006).

The analytical and advisory services will incorporate a broad perspective on health interventions. Countries will set their own priorities and make trade-offs based on local needs, desired outcomes, resource constraints, institutional capacity, and local values. In particular, the World Bank can provide advisory services (and, where appropriate, investment or development policy lending based on client demand) to help ensure the sustainability of health financing through the appropriate definition of benefits packages, supply- and demand-side reforms aimed at cost containment, health technology assessments, availability and affordability of pharmaceuticals, and other measures as needed.

Integration into Lending Operations

Depending on country requests, the Bank will consider increasing its support for country-led efforts to prevent and control NCDs. The step-wise framework of interventions recommended by WHO (2005a) provides a useful basis for action. The Bank will support approaches that are consistent with the emerging consensus on the alignment and harmonization of aid with country operations and integration into country strategies with predictable and sustainable financing.[2]

In addition to the provision of analytical and advisory services, the Bank will be more proactive in stimulating informed discussions about best buys in interventions against NCDs and in ensuring that clients are aware of these interventions when planning large-scale operations to be financed in part by grants, credits, or loans from the Bank. Chapter 2 and appendix 2 contain more detailed information about these interventions. In low-income countries, the need is for a gradual integration of selected, highly cost-effective interventions against NCDs into health services in a way that can be sustained within the resource envelope of domestic and external financing. In both low- and middle-income countries, the Bank will assist countries by disseminating the key messages of this report.

World Bank lending operations can reflect the findings of this report through at least three approaches. The first is the inclusion of NCDs in multisectoral programs that include outcome and impact indicators of NCD prevention and control. The second approach consists of health system operations that help countries prevent NCDs as much as possible while also preparing to deal with the rising burden of NCDs. The third approach consists of NCD-specific projects in countries where NCDs are important and governments request such operations.

Improving the Knowledge Base

What are the costs and benefits of treating NCDs? Where are the market failures and what should be done to address them? Are greater public subsidies for treating NCDs through public health care systems likely to benefit the rich rather than the poor? These are critical questions for efforts to tackle NCDs on a large scale, yet they are difficult to answer. The exercise on which this report is based began with critical questions about NCDs, but data to answer the questions in many cases simply did not exist. The following are some key questions and alternatives approaches to addressing them:

- *What are the costs of NCDs?* Lumping all NCDs into a single disease category is problematic, as their cost profiles can vary considerably by disease, by country, and even within countries. As a first step, the cost profiles of different NCDs among those affected can help answer many questions about the stage or stages at which treatment should be targeted in environments with significant resource constraints. This would also help countries determine whether their systems have ways to reduce costs, for example, by adopting more cost-effective interventions, changing the way services are delivered, or introducing economies of scale in laboratory procedures.
- *What are the benefits of preventing and treating NCDs?* A second basic question relates to the benefits of interventions, including prevention and treatment, but going beyond the clinical context as done by a recent study on HIV treatment (Thirumurthy, Graff-Zivin, and Goldstein 2005), which shows that the benefits of HIV treatment to the individuals in terms of labor supply are lower than the costs of the program. The authors also report that treatment had large positive impacts on school enrollment by children in the family, presumably because the now healthy parents were able to send their children back to school. Thus, evaluating treatment benefits solely on the basis of individuals' outcomes could lead to the wrong policy conclusions.
- *What are the problems that people face in treating NCDs?* Anecdotal information, but little or no empirical data, is available on whether individuals diagnosed with an NCD or risk factor would follow a treatment. Even when information has been provided, individuals may not be able to afford or borrow sufficiently to finance their treatments. The new literature on behavioral economics suggests that problems with bounded rationality (that is, limits on the capacity of individuals to process information, deal with complexity, and pursue rational aims) and self-commitment may play a role. Each of these is a possibility, but little pertinent empirical evidence is currently available.
- *What are the distributional impacts of NCD services?* Understanding the costs and benefits and the market failures in treatments relates to the efficiency aspects of the treatment of chronic illnesses. A second issue is equity. Governments, whether they provide the services or not, need to know the proportion of public expenditure that is spent on the rich and the poor.

Several knowledge generation activities follow on from this framework, among which the following are considered priorities:

- *Knowledge generation activity number 1: long-term monitoring of households.* Both the cross-sectional living standards measurement studies and randomized studies add useful information to our current knowledge. Yet understanding the structure of market failures that prevent treatment or better health outcomes related to NCDs is typically hard, particularly as these require consistent care over time. Small-scale (500 households or so) monitoring studies that follow households over three to five years can help answer at least two of the issues discussed earlier, namely, the costs and benefits of treatment to households that have a member with an NCD and the behavioral issues that people with an NCD face by themselves and within their households.
- *Knowledge generation activity number 2: monitoring and impact evaluation of large-scale programs for control of NCDs.* Demonstrating high levels of efficacy of interventions under ideal conditions is important, but is not sufficient to justify the widespread introduction of an intervention. The efficacy of an intervention measured in a pilot setting can rarely be attained when the intervention is implemented in routine circumstances on a large scale. Therefore, monitoring and evaluating the effectiveness of large-scale programs for the control of NCDs in low- and middle-income settings are important. In collaboration with partner agencies and financiers, the Bank will explore opportunities to commission studies to meet the needs identified earlier. For these studies to be done or commissioned by the Bank is not essential, but having them done or commissioned by institutions with comparative advantages in each area is essential. The options include limited funding by the Bank itself, financing from country budgets with the caveat that publicly funded research is highly constrained in most low-income countries, and financing by other institutions such as foundations and bilateral agencies.

Key Messages

The key messages of this chapter are as follows:

- The Bank will focus its policy discussions with countries on those areas in which it has a comparative advantage in the prevention and control of NCDs. Lending operations will be demand driven. In most cases, they will be undertaken in the context of health sector programs and multisectoral programs that have impacts on the NCD outcomes framework.

- The emphasis will be on affordable and highly effective interventions at the levels of the population and the individual.
- Future Bank support for the control of NCDs will focus on achieving sustainable outcomes in prevention and treatment, with an emphasis on those aspects in which the Bank has a comparative advantage.
- The Bank's approach will be selective and tailored to each context.
- Knowledge generation is an important part of the Bank's agenda pertaining to the control of NCDs.

Notes

1. For further details, see World Bank. "Showcasing Five Years of World Bank Work on Mental Health." World Bank. http://web.worldbank.org/WBSITE/ EXTERNAL/TOPICS/EXTHEALTHNUTRITIONANDPOPULATION/ EXTMH/0,,contentMDK:20468291~menuPK:384019~pagePK:148956~ piPK:216618~theSitePK:384012,00.html. Date consulted: December 3, 2006.

2. High-Level Forum on the Health MDGs. "Summary of Conclusions and Action Points: Post-High Level Forum on the Health MDGs." June 12–13, Tunis. World Bank and World Health Organization. http://www.hlfhealthmdgs.org/ HLF4Tunis/TunisMeetingReport2006Final.pdf. Date consulted: November 15, 2006.

The Basis for Public Intervention in the Control of Noncommunicable Diseases

This appendix contains additional background, mostly of a technical nature, on topics covered in chapters 1 and 2.

Accelerated Mortality Reduction Scenario for Noncommunicable Diseases

The World Health Organization's (WHO's) 2002–30 burden of disease projections are based on historical trends that may or may not persist in the future. As noted in chapter 1, if a wide range of noncommunicable disease (NCD) interventions is successfully adopted in the years ahead, more rapid progress in addressing NCD-related morbidity and mortality may be achieved. What would be a feasible target for NCD mortality reduction? This section provides some additional background to the scenario presented in the main text.

Figure 1.4 showed the implications of doubling historical rates of NCD mortality reduction worldwide during 2005–15. That is, it doubled historical annual decreases in age- and gender-specific NCD mortality rates. The only exception was for males aged 70 and older, for which the baseline projection is a 0.5 percent annual increase in mortality because of strong aging trends. As doubling this positive value would imply a deteriorating trend, the scenario instead incorporates a 0.5 percent annual decrease in mortality for this group, which is close to the doubled rate for females aged 70 and older. Figure A1.1 shows the annual decreases in age- and gender-specific NCD mortality rates in the baseline (that is, historical trends) and doubling scenarios. For information, the figure also includes the additional 2 percent scenario contained in Strong and others (2005) and advocated by WHO (2005a). That scenario subtracted an additional two percentage points from the historical trends.

As noted in the main text, the best-case scenario achieved historically over sustained periods of time has been the 3 percent annual reductions achieved in cardiovascular disease mortality rates in several high-income countries. The doubling scenario was identified as a plausible compromise that significantly improves upon historical rates, but acknowledges that the experiences of high-income countries with excellent medical care are likely to be beyond the reach of most low- and middle-income countries in the immediate future. The doubling scenario would mean that roughly 13 million deaths could be averted for all age groups cumulatively over 2005–15. The corresponding number for the additional 2 percent scenario is 36 million.

As in Strong and others (2005), the estimates here use deaths instead of disability-adjusted life years as the unit of measurement. The calculation of disability-adjusted life year reductions associated with the scenario presented here was beyond the scope of this report, although this is not intended to diminish the potential gains in morbidity reduction that can be achieved through improved NCD outcomes.

Evidence on the Economic Burden of NCDs

The section on "Economic Rationale: Efficiency, Equity, and Budget Implications" in chapter 2 briefly described various findings in the literature on the economic burden of NCDs, particularly in the form of cost of illness studies, and the broader household impact of chronic disease and risk factors. Tables A1.1–A1.4 provide additional information. Note that the literature contains large gaps with regard to explicitly addressing NCDs and their economic burden. More commonly, the literature discusses health in general and leaves readers to infer the possible impact of NCDs in particular (see, for example, Gertler, Levine, and Ames 2004; Russell 2005). Closing this gap should be a priority for future research.

Figure A1.1. Annual Change in Age- and Gender-Specific NCD Death Rates, 2005–15, Alternative Scenarios

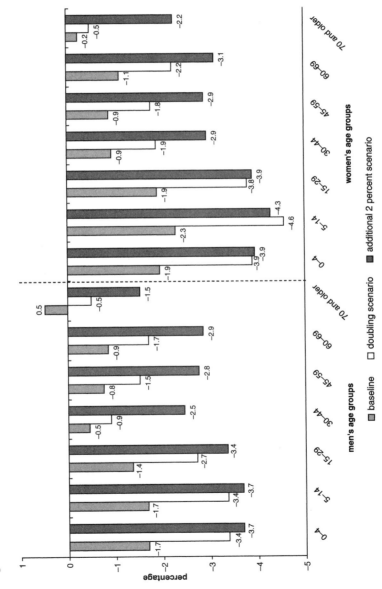

Source: Lopez and others 2006; Strong and others 2005; authors' calculations.

Table A1.1. Cost of Illness Studies for Noncommunicable Diseases and Risk Factors

Economy or group of economies	Condition	Year of estimate	Total costs as a percentage of gross domestic product	Percentage of costs that are indirect	Source
Australia	Tobacco use	1992	3.4	48.7	Collins and Lapsley 1996
Canada	Tobacco use	1991, 1992	1.4–2.2	—	Kaiserman 1997; Xie and others 1996
Canada	Obesity	2001	0.7	69.8	Katzmarzyk and Janssen 2004
China	Tobacco use	1989	1.5	74.4	Hu and Mao 2002
China	Obesity	1995	2.1	23.8	Popkin and others 2001
European Union–25	Cardiovascular disease	2003	1.9	42.8	British Heart Foundation (unweighted averages)[a]
European Union–25	Stroke	2003	0.5	61.4	British Heart Foundation (unweighted averages)[a]
Finland	Tobacco use	1995	0.8	—	Pekurinen 1999
France	Alcohol use	1997	1.4	56.5	Fenoglio, Parel, and Kopp 2003
France	Tobacco use	1997	1.1	49.9	Fenoglio, Parel, and Kopp 2003
Germany	Alcohol use	1995	1.1	—	Horch and Bergemann 2003
Germany	Obesity	1998	0.2	48.2	Sander and Bergemann 2003
Hungary	Tobacco use	1998, 2002	3.2–4.0	—	GKI Economic Research Institute 2004; Szilagyi 2004
India	Tobacco use	1990–91	0.02	—	Rath and Chaudry 1995
India	Obesity	1995	1.1	67.3	Popkin and others 2001
Korea, Rep. of	Tobacco use	1993–98	0.6–1.2	—	Kang and others 2003
Latin America (24-country average)	Diabetes	2000	3.5	72.4	Barcelo and others 2003
Mexico	Diabetes	1995	0.8	—	Villarreal-Rios and others 2002

Country	Condition	Year			Source
Mexico	Hypertension	1999	0.7	—	Villarreal-Rios and others 2002
Myanmar	Tobacco use	1999	0.1	—	Kyaing 2003
Peru	Tobacco use	1997	0.77	—	Chaloupka and Jha 2000
Switzerland	Alcohol use	2001	0.1	—	Frei 2001
Switzerland	Obesity	2002	0.6	—	Schmid and others 2005
Taiwan, China	Tobacco use	2001	0.5	77.8	Yang and others 2005
Tanzania	Diabetes	1992	0.5	—	Chale and others 1992
United Kingdom	Cardiovascular disease	1999	1.0	75.5	Liu and others 2002
United States	Tobacco use	1997–2001	1.7	55.1	Centers for Disease Control and Prevention 2005
United States	Obesity	2000	1.2	47.9	Department of Health and Human Services 2001
United States	Depression	2000	0.8	68.6	Greenberg and others 2003
United States	Diabetes	2002	1.3	30.7	American Diabetes Association[b] 2006
United States	Cardiovascular disease	2006	3.5	36.1	American Heart Association 2006
United States	Hypertension	2006	0.6	25.2	American Heart Association 2006
United States	Stroke	2006	0.5	35.6	American Heart Association 2006
Venezuela, R. B. de	Tobacco use	1997	0.3	—	Pan American Sanitary Bureau 1998

Source: Suhrcke and others 2005.

Note: — = not available.

a. British Heart Foundation. "British Heart Foundation Statistics." British Heart Foundation. http://www.heartstats. org/ eucosts. Date consulted: August 15, 2005.

b. American Diabetes Association. "Direct and Indirect Costs of Diabetes in the United States." American Diabetes Association. http://www.diabetes.org/diabetes-statistics/costs-of-diabetes-in-usjsp. Date consulted: November 15, 2006.

Table A1.2. Estimates of the Annual Per Capita Burden of Cardiovascular Disease, Selected Countries, 2000

(U.S. dollars)

Country	Low estimate	High estimate
Brazil	15.79	21.32
China	5.64	7.62
India	4.78	6.45
Portugal	57.64	77.82
Russia	69.34	93.61
South Africa	22.88	30.88
United States	205.91	277.98

Source: Leeder and others 2004.

Note: Estimates are in potentially productive years of life lost converted to per capita figures based on gross domestic product and population estimates from the World Bank. High estimates are based on alternative studies that used different measures of mortality to produce about a 30 percent increase in potentially productive years of life lost. See Zhou and others 2003.

Table A1.3. Estimated Prevalence of Diabetes among Those Aged 20–79 and Direct Medical Costs Attributable to Diabetes by Region, Selected Years

Region	Prevalence (%) 2003	Prevalence (%) 2025	Direct medical costs, 2003 (US$ billions) Low estimate	High estimate
Developing countries	4.5	5.9	12.3	23.1
East Asia and the Pacific	2.6	3.9	1.4	2.7
Europe and Central Asia	7.6	9.0	2.9	5.3
Latin America and the Caribbean	6.0	7.8	4.6	8.7
Middle East and North Africa	6.4	7.9	2.3	4.3
South Asia	5.9	7.7	0.8	1.6
Sub-Saharan Africa	2.4	2.8	0.3	0.5
Developed countries	7.8	9.2	116.4	217.8
World	5.1	6.3	128.7	240.9

Source: International Diabetes Federation 2003. Narayan and others 2006.

Extent to Which NCDs Matter to the Poor

Chapter 2 provided a brief overview of findings on the extent to which NCDs matter to the poor. This appendix includes graphical representations of the results described earlier (results are drawn primarily from Smith 2006b).

The earlier discussion pointed out that if the burden of disease is measured as total deaths, NCDs appear to be highly important to the world's poor (figure A1.2). NCDs account for about 75 percent or more of the disease burden in all country income groups except the poorest. Even in

Table A1.4. Household Impacts of Chronic Diseases and Risk Factors

Country	Study	Year(s) of study	Condition	Adverse impact
Bangladesh	Kibriya and others 1999	—	Diabetes	6–12 months wages; or US$160 per year.
Bangladesh	Efroymson and others 2001	1991–96	Tobacco use	Male smokers spent 18 times more money on cigarettes than on health and 20 times more than on education, or twice as much as health, education, clothing, and housing combined. This is equivalent to 500 more calories for children's diet: If money were spent on food instead of tobacco, 10.5 million malnourished individuals could have an adequate diet, saving 350 children each day.
China	Hu and others 2005	2002	Tobacco use	The urban poor spend 6.6 percent of their household income on cigarettes.
Egypt	Nassar 2003	1995–2000	Tobacco use	5–6 percent of household income.
India	Shobhana and others 2000	—	Diabetes	15–25 percent of household income for treatment.
India	Bonu and others 2005	1995–96	Tobacco use	OR = 1.35 of borrowing and for distress selling during hospitalization for individuals who use tobacco. OR = 1.38 for nonusers who lived in household with smoking. OR = 1.51 for nonusers in households with both tobacco and alcohol use. Population-attributable risk for borrowing due to tobacco use = 16 percent.
India	Bonu and others 2004	1998–99	Tobacco use	Children are less likely to be immunized and more likely to have acute respiratory infection, to be malnourished, and to die before age one. OR = 1.21 less likely from smoking. OR = 1.15 more likely respiratory illness. OR = 1.21 more likely underweight. 7 percent of infant mortality is attributed to tobacco.
Indonesia	Adioetomo, Djutaharta, and Hendratno 2005	1999	Tobacco use	6.2 percent of household income.
Morocco	Aloui 2003	1998–99	Tobacco use	2.4 percent of household expenditure.

(continued)

Table A1.4. Household Impacts of Chronic Diseases and Risk Factors (*continued*)

Country	Study	Year(s) of study	Condition	Adverse impact
Myanmar	Kyaing 2003	1999	Tobacco use	2.7 percent of household expenditure; 4.4 percent for the lowest quintile.
Nepal	Karki, Pant, and Pande 2003	2001	Tobacco use	9.6 percent of lower household expenditure.
Russia	Suhrcke and others 2005	2002	Chronic disease	5.6 percent of lower median per capita income.
Tanzania	Neuhann and others 2001	1996–98	Diabetes	25 percent of minimum wage; costs exceed per capita health expenditure by a factor of 20.

Source: Suhrcke and others 2005.

Note: — = not available; OR = odds ratio.

Figure A1.2. Causes of Death by World Bank Income Group, 2005

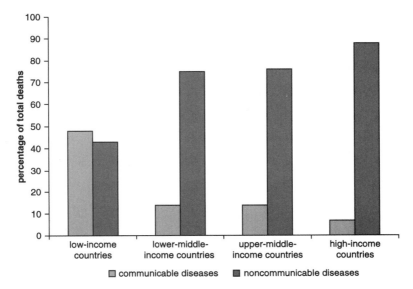

Source: Lopez and others 2006.

low-income countries, NCDs are projected to be the most important cause of death by 2015.

When total deaths are shown, the implicit counterfactual is that all deaths can be averted; however, as shown in figure A1.3, an alternative metric whereby NCDs appear less important is excess deaths. This yardstick addresses the gap between mortality in the world's richest countries and the rest of the world, and thus the implicit counterfactual is the mortality profile that prevails in the world's richest countries. Specifically, excess deaths are calculated by subtracting current deaths due to NCDs and other causes among the world's poorest 80 percent from the number of deaths that would occur if their current population structures had the same age- and gender-specific death rates that now prevail in the world's richest 20 percent (see Gwatkin and Guillot 2000; Smith 2006b).

As the figure indicates, in the world's two poorest quintiles—primarily countries in Africa and South Asia—NCDs account for less than a third of excess deaths. This is in contrast to total deaths, for which India, for example, has an almost equal balance between total deaths due to NCDs as opposed to other causes. The difference between total and excess deaths attributable to NCDs is particularly stark in several large

Figure A1.3. World Income Percentiles and NCDs as a Percentage of Excess Deaths by World Bank Region, 2005

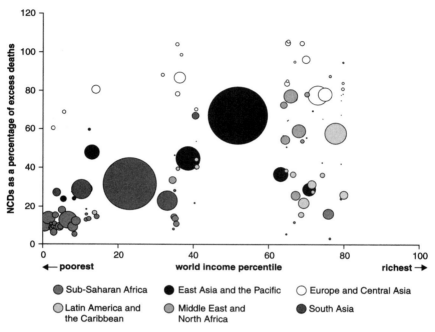

Source: Smith 2006b.

middle-income countries in the fourth quintile. The gap is 25 to 40 percentage points in Algeria, Colombia, Peru, Thailand, and the República Bolivariana de Venezuela. Many of the poor countries where NCDs are important when looking at excess deaths are in the Europe and Central Asia region. In China, NCDs account for about 77 percent of total deaths and 67 percent of excess deaths.

The reason for the gap between the NCD share of total deaths and of excess deaths is the relative size of the difference between underlying mortality rates of the rich and poor for NCDs compared with communicable diseases. As figure A1.4 shows, while the rich-poor gradient is significant for NCDs, it is far smaller than the equivalent gradient for communicable diseases. For NCDs the mortality rate is twice as high for the poor than for the rich; for communicable diseases the ratio is 20 to 1. Whether the data are presented for NCDs in isolation or together with communicable diseases can affect the interpretation of the importance of NCDs.

Figure A1.4. Ratio of Age-Standardized Death Rates in Low- and Middle-Income Countries to Those in High-Income Countries, 2005

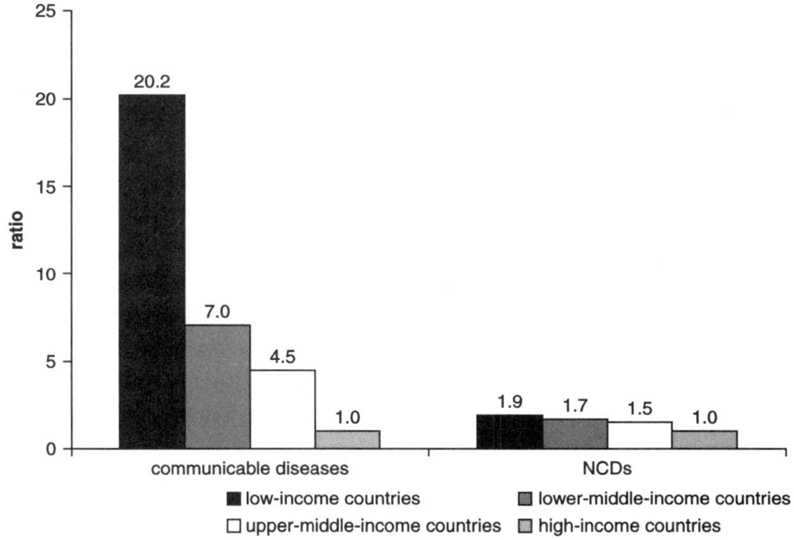

Source: Authors' calculations based on Lopez and others 2006; Mathers and Loncar 2005.

Despite interest in the gradient between rich and poor *within* a country, fewer data are available on this issue. Some evidence suggests that for obesity, the income gradient "twists" as countries, grow richer (Monteiro and others 2004). That is, in poorer countries, obesity is a greater problem for the rich, whereas in richer countries it is more relevant to the poor. This inflection typically appears to take place in the lower-middle-income bracket. This view is supported by evidence from the Europe and Central Asia region that suggests that within countries the poor have both a higher prevalence of NCDs and higher risk factors than the rich (Suhrcke and others forthcoming), but the relationship between risk factors and socioeconomic status appears to vary widely across different world regions (Blakely and others 2005).

Finally, in relation to the distribution of NCD risk factors across income groups, figure A1.5 shows how the presence of four risk factors—adult smoking prevalence, systolic blood pressure, cholesterol, and body mass index—varies across countries. Raw data are presented as standard deviations below (better than) or above (worse than) international averages. The figure indicates that in general, risk factors tend to become worse as countries develop, reflecting the effects of urbanization, dietary changes, and other lifestyle issues. As these are raw data, and all four risk factors are weighted equally, the figure should not be interpreted as a measure of absolute or relative risk in the medical sense.[1]

NCDs and Health Financing

A section in chapter 2 discussed the potential relationship between a larger NCD burden and health expenditures and highlighted upstream and downstream linkages with aging, technology adoption, insurance coverage, and economic growth. The key message was that the aging channel was likely to be a considerably less important determinant of health spending increases than the pressures on age-specific expenditures caused by the other factors. The section emphasized that greater demand for expensive technologies and insurance coverage, both of which could be expected to accompany a growing NCD burden, were key channels that merit policy attention.

Historical experience in a wide range of middle- and high-income countries suggests that age-specific expenditures often increase at a rate

Figure A1.5. Income Percentile and NCD Risk Factors

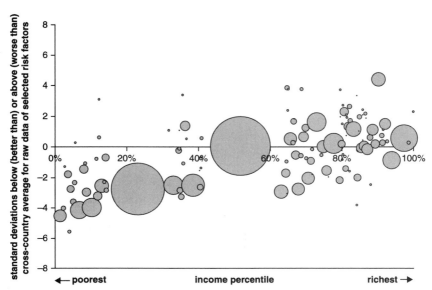

Source: Authors' calculations using data from Lopez and others 2006; WHO. "WHO Global InfoBase Online." WHO. http://www.who.int/ncdsurveillance/infobase/web/InfoBaseCommon/. Date consulted: November 14, 2006.

one to two percentage points faster than gross domestic product growth. Figure A1.6 illustrates that if age-specific expenditures rise at a rate 2 percentage points faster than gross domestic product because of the potential pressures identified earlier, the resulting increase in health spending would be much larger than the impact of aging alone. If the difference was 1 percentage point, the key message would remain. These estimates are approximate and are not intended as formal projections of the growth of health spending in the future (note that projections in World Bank 2006a are considered to be demographic shifts only). Nevertheless, they serve to emphasize the potential impact of NCDs on health spending through age-specific expenditure growth.

The positive message emerging from these estimates is that age-specific expenditures can be substantially influenced by policy, whereas aging cannot. Perhaps the most important policy instrument in this respect is the definition of nascent benefits packages, that is, whether these are provided in the form of social insurance schemes or tax-financed public provision. Decisions must be made about when, for example, anticholesterol drugs, CT scans, mammography, and so on become widely prescribed and applied within publicly funded financial protection mechanisms.

Figure A1.6. Potential Changes in Total Health Spending as a Percentage of Gross Domestic Product, Regional Averages

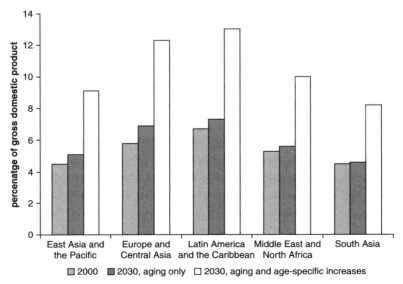

□ 2000   ■ 2030, aging only   ☐ 2030, aging and age-specific increases

Source: Smith 2006a.

An important consideration will be how soon they can be afforded given the revenue stream. As the discussion of technology and insurance highlighted, these are the issues that are likely to play a central role in determining the impact of NCDs on health budgets. Specific approaches could include health technology assessments and the familiar reforms to patient cost sharing, provider payment mechanisms, possible insurance competition, and so on.

An additional policy issue relates to sustainability and the funding of future obligations. Many health financing mechanisms, including tax-financed systems and many social insurance schemes, are financed in a pay-as-you-go manner, in which current contributions fund current beneficiaries. However, in aging societies, revenues will fall while outlays increase, which can lead to insolvency. This highlights the importance of ensuring that health financing systems—whatever form they take—are sustainable over the long-term in the face of a rising burden of NCDs. Despite insufficient evidence to draw clear policy conclusions, medical savings accounts are another option that may be considered.[2]

Notes

1 The report team is engaged in ongoing work to develop a more accurate risk factor index.

2 These are personal savings accounts that are restricted to spending on medical care (see World Bank 2006a for a brief overview).

The Evidence Base for the Prevention and Control of Noncommunicable Diseases

During the second half of the 20th century, most of the scientific research into noncommunicable diseases (NCDs) was oriented toward establishing causal relationships between potential contributory factors and disease. A large body of knowledge was generated concerning specific risk factors as well as broader determinants of health. This information has pointed toward areas of prevention and health promotion, yet knowledge, and even understanding, of causality does not immediately translate into a preventive strategy. The long lag time between the research that established that tobacco use was a major cause of morbidity and mortality in the 1950s and the enactment of preventive interventions in the 1980s and 1990s speaks to a complex pathway.

Preventive interventions for NCDs require more than deciphering the causal relationships and biological explanations of disease. They also require an understanding of human behavior and of relationships among political contexts, economic interests, and public health objectives. Perhaps the most crucial constraint to the effectiveness of prevention has been the lack of proper evaluation of interventions. Programs were often adopted on the basis of a simple cause-and-effect rationale, only for the adopters to find out, after spending resources, that the programs did not work as expected. Examples of this are running school-based tobacco control programs to prevent the uptake of smoking and promoting early detection of breast cancer through breast self-examination among women. Impact evaluations demonstrated that both these approaches were ineffective after they had been widely adopted (Thomas and others 2002; Yach and Wipfli 2006).

In the case of biological interventions, such as drug treatments, chemoprevention, and immunoprevention, the intervention in question must compare favorably with usual care or no intervention. Therefore, comparison of groups that are as similar as possible with and without the intervention is a precondition for recommending use of the intervention. The key to comparability is similarity of the groups, which is achieved through randomization. Ideally, the same standards should be observed for behavioral and organizational prevention and control strategies. For the purpose of this work, evidence that a proposed intervention works was taken to be that for which several evaluation studies have consistently showed the same direction of the effect of a given intervention. Published reviews were searched systematically in various databases and additional studies not contained in the review or that would help answer the questions were also retrieved. The results are presented in a summary that can be understood by nonspecialists.

The evidence is presented at two different levels of action: intersectoral, in which public policies are developed, and intrasectoral, in which interventions occur within the health care system. To ensure transparency, consistency, and attention to developing countries, as much as possible, cost-effectiveness ratios used in this appendix were taken from Jamison and others (2006a), unless otherwise specified.

Premature Mortality

Mortality from NCDs increases with age, but the toll of premature mortality among adults has important consequences for the labor force. To avoid the variability that exists in registering the cause of deaths, figure A2.1 presents the probability that a 15-year-old will die before age 60 (premature mortality) according to gross national income per capita for 2004 in 162 countries. Not surprisingly, among both males and females, mortality is highest in low-income countries and decreases as income per capita increases.

To better understand the causes of premature mortality, figure A2.2 presents estimates of unweighted, discounted (3 percent) disability-adjusted

Figure A2.1. Premature Mortality among Adults Aged 15–59 According to Gross National Income Per Capita in 162 Countries, 2004

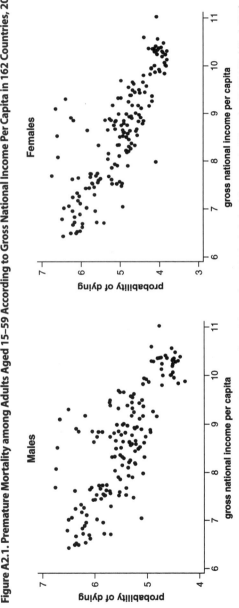

Sources: WHO 2006a. "World Health Statistics 2006." WHO. http://www.who.int/whosis/whostat2006/en/index.html. Date consulted: November 15, 2006; World Bank 2006f.

Note: Gross national income per capita and the probability of dying are expressed as natural logarithms.

Figure A2.2. Premature Mortality: Disability-Adjusted Life Years (DALYs) Lost Attributable to the Most Frequent Risk Factors for Disease by World Bank Region, 2001

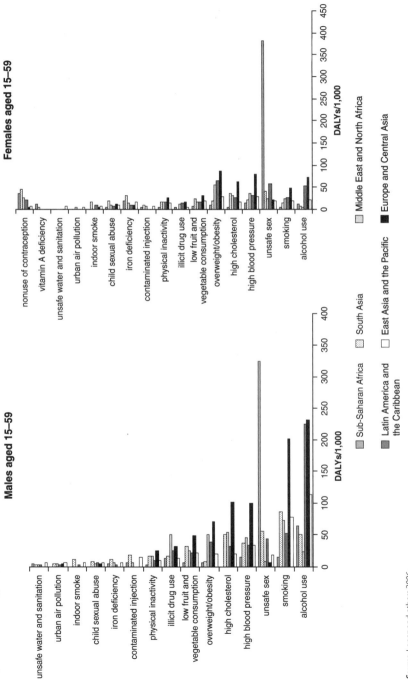

Source: Lopez and others 2006.

life years (DALYs) lost for males and females aged 15–59 attributable to leading risk factors by World Bank region. Worldwide, the most important cause of premature mortality is clearly unsafe sex among males and females in Sub-Saharan Africa, whereas alcohol use and other risk factors for NCDs appear to take a larger toll in other regions. Figure A2.3 presents the same information but excluding Sub-Saharan Africa, which allowed the unmasking of other conditions that present a high risk of premature deaths for adults.

Among males, the leading risk factor is hazardous consumption of alcohol in Europe and Central Asia followed closely by Latin America and the Caribbean. The high number of DALYs also attributable to smoking, high cholesterol, high blood pressure, and overweight and obesity among males and females in Europe and Central Asia speaks to a significant toll of NCDs. Elsewhere among females, these NCD risk factors are an important cause of DALYs, but in Latin America and the Caribbean and in South Asia, unsafe sex and lack of access to contraception are also significant causes of premature mortality. Mortality attributable to smoking is increasing in developing countries, where tobacco control policies have recently or not yet been enacted (box A2.1).

Public Policy

The populations of low- and middle-income countries are increasingly being exposed to the common risk factors, such as tobacco, hazardous use of alcohol, inadequate diet, and lack of physical activity, for the leading NCDs (WHO 2002b). As developed countries have implemented successful tobacco control policies, tobacco use has shifted to developing countries. In the last 20 years, the prevalence of smoking has increased from 30 to 50 percent among men in developing countries, whereas in developed countries the proportion of men who smoke has decreased from 50 to 34 percent (Guindon and Boisclair 2003).

As a consequence of rapid urbanization and concurrent social changes, such as the incorporation of women into the workforce, developing countries have shifted from a simple and monotonous diet to consuming more animal-source foods, fats, sugar, and processed foods (Popkin and Gordon-Larsen 2004). This process is bolstered by the global commercialization of food that is now possible though improvements in technology. The results are higher and increasing rates of high blood pressure, high cholesterol, obesity, and NCDs.

Figure A2.3. Premature Mortality: Disability-Adjusted Life Years (DALYs) Lost Attributable to Most Frequent Risk Factor for Disease, by World Bank Regions excluding Sub-Saharan Africa, 2001

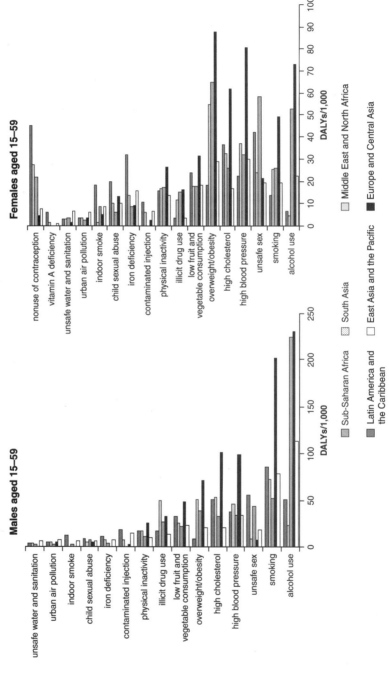

Source: Lopez and others 2006.

Box A2.1

Trends in Mortality Attributable to Smoking

In those high-income and former socialist economies with more complete and reliable mortality statistics than those elsewhere, one can measure the effects of increased smoking prevalence and subsequent decreases that have been observed among large numbers of adults. The changes are best documented by examining lung cancer mortality among young adults, because lung cancer is rarely misclassified with other causes of death at young ages and is almost entirely attributable to smoking, and is an indicator of the trend in mortality of all smoking-related causes.

In the United Kingdom, the age-standardized lung cancer mortality rate among males aged 35–44 per 100,000 fell from 18 in 1950 to 4 by 2000. In contrast, comparable male lung cancer rates in France show the reverse pattern. In France, the increase in smoking occurred some decades later than in the United Kingdom, and declines in smoking began only after 1990. Similarly, a large increase in female lung cancer at young ages was avoided in the United Kingdom, but female lung cancer at young ages continues to rise in France.

Source: Jamison and others 2006a.

Behaviors leading to tobacco use, hazardous use of alcohol, inadequate diet, and lack of physical activity are not only a matter of rational individual choice, but a more complex process whereby the social environment can induce choices (Emmons 2000). The following sections discuss public policies to reduce the behavioral risk factors. The information is organized according to the main types policy levers, where appropriate:[1] (a) economic incentives and disincentives, (b) informational environments, (c) direct regulation, (d) indirect regulation, and (e) deregulation. These are policy instruments for government intervention that are consistent with a population-based approach.

Tobacco Control

No other legal consumer product is as dangerous as tobacco. Evidence of the health hazards of tobacco use has long been established (Doll and Hill 1954; U.S. Surgeon General's Advisory Committee on Smoking and Health 1964). Cigarettes are the most widely used tobacco product, but tobacco use also includes pipe smoking, tobacco chewing, hand-rolled cigarettes, and local forms of tobacco consumption that vary across cultures. According to the World Health Organization (WHO), 4.9 million deaths in 2000 can be attributed to tobacco (WHO 2002b). The figure is increasing in developing countries, which currently account for 56 percent of the tobacco diseases burden (WHO 2002b).

In 1999, a World Bank (1999, p. 34) report addressed the economics of tobacco control. One of its main conclusions was that "it appears unlikely . . . that smokers either know their full risk or bear the full cost of their choice. Governments may consider that intervention is therefore justified, primarily to deter children and adolescents from smoking and to protect nonsmokers, but also to give adults all the information they need to make an informed choice." The report specified that interventions to control demand are more effective than supply-side interventions.[2]

Economic disincentive: increasing the price of tobacco products through excise taxation—Increasing the unit price of tobacco products through excise taxation is the most cost-effective intervention for tobacco control (Ranson and others 2000; Shibuya and others 2003). The World Bank originally estimated a price elasticity of –0.4 for developed countries and –0.8 for developing countries. A systematic review (Hopkins and others 2001) of evaluations of such interventions, mostly in developed countries, reported a median price elasticity for prevalence of tobacco use of –0.15. For tobacco consumption among those who continued to smoke, the median price elasticity was –0.19. Gallus and others (2006) estimated price elasticities for countries in the European Union of –0.43 and for countries not in the European Union of –0.87, closer to the World Bank's original estimates.

Following the publication of the World Bank report and working toward the Framework Convention on Tobacco Control sponsored by WHO, investigators undertook several World Bank–sponsored studies on the economics of tobacco control in developing countries using data from household surveys. All the studies used the same methodology (Wilkins, Yurekli, and Hu 2003) and consistently reported a significant decrease in consumption with a 10 percent rise in real price, but with a wider variation than the original World Bank (1999) estimates (table A2.1).

Studies that analyzed data by socioeconomic group document that responsiveness to price increase is higher among poor smokers (Hu and others 2006; Townsend, Roderick, and Cooper 1994; Van Walbeek 2005). Subsequent to tax increases, those of lower socioeconomic status smoke fewer cigarettes per day and cheaper brands than affluent smokers.

Table A2.1. Expected Decrease in Cigarette Consumption per 10 Percent Rise in the Real Price of Cigarettes, Selected Developing Countries, Circa 2000

Country	Expected decrease (%)
Asia	
Bangladesh	2.7
China	5.4
Indonesia	3.4
Nepal	8.8
Sri Lanka	5.3
Thailand	3.9
Eastern Europe	
Bulgaria	8.0
Estonia	3.4
Turkey	1.9
Latin America	
Argentina	2.7
Bolivia	8.5
Brazil	2.5
Chile	2.2
Uruguay	4.9
Middle East	
Egypt	4.0
Morocco	5.1

Sources: Adioetomo, Djutaharta, and Hendratno 2005; Alcaraz 2005; Ali, Rahman, and Rahman 2003; Aloui 2003; Arunatilake and Opatha 2003; Debrott Sanchez 2005; Gonzales-Rozada 2005; Hu and Mao 2002; Iglesias and Nicolau 2005; Karki, Pant, and Pande 2003; Nassar 2003; Onder 2002; Ramos and Curti 2005; Sayginsoy 2002; Taal 2004. These reports are available on line at http://www.worldbank.org and for Latin America at http://www.paho.org.

Adolescents and young adults are particularly sensitive to price increases (Lewit and others 1997; Liang and Chaloupka 2002). This is important, because most smokers initiate tobacco use before age 25 and become addicted during the first few years of use (Clark and others 2005). In the United States, expenditure on tobacco marketing exceeds US$15.5 billion per year, 71.4 percent of it through price discounts,[3] which speaks to the importance of price interventions.

Policy makers are concerned that by increasing tobacco taxes, and hence the price of tobacco, illicit trade in tobacco could increase, and this argument is widely used. At the same time, this is a practice condoned by tobacco companies, as shown in court records of proceedings during which tobacco company executives were found guilty of complicity in smuggling operations (Warner 2000). The level of illicit tobacco trade has been correlated with the corruption perception index, also known as the transparency index,[4] indicating that smuggling is more likely to occur in those countries where corruption is high (Merriman, Yurekli, and Chaloupka 2000). Figure A2.4 shows the relationship between the reverse transparency index and cigarette smuggling. According to Merriman, Yurekli, and Chaloupka, the level of transparency explains the amount of smuggling that occurs as much as price and taxes.

Several countries have significantly reduced illicit trade. Spain, for example, reduced illicit trade from 16 to 2 percent in five years (1996–2001) by strengthening law enforcement, which included seizing smuggled tobacco products and levying a fine covering the costs of the seizure (Wilkins, Yurekli, and Hu 2003). Malaysia and the United Kingdom have taken a proactive approach by marking domestic cigarettes packages with information and special ink to identify smuggled and counterfeit products (Joossens and Raw 2000).

Smuggling is an important problem, but rather than forgoing the well-established public health and fiscal benefits of high tobacco prices by lowering the price of tobacco in an attempt to reduce smuggling, it should be addressed as a law enforcement issue. Canada learned this from experience. In the 1990s, the Canadian government reduced the

Figure A2.4. Reverse Transparency Index and Estimated Smuggling as a Share of Tobacco Consumption, Selected Countries, 2000

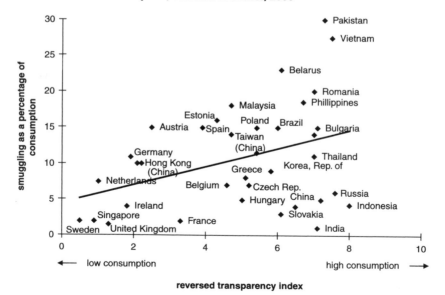

Source: Merriman, Yurekli, and Chaloupka 2000.
Note: $R^2 = 0.2723$. The reverse transparency index explains 27.23 percent of the variations in smuggling as a percentage of consumption.

tobacco taxes to control illicit trade as advocated by the tobacco companies. As a consequence, the year after the tax cuts the government's revenues fell by Can$1.2 billion and smoking among children increased (Hamilton and others 1997).

A country's institutional capacity to control illicit tobacco trade needs to be considered when increasing the price of tobacco products. At least in part, the control of illicit trade could be self-financed through fines. In addition, data show that despite smuggling, tax increases do have an effect on tobacco consumption and do increase revenues (Gruber, Sen, and Stabile 2003).

Informational environment—The informational environment for tobacco control at the population level is mainly shaped through antitobacco mass media campaigns, advertisements against tobacco use, advertising bans, and warning labels on tobacco products. Evaluation of these interventions poses several methodological challenges, such as assessing the exposure and intensity of the campaign, determining whether the control group has been contaminated, and separating the campaign's effects from those of other interventions. Three out of five published experimental studies that met quality criteria for a systematic review reported a reduction in smoking prevalence following a media campaign (Farrelly, Niederdeppe, and Yarsevich 2003). Two review papers state that media campaigns can improve outcomes when used in conjunction with other interventions (Hopkins and others 2001; Sowden and Arblaster 2000). Antitobacco media campaigns that have documented reductions in the prevalence of tobacco use have been carefully planned, adequately funded, and based on solid theoretical grounds and formative research (Farrelly, Niederdeppe, and Yarsevich 2003; Hopkins and others 2001).

Despite some controversy about the methods used to evaluate the effect of bans on advertising tobacco, it continues to be one of the most heavily advertised products in the world. In the United States before the advertising ban in 1970, most of the advertising budget was spent on television and radio. Since then, newspapers and magazines have been the preferred advertising channel, and the total marketing budget has continued to increase. A study with data from 22 high-income countries (Saffer and Chaloupka 2000) estimated that a total advertising ban could reduce smoking among adults by 6.3 percent.

Another information strategy is the placement of warning labels on cigarette packages, advertisements, and points of sale. Most evaluations have shown positive results in terms of people reading, recalling, and understanding the messages (Strahan and others 2002). A study conducted in Canada at the time when warning labels were increased to cover 50 percent of the package, front and back, and included vivid images and clear messages, demonstrated a positive relationship between the depth of cognitive processing of the messages and the intention to quit or actual quitting of tobacco use among adults (Hammond and others 2003).

Regulation to reduce harm to others: secondhand smoke—Regulations restricting or banning smoking in the workplace have decreased the number of cigarettes smoked, increased attempts to quit among smokers, and reduced the prevalence of tobacco use (Farrelly, Evans, and Sfekas 1999; Fichtenberg and Glantz 2002). An analysis of the 50 states and the District of Columbia in the United States (McMullen and others 2005) found that the extent of legislation related to exposure to clean indoor air had a positive association with the proportion of indoor workers reporting a smoke-free workplace and an inverse association with the prevalence of smoking among 12- to 17-year-olds. A large body of evidence indicates that eliminating involuntary exposure to tobacco smoke is an effective component of tobacco control policies (Department of Health and Human Services 2006).

Around the world, the hospitality industry has raised concerns about the potential loss of income to its businesses if it adopts a smoke-free policy. In reviews of the studies evaluating the effect of smoke-free policies, none of the studies that met the quality criteria found a decrease in revenue for bars and restaurants (Jossens 2005; Scollo and others 2003). The studies that found a negative effect did not measure objective outcomes, were based on opinions, and most were funded by the tobacco industry. Empirical evidence (Bartosch and Pope 2002), including an analysis of the long-term effects in California (Cowling and Bond 2005), which put smoking bans into effect in restaurants in 1992 and in bars in 1995, showed that taking existing trends into account, revenues for bars and restaurants actually increased after a ban on smoking.

Deregulation: over-the-counter nicotine replacement therapy—Several analyses demonstrate the effectiveness of nicotine replacement therapy, physician's advice, and use of the antidepressant bupropion on smoking cessation (Hughes, Stead, and Lancaster 2004; Silagy and others 2004). Individual interventions such as these tend to have lower population impact and be less cost-effective than public policy (table A2.2).

Table A2.2. Cost-Effectiveness of Interventions to Control Tobacco Addiction
(US$/DALY)

Intervention	Cost-effectiveness ratio	Comments
33 percent price increase by means of tobacco taxes	22	These estimates are based on a price elasticity of demand of 8 percent (p. 875)
Interventions in the information environment, restrictions to reduce smoking in the workplace and public places, and interventions to reduce smuggling of tobacco products	353	There is evidence of effectiveness for each of these interventions (p. 876)
Nicotine replacement therapy for smoking cessation	396	Individual approach, with the potential to avert only 23 percent of the deaths averted by tax increases (p. 76)

Source: Jamison and others 2006a.

Nonetheless, if affordable, deregulation of nicotine replacement therapy to be sold over the counter and efforts to reduce its price can be useful for smoking cessation programs (Hughes and others 2003).

International treaty—Since its initial stages when WHO convened the parties involved, the World Bank has supported the international treaty known as the Framework Convention for Tobacco Control. The World Bank has worked with countries on economic analyses for tobacco control and made the information from this work widely available.[5] The treaty came into force in February 2005, and countries that have ratified the convention are obligated under international law to enact its provisions. All signatories participate in the conference of parties, which meets regularly to monitor the progress of the treaty's provisions and facilitate their implementation. The challenge now is to bridge the gap between ratification and implementation by gaining a better understanding of the political economy of the development of policies for tobacco control and helping countries execute the convention.

Hazardous Use of Alcohol

Hazardous alcohol use constitutes an important risk factor for premature mortality in many developing countries. Among men aged 15 to 59, it accounts for 23.1 percent of DALYs in Europe and Central Asia, 22.5 percent in Latin America and the Caribbean, and 11.3 percent in East Asia. The alcohol-related burden of disease is much lower for women: 7.3 percent in Europe and Central Asia, 5.3 percent in Latin America and the Caribbean, and 2.2 percent in East Asia. Hazardous use is defined as an average rate of consumption of alcohol of more than 20 grams daily for women and 40 grams daily for men (Lopez and others 2006; Room, Babor, and Rehm 2005). Even though this is a significant quantity of alcohol, it does not account for the various patterns of drinking, nor does it reflect that even small quantities of alcohol can impair neuro-logical functions and reasoning enough to cause harm. Examples of this are motor vehicle accidents and injuries from violence caused while under the influence of alcohol (Room, Babor, and Rehm 2005).

Patterns of drinking are cultural and context specific and vary greatly across societies, as does the type of alcohol that people prefer. For example, among drinkers in southern Europe, where social drinking frequently takes place in conjunction with meals, 41 percent prefer wine and another 41 percent prefer beer, whereas in Eastern Europe, 68 percent of drinkers prefer spirits and the predominant pattern is binge drinking (Chisholm and others 2004; Nicholson and others 2005). In some areas, alcohol drinking is more clearly linked to festivities, such as the carnivals in Brazil and in Trinidad and Tobago, whereas in others it is predominant in spe-cific population groups, for example, indigenous populations in Canada and the United States (Room, Babor, and Rehm 2005). In the Americas, more than 50 percent of drinkers prefer beer (Chisholm and others 2004). Therefore, interventions need to vary according to the context and estimates of cost-effectiveness can only point toward potential areas of action, particularly when these estimates rely on mathematical modeling rather than on empirical data.

Economic disincentives—Alcohol consumption is sensitive to price increases. In general, younger people are most responsive, but hazardous drinkers also decrease their alcohol consumption. The price elasticity of demand, however, varies substantially according to prevailing drinking patterns in the population (Babor and Caetano 2005). Unintended consequences of price increases are home production of alcoholic drinks and illicit trade, yet various econometric studies conclude that the benefits of increasing alcohol prices far outweigh the costs (Osterberg 2004). The effect of excise taxation is not as important if the prevalence of alcohol use is low, but it contributes to government revenues if the revenue collection system is efficient.

Informational environment—Although many countries frequently provide information to the public on the hazards of alcohol use (Babor and Caetano 2005), this has not been found to influence consumption patterns. Other information strategies for which evidence of effectiveness is inconclusive include public service announcements, advertisement restrictions, advertisements against alcohol consumption, warning labels, and school-based programs. Nevertheless, communication strategies can be useful for gaining popular support for regulations (Osterberg 2004).

Regulations—Several regulations aimed at decreasing the availability of alcohol have shown some level of effectiveness, while others have been counterproductive. Total prohibition has been enforced in several countries and is an established practice in Islamic countries, but in the absence of social acceptance of prohibition, illegal alcohol production and smuggling have meant that the harm has been greater than the benefits (Jernigan and others 2000).

Evidence with regard to restrictions on the number of outlets and their location is inconclusive (Osterberg 2004), but restrictions on the hours and days of operation have been shown to decrease alcohol consumption and related injuries in Sweden (Norstrom and Skog 2005). Alcohol strikes—defined in Finland as the restriction of sales during popular games or festivities—have been shown to reduce drinking among heavy drinkers, public disturbances, violent crimes, and alcohol-related hospital admissions (Cook and Moore 2002). These findings need to be further evaluated, but could be applicable in many circumstances.

The minimum drinking age in many countries coincides with the legal age of adulthood, except in the United States, where setting the minimum drinking age at 21 while the legal age of adulthood remained at 18 had an effect on consumption and alcohol-related injuries. Studies in several states show that increasing the drinking age from 18 to 21 reduced motor vehicle crashes by 10 percent (Shults and others 2001).

Licensing places that can sell alcohol, such as bars and restaurants, has been an important policy in the industrial countries, in particular to enforce restrictions of sales to minors and to intoxicated individuals. Some indications suggest that holding both owners and patrons legally liable for infringing the law and risking the alcohol sales license may limit hazardous drinking in public places (Babor and Caetano 2005).

Indirect regulation—Because one of the main causes of death from alcohol is motor vehicle accidents, legislation that discourages drunk driving is critical to alcohol control. In the United States, as states reduced the legal alcohol level allowed for drivers from 0.10 grams per deciliter (g/dl) to 0.08 g/dl, fatalities decreased by 7 percent (Jernigan and others 2000). The level of blood alcohol concentration at which driving is against the law varies by country and jurisdiction, ranging from 0.08 g/dl in most industrial countries to zero in Japan. Young motorists, motorcycle drivers, and commercial drivers are at higher risk for motor vehicle accidents in general. A recent report by WHO and the World Bank recommended setting the limit for blood alcohol concentration at 0.05 g/dl in general and 0.02 g/dl for young people and motorcycle drivers (WHO and World Bank 2004). The level at which alcohol affects an individual's motor skills, sense of balance, visual acuity, and reasoning varies from person to person. WHO and the World Bank (2004) have documented that the relative risk for involvement in a crash increases significantly at 0.04 g/dl and above.

The effectiveness of drunk driving legislation is directly related to the level of enforcement. Taking random breath samples from motorists has been found to decrease fatalities by 6 to 10 percent (Chisholm and others 2004). Several economic evaluations have reported that random breath testing is the most effective strategy to decrease fatalities from drunk driving. Severe penalties also contribute to decreased drunk driving, of which the most effective have been found to be suspension of the driver's license (Osterberg 2004).

Deregulation—Considerable evidence indicates that when government-owned alcohol monopolies are privatized, alcohol consumption increases (Osterberg 2004). This is likely to occur because government-owned outlets tend to be few, have shorter operating hours, and are more likely to control sales to minors (Babor and Caetano 2005). A review of cost-effective interventions to reduce high-risk alcohol use is presented in table A2.3.

Food and Nutrition

Substantial evidence exists that high consumption of energy-dense food and low consumption of fruits and vegetables increase the risk for chronic diseases (International Agency for Research on Cancer 2002b; WHO 2002b). Worldwide, low intake of fruits and vegetables accounts for 26.7 million DALYs and obesity accounts for 33.4 million DALYs, and together are comparable to the burden of disease of undernutrition-related deficiencies. Iron deficiency accounts for 35.1 million DALYs, vitamin A deficiency for 26.6 million DALYs, and zinc deficiency for 28.0 million DALYs. Although undernutrition-related deficiencies

Table A2.3. Cost-Effectiveness of Interventions to Reduce High-Risk Alcohol Use by World Bank Region

Intervention	Coverage (%)[a]	Europe and Central Asia	Latin America and the Caribbean	Sub-Saharan Africa	East Asia and the Pacific	South Asia
Cost-effectiveness relative to no intervention (US$/DALY averted)						
Excise tax on alcoholic beverages (current situation)	0.95	141	225	104	516	2,671
Excise tax on alcoholic beverages (25 percent increase)	0.95	127	202	100	447	3,654
Excise tax on alcoholic beverages (50 percent increase)	0.95	**116**	**184**	**95**	394	4,641
Reduced access to alcoholic beverage retail outlets	0.95	216	340	152	146	827
Comprehensive advertising ban on alcohol	0.95	185	380	134	**123**	1,123
Random breath testing of motor vehicle drivers	0.80	1,856	1,542	973	984	531
Brief advice to heavy drinkers by a primary care physician	0.50	270	502	204	224	**462**
Combination: highest tax + brief advice	n.a.	216	350	143	269	845
Combination: highest tax + advertising ban + random breath testing + brief advice	n.a.	381	546	229	383	707
DALYs averted/US$ million expenditure						
Excise tax on alcoholic beverages (current situation)	0.95	7,107	4,435	9,633	1,937	374
Excise tax on alcoholic beverages (25 percent increase)	0.95	7,847	4,953	10,007	2,239	274
Excise tax on alcoholic beverages (50 percent increase)	0.95	**8,590**	**5,442**	**10,553**	2,536	215
Reduced access to alcoholic beverage retail outlets	0.95	4,638	2,940	6,580	6,856	1,209
Comprehensive advertising ban on alcohol	0.95	5,417	2,631	7,442	**8,139**	891
Random breath testing of motor vehicle drivers	0.80	539	648	1,027	1,016	1,882
Brief advice to heavy drinkers by a primary care physician	0.50	3,705	1,992	4,891	4,460	**2,163**

(continued)

Table A2.3. Cost-Effectiveness of Interventions to Reduce High-Risk Alcohol Use by World Bank Region (Continued)

Intervention	Coverage (%)[a]	Europe and Central Asia	Latin America and the Caribbean	Sub-Saharan Africa	East Asia and the Pacific	South Asia
Combination: highest tax + brief advice	n a.	4,627	2,859	7,016	3,718	1,184
Combination: highest tax + advertising ban + random breath testing + brief advice	n.a.	2,621	1,833	4,364	2,612	1,415

Source: Jamison and others 2006a.
Note: n.a. = not applicable. Bold figures indicate the most cost-effective strategy for reducing high-risk alcohol use based on the model for the region.
[a] Refers to the modeled percentage of all high-risk drinkers exposed to the intervention.

account for 10 times the number of DALYs than overnutrition-related risk factors in low-income African countries, the relationship starts to reverse in middle-income countries. In middle-income countries, DALYs attributable to vitamin A and zinc deficiencies are nearly one-seventh of those attributable to obesity and low intake of fruits and vegetables.[6]

Two features that present policy challenges characterize changes in the patterns of overweight and obesity in developing countries. The first is that the obesity epidemic in developing countries is occurring at a faster pace than economic development (Monteiro and others 2004; Popkin 2002; Popkin and Gordon-Larsen 2004), finding countries unprepared. The second characteristic, and possibly a consequence of the first, is that overnutrition and undernutrition may occur in the same household (Doak and others 2000).

Figure A2.5 shows the nutritional status per 100 households in three large countries: Brazil, China, and Russia. Overweight and obesity represent the largest proportion of the nutritional problem in Brazil and Russia,[7] whereas in China, 38 percent of the households were classified as normal. Although in China this does not necessarily represent a lower risk, as Asian populations have higher risk at lower levels of body mass index (WHO Expert Consultation 2004). In all three countries, between 8 and 11 percent of households had at least one overweight or obese member and at least one underweight member. A study of 27 developing countries (Garrett and Ruel 2005) reported a similar proportion of pairs of stunted children and overweight mothers. The authors report that this phenomenon was higher in Latin America and correlated positively with gross domestic product, but not with urban

Figure A2.5. Prevalence of Overweight and Obesity and Underweight by Household in Three Large Countries: Evidence of the Double Burden of Disease

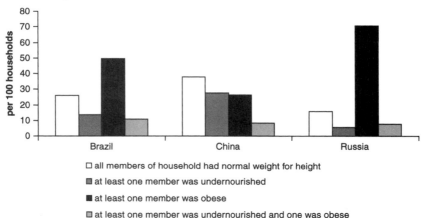

Source: Doak and others 2000.

residence. Originally, obesity in low-income countries was interpreted as being more prevalent among higher socioeconomic groups. More recently, a trend analysis of survey data in Brazil (Monteiro, Conde, and Popkin 2004) showed that undernutrition among women declined by half during 1975–89, both in the poorest 25 percent of the population and in the richest 25 percent. During 1989–97, undernutrition did not change in either group, but obesity increased by 59 percent among the poorest 25 percent of women and decreased by 23 percent among the richest 25 percent of women.

The rapid changes in the prevalence of obesity across different socioeconomic groups can be understood by looking at the agro-food system as a whole and not only through the lens of nutrition and individual behaviors and their biological consequences. Over the past 20 years, food production and distribution have changed significantly. Technology has permitted the development of specialized agro-industry on a large scale. The biological adaptation of crops; the reduction of production costs; and the improvement of conditions for trade, such as transportation and removal of trade barriers, have given way to the globalization of food markets (Hawkes 2006). Countries often set most of their regulatory measures to comply with trade agreements and to facilitate exports of agricultural products. In most countries, fruits and vegetables remain mostly for local consumption, hence governments have had few incentives to regulate, support, or set standards for these products. In contrast, grains and oilseeds have dominated agricultural trade, and processed foods and beverages are also important. These goods are traded in international markets and represent a larger share of retail than fruits and vegetables, yet the availability of low-priced processed foods, usually energy dense, is precisely what spearheads the increasing rates of overweight and obesity, particularly in urban environments. Prepared foods are an attractive option for busy working adults, even those in lower socioeconomic groups (Cutler, Glaeser, and Shapiro 2003; Popkin and Gordon-Larsen 2004). Although open produce markets still exist in most developing countries, cities are increasingly limiting the locations and hours of operation of such markets, which decreases access, especially for people with no means of transportation.

Globally, the lead in food distribution has been taken by large supermarket chains, which in turn have changed procurement and retail practices, moving toward centralized purchase and distribution with sophisticated logistic systems (Reardon and others 2003). Although fruits and vegetables represent a small share of the total food retailed by supermarkets, the produce section is key to marketing and to the store's competitive position (Cacho 2003). Large distributors, usually owned by the same supermarket company, set their own standards for purchasing fruits and vegetables, thus small farmers, who cannot meet the standards and compete, are driven out of the market (Reardon and Berdegue 2002).

For distributors, selling to small-scale stores is too costly, and for such stores stocking perishable goods is costly as well. At the same time, the location of large-scale stores or supermarkets is not random. Supermarkets are more profitable in high-income neighborhoods, which leave small food stores to serve poor neighborhoods. In areas with no supermarkets, the consumer has limited choices consisting mainly of dense-energy foods and few fruits and vegetables (Rex and Blair 2003). This may explain the findings of a large study in the United States that reported higher prevalence of overweight and obesity in urban areas with no supermarkets (Morland, Diez Roux, and Wing 2006). In this study, individuals living in neighborhoods that only had grocery or convenience stores (or both) had a 14 to 18 percent higher prevalence of overweight and a 48 to 60 percent higher prevalence of obesity than those living in urban areas with supermarkets after adjusting for individual-level variables related to obesity. The results of economic research are consistent with those of epidemiological studies and further suggest that people's food choices are constrained by availability and price

(Andrieu, Darmon, and Drewnowski 2006; Chou, Grossman, and Saffer 2004; Cutler, Glaeser, and Shapiro 2003; Drewnowski and Darmon 2005; French 2003; Glanz and others 1998; Khan and others 2004; Mancino 2003).

Economic incentives and disincentives: searching for balance— Analyses from developed countries have pointed toward increased consumption of energy-dense snacks as a factor in the causal chain of obesity (Cutler, Glaeser, and Shapiro 2003; Nielsen and Popkin 2004). Public health advocates have proposed taxing these snacks, among other price interventions (Nestle and Jacobson 2000). An economic analysis assessing the effects of taxing snack foods in the United States found that an excise tax of 1 percent per pound or a 1 percent price increase would not appreciably alter consumption, but it would generate US$40 million to US$100 million per year in tax revenues (Kuchler, Tegene, and Harris 2004). An analysis by the Food and Agriculture Organization of the United Nations (Schmidhuber 2004) predicted low demand elasticity for snacks in high-income groups and high demand elasticity in low-income groups. A study in China (Guo and others 1999) documented consumers' reaction to changes in the price of various foods items. It showed that pork consumers in the lowest income strata were three times more responsive to a price increase than consumers in the highest income strata. Thus subsequently, consumption of vegetable oils and unsaturated fats increased only among the rich as the poor did not have other alternatives and suffered the undesired consequence of decreased protein intake. In places that have concurrent overnutrition and undernutrition, taxing specific food items requires careful analysis, otherwise it may have little effect on obesity and may increase undernutrition.

Goodman and Anise's (2006, p. 20) review of economic instruments to reduce consumption of foods high in saturated fats and other energy-dense foods concluded that "the price inelasticity of foods may dampen the effect of economic instruments." The authors reported that they did not find empirical evaluations, only limited observational studies, such as the Guo and others (1999) study. Modeling exercises in Europe, however, suggest that increasing the price of nutrients could have a much larger effect than increasing the price of certain food items. One study stated that putting a tax on sugar would have a much larger effect than taxes on fat or subsidies on dietary fiber, particularly among younger and older consumers and those belonging to low socioeconomic groups. A report commissioned in the United Kingdom agrees with these findings and warns of the potential regressivity of a fat tax, as total energy intake would not be significantly modified.

The market is responding differently to the externalities of the obesity epidemic: insurance companies offer discounts for people with normal body weight, employers provide access to exercise facilities to prevent obesity and NCDs, car insurers and airlines have instituted special policies for the obese, and even the U.S. Internal Revenue Service reimburses taxpayers for treatment of obesity if not covered by health insurance.[8] The question is whether taxing risk, directly or indirectly through insurance premiums or use of private services, would be more effective and efficient than taxes on specific food items or nutrients. A caveat is that such a tax may be regressive, as excess weight results from a diet of poor nutritional value, which is more prevalent among the poor, but it could provide an incentive if young adults of normal weight committed to maintaining a healthy weight in exchange for long-term lower health insurance premiums.

Informational environment—Three strategies can be effective in shaping the informational environment toward a quality diet: the provision of information and education to the population at large, the provision of information at the point of purchase and food labeling, and the restriction of advertising and of health claims. According to several systematic reviews (Ammerman and others 2002; Pignone and others 2003; Pomerleau and others 2005), direct education, delivered either by telephone or in person, is the most effective intervention; however, individual interventions can be resource intensive, have a lower population impact, and are not always feasible in low- and middle-income countries.

Research has shown the benefits of point-of-purchase information, such as labeling healthier food selections in supermarkets and providing information about low calorie and low fat meals in restaurants, cafeterias, and vending machines (Matson-Koffman and others 2005). Nutrition labels on food packages have become widespread, but these are voluntary, and in most countries are not subject to standards. Ten countries where nutrition labels are mandatory based their decision on cost-benefit analyses. Their studies concluded that under the assumption that food labels contribute to consumers' choices, the savings in health care costs outweigh the cost of labeling (Hawkes 2004). However, the predominant users of nutrition labels to inform choices are young women and people with higher levels of education. Two systematic reviews found that consumers regarded labels as complex (Baines and Lata 2004; Cowburn and Stockley 2005). These results suggest that labeling is insufficient and that additional educational interventions are needed. In addition, in countries with low literacy rates, some form of graphical representation may be more useful.

Several developed countries are undertaking measures to regulate advertising to children. Food advertising to children has been banned in Quebec, Canada, since 1980; in Sweden since 1991; and in Norway since 1992. Although no formal evaluation of the impact of these bans has been published (Hawkes 2004), an extensive review of the literature on children's preferences concluded that children aged 2 to 11 were highly influenced by television advertising, but that older children were less affected (Committee on Food Marketing and the Diets of Children and Youth and others 2006).

Direct regulation—The Codex Alimentarius Commission of the Joint Food and Agricultural Organization of the United Nations and WHO Food Standards Program addresses food labeling and health claims. The Codex Alimentarius is a set of international standards, guidelines, and texts pertaining to food products developed to protect the consumer. The World Trade Organization recognizes the Codex Alimentarius as a reference for international trade and trade disputes. The Codex Alimentarius does not bind countries to a mandatory food label and is enforced only if a nutrition claim arises. European Union countries base their regulations on the European Commission's regulation on nutrition labeling (Council Directive 90/496/EEC as amended by Commission Directive 2003/120/EC).[9]

Based on results from etiologic research and on experience in the United States and Europe, academics and advocacy groups proposed that legislation to replace saturated fats with unsaturated fats, including sources of omega-3 fatty acids, would reduce the risk of ischemic heart disease by reducing low-density lipoprotein cholesterol. Table A2.4 presents the potential cost-effectiveness of such measure under two assumptions of cost. European manufacturers have already altered production methods to eliminate trans-fatty acids. and in the United States, the requirement to label trans-fatty acid content has led food manufacturers to follow suit. Given the biological rationale, such modification is sensible if it includes oils used for cooking, but additional evaluations are necessary to assess whether it actually leads to significant reductions in ischemic heart disease and diabetes. Conservative cost-effective estimates derived from modeling

**Table A2.4. Incremental Cost-Effectiveness Ratios for Legislation Substituting
2 Percent of Energy from Trans Fat with Polyunsaturated Fat by World Bank Region**
(US$/DALY averted)

| | Intervention cost | |
Region	US$0.50/adult	US$6/adult
East Asia and the Pacific	73	1,583
Europe and Central Asia	65	1,670
Latin America and the Caribbean	40	1,865
Middle East and North Africa	25	2,259
South Asia	38	1,014
Sub-Saharan Africa	53	1,344

Source: Jamison and others 2006a.

assume a 7 percent reduction in ischemic heart disease at a cost as low as US$38 per DALY if the intervention is a low-cost one.

Researchers have proposed the reduction of salt content in foods, which could be beneficial in places where consumption of processed foods is high. Such regulations could have important economic consequences for trade, food production, and agricultural policies. In general, regulatory mechanisms, whether on their own or attached to legislation, tend to be politically difficult, because stakeholders resist them (Hawkes 2006). Even though industry may already have the technology, modifying a product has a cost, thus it is more conservative to err on the side of higher costs for the intervention when estimating cost-effectiveness.

Deregulation—An example of deregulation, while not planned, took place in Poland. In the 1990s, as part of its economic reforms, the country eliminated subsidies for dairy products and other animal fats. At the same time, the market was opened to imports of fruits and vegetables. Zatonski, McMichael, and Powles (1998) reported a significant decrease in mortality from ischemic heart disease following this period and attributed the decrease to dietary changes following the deregulation. Zatonski and Willett (2005) further compared the relationship between an increased ratio of dietary polyunsaturated fat to saturated fat and the risk of ischemic heart disease in a U.S. cohort study and reported remarkably similar trends through 2002; however, their results have been questioned on the basis of a lack of consistency of this association across studies that assessed individual risk (Ravnskov 2005). The data from Poland show that reducing cardiovascular disease (CVD) is feasible over a short period of time. The inconsistency with individual-level data highlights the methodological difficulties of establishing relationships that occur at different levels of social organizations, from agricultural policy to individual risks.

Physical Activity

Solid scientific evidence of the health benefits of regular physical activity is available (Department of Health and Human Services 1996). Increasing and sustaining regular physical activity in adults at any age increases disability-free life expectancy and reduces the risk of CVD, diabetes, colon cancer, and osteoporosis. Moderate physical activity has therapeutic effects on high blood pressure and depression and increases cognitive functions in middle-aged adults (Kahn and others 2002; Singh-Manoux and others 2005; Whelton and others 2002).

Experimental and quasi-experimental studies in communities and workplaces have shown that using prompts at points of decision, such as stairs, increases the odds of physical activity (Matson-Koffman and others 2005). Randomized trials indicate that direct intervention and supervision improve physical activity in previously sedentary individuals (Hillsdon, Foster, and Thorogood 2005). Research on work site promotion of physical activity has shown inconsistent results (Dishman and others 1998; Matson-Koffman and others 2005), yet the inconsistency appears to be more an issue of the actual intervention than of the work setting. Note that these are all individual-level interventions with a low population effect.

Population surveys report that only 25 to 30 percent of adults in developed countries and in urban areas of middle-income countries engage in regular physical activity (WHO 2005b). Encouraging physical activity should be a major public health intervention, yet worldwide, population policies to promote physical activity are scarce, and if present are rarely evaluated. In an extensive literature review, Sallis, Bauman, and Pratt (1998) stated that environmental interventions that facilitated physical activity should be in place before other informational and behavioral programs were attempted. A facilitating environment includes urban designs in which people can walk or bike, access to exercise facilities, transportation policies that encourage use of public transport and nonmotorized forms of transit, and neighborhood safety. Overall, quasi-experimental studies that have evaluated enhanced access to places for physical activities combined with educational interventions have reported increased physical activity in the target population (Kahn and others 2002). Outcome measurements across these studies varied, so obtaining an average estimate of the effect is difficult. An assessment conducted in eight European cities in developed and emerging economies (Shenassa, Liebhaber, and Ezeamama 2006) found that perceived neighborhood safety was associated with 40 percent higher odds of occasional and frequent physical activity among women and 39 percent increased odds of occasional physical activity among men. Consistent with data from elsewhere, in these European cities men reported being more physically active than women.

The approach to physical activity may differ in developed and developing countries. In low- and middle-income countries, the predominant modes of transport are walking, cycling, motorcycling, and using public transport. WHO and World Bank (2004) reported that while the industrialized countries average two or three people per car, countries such as China and India average 220 to 280 people per car. Those of lower socioeconomic status are more likely to walk to work and walk longer distances (World Bank 2006e). The caveat, however, is that the urban environment is not pedestrian oriented and that public transportation is deficient. As a consequence, people may have to walk distances that are too far under unsafe conditions. Motor vehicle accidents are the second leading cause of death for 5- to 29-year-olds worldwide. The risk of fatal road traffic injury is higher for pedestrians, cyclists, and motorcyclists than for car occupants (WHO and World Bank 2004). Therefore efforts to increase physical activity must be introduced in connection with urban and transport interventions.

Research attempting to understand the factors that influence physical activity and how it can be stimulated is beginning to emerge. It includes examination of the environmental changes necessary to induce physical activity, particularly in urban settings; of the use of leisure time; of occupation and conditions at the workplace; of transportation; and of home-based activities. Along these lines, Pratt and others (2004) have proposed an economic framework for understanding what influences physical activity and identifying potential interventions.

Key Messages

The main conclusions of the review on public policies that affect the occurrence of chronic NCDs are as follows:

- The harmful effects of tobacco are well known and what works for tobacco control is well established. Despite worldwide, country-by-country epidemiological and economic analyses and an international treaty, implementation is absent or weak in most countries. Increasing the price of tobacco products through taxes remains the most cost-effective intervention, yet a better understanding of the political economy is necessary to develop policies for tobacco control.

- Increasing the price of alcohol via excise taxation has been found to be a highly cost-effective strategy. In many countries, however, enormous benefits could be derived from legislation to prevent driving while under the influence of alcohol.
- The situation for food and nutrition policies is complex in developing countries, and consideration must be given to both overnutrition and undernutrition. The issue has to be addressed from the perspective of the agro-food system. Economic instruments such as price and subsidies are unlikely to have a significant effect. Information-based strategies, such as food labeling and point-of-purchase information, can support behavior change, but are insufficient. Legislation to reduce the content of trans-fatty acids in processed foods is a promising strategy that is already taking place in the industrial countries.
- The evidence on the enormous health benefits of regular physical activity is increasing, but understanding of how to bring about substantial increases in physical activity in the population is limited, although the importance of the urban environment is undeniable. Pedestrian-oriented cities and appropriate transport policies would mostly benefit the poor.

Despite the large body of evidence on the causal relationship of tobacco consumption, alcohol consumption, diet, and physical activity to the incidence of and mortality from NCDs, this review found empirical evidence of effective policy-level interventions mostly for tobacco control and hazardous use of alcohol. A publication bias may be possible, as the review was based on published literature. Perhaps many experiences, particularly in developing countries, are either not published or are published as descriptive accounts, as impact evaluation is infrequent. Therefore, most of the evidence presented here comes from developed countries.

The applicability of developed country evidence to developing countries could be questionable, yet many of the processes are of global scope, such as those influencing agro-food systems that lead to limited availability of food for a healthy diet to the urban poor or those pertaining to the effectiveness of price increases to reduce tobacco use. Not all the policy issues described are limited to health; indeed, most of the solutions come from other sectors. Accordingly, the next steps require collaborative work to assess the effect of various policies on health in low- and middle-income settings.

Incorporating Prevention into Primary Care

Health care plays an important role in preventing and reducing premature mortality from NCDs. Analyses from developed countries estimate that health care accounts for 35 to 60 percent of the reduction in ischemic heart disease mortality that has taken place over the last 30 years (Bennett and others 2006; Capewell and others 2000; Capewell, Morrison, and McMurray 1999; Goldman 2004; Hunink and others 1997; Kuulasmaa and others 2000; Laatikainen and others 2005; Park, Safdar, and Schmidt 2002; Peeters and others 2003; Tunstall-Pedoe and others 1999) and all of the 30 to 80 percent reduction in mortality from cancer brought about by cancer screening and treatment (International Agency for Research on Cancer 2002a, 2005). Therefore, individuals who cannot access these services die from preventable causes.

Demographic changes currently under way in low- and middle-income countries lead to an absolute increase in the adult population and rapid growth of urban areas; hence, an increase in the number of people with chronic diseases is practically inevitable. What tools are currently available to deal with the imminent burden of chronic diseases? This section discusses the evidence for effective interventions against two major disease categories not on the basis of the actual diseases, but on the basis of the challenges that they present to health systems. The last two sections deal with cross-cutting issues regarding health care delivery and the need for stewardship within the health sector.

The Continuum of Care: Cardiovascular Prevention

Cardiovascular risk is a continuum of interdependent factors that cumulatively increase the probability of having a fatal or nonfatal cardiovascular event. The most frequent events are myocardial infarction and angina (ischemic heart disease) and stroke (cerebrovascular disease) (WHO 2002b). With the exception of age, risk factors can be prevented, reduced, or eliminated. Biological risk factors are initially asymptomatic. Many individuals do not know they have them and learn of their condition when it has advanced and disease is already likely to have caused damage.

The main biological risk factors are hypertension; hypercholesterolemia (the most common form of hyperlipidemia); age; and a condition known as metabolic syndrome, which is characterized by the presence of abdominal obesity (Grundy and others 2005). The various interrelationships of the cardiovascular risk complex are depicted in figure A2.6. Tobacco use also contributes independently to cardiovascular risk. Diet and physical activity are behaviors that lead to the development or prevention of biological risk factors. Although genetics also play an etiologic role, the exact mechanisms and interrelations with external risk factors are not yet clear. An individual's level of risk is conditioned by the presence and intensity of independent risk factors and is expressed as absolute risk or the probability of having a cardiovascular event in the following 10 years (Anderson and others 1991).

Hypertension—Potentially, one of the most effective ways to decrease mortality from CVD is to control high blood pressure. Clinical trials have estimated that adequate treatment of hypertension can decrease deaths from stroke by 30 percent, deaths from ischemic heart disease by 20 percent, and overall cardiovascular mortality by 19 percent

Figure A2.6. Pathways to Cardiovascular Risk

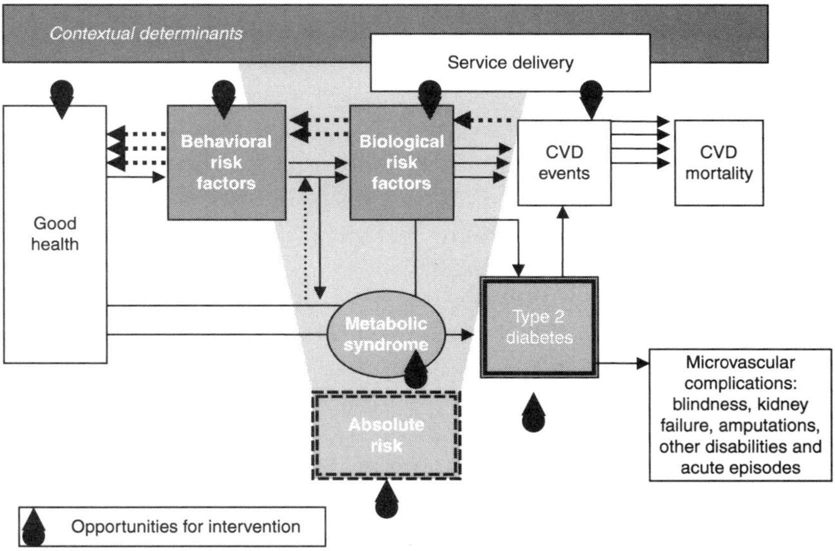

Source: Authors.
Note: This is a graphical representation of the natural history of CVD, interrelationships between causes or risk factors and potential points of intervention. The progression toward cardiovascular mortality is shown by continuous arrows; the regression is shown by dashed arrows. When people are in good health or with only one risk factor, then contextual determinants are critical. Primary care interventions become the cornerstone of risk management when progression occurs, yet contextual determinants continue to exert influence.

(Neal and others 2000; Psaty and others 2003). An accepted value for defining hypertension is having systolic blood pressure of 140 millimeters of mercury or above and diastolic blood pressure of 90 millimeters of mercury or above (Department of Health and Human Services; National Institutes of Health; and National Heart, Lung, and Blood Institute 2003). Research during the last decade has revealed that "the relationship between blood pressure and risk of cardiovascular (CVD) events is continuous, consistent, and independent of other risk factors. The higher the blood pressure, the greatest the chance of heart attacks, heart failure, stroke, and kidney disease" (Department of Health and Human Services; National Institutes of Health; and National Heart, Lung, and Blood Institute 2003, p. 2). Blood pressure increases with age and this trend is more pronounced after age 55 (Port and others 2000). Given the continuous nature of hypertension and its interrelationship with age and other risk factors, health professionals now recommend that it be managed not as an isolated condition, but as part of cardiovascular risk as a whole, based on absolute risk (Giles and others 2005).

Worldwide, more than 20 percent of adults have high blood pressure. In developed countries, reported prevalence ranges from 27.6 percent in North America to 55.3 percent in Germany (Wolf-Maier and others 2003). As reliable data from developing countries become available, most reports estimate prevalence among adults as between 15 and 40 percent (Ordunez and others 2001; WHO 2005b), which makes hypertension one of the most frequent risk factors for CVD in the developing world.

Population-based surveys that have measured blood pressure report that in North America, nearly 70 percent of people with hypertension are aware of their condition, but that only 60 percent of those with diagnosed hypertension are treated (Hajjar and Kotchen 2003; Wolf-Maier and others 2003). An analysis of studies in six European countries reported that, on average, 26.8 percent of those with hypertension receive treatment (Wolf-Maier and others 2003). In China, India, and low- and middle-income countries of Europe and Latin America, awareness of having hypertension ranges between 35 and 46 percent, and among those diagnosed with hypertension, 20 to 40 percent receive treatment (Gu and others 2002; Macedo and others 2005; Ordunez and others 2001; Panagiotakos and others 2003; Reynolds and others 2003; Zachariah and others 2003).

Lifestyle factors such as diet and physical activity play a larger role in blood pressure control than previously thought. In China, those people who introduced lifestyle modifications to their treatment regime had

59 percent higher control rates than those who did not (Gu and others 2002; Li and others 2003). In Greece, control rates for people with hypertension who followed a Mediterranean diet were 39 percent higher than for those with other diets (Panagiotakos and others 2003). An important benefit is derived from physical activity, in particular, aerobic exercise. A meta-analysis that included 53 randomized trials where the only difference between intervention and control groups was aerobic exercise showed significant reductions in systolic and diastolic blood pressure regardless of weight loss (Whelton and others 2002). Evidence also indicates that physical activity reduces insulin resistance and the serum concentration of total cholesterol in people with hypertension (Brett, Ritter, and Chowienczyk 2000; Brown and others 1997).

Hyperlipidemias—People with hyperlipidemias (most often high cholesterol) are at increased risk of ischemic heart disease, stroke, and other vascular diseases. Estimates indicate that worldwide, hyperlipidemias account for 47 percent of ischemic heart disease and 26 percent of strokes. Data from clinical trials indicate that by reducing a subtype of cholesterol (measured through low-density lipoprotein) by 1 millimole per liter (39 milligrams per deciliter) through treatment with statins, first coronary events (myocardial infarction or angina) can be reduced by 23 percent, stroke can be reduced by 17 percent, and major vascular events can be reduced by 21 percent (Baigent and others 2005).

Hypertension and hypercholesterolemia are independent risk factors for CVD, but they are often both present in the same person. The presence of behavioral risk factors, a diet low in fruits and vegetables, and a lack of physical activity usually precede this comorbidity.

Absolute risk—The concept of absolute risk evolved from the Framingham study of CVD. For more than 30 years, this study has followed a random sample of individuals residing in Framingham, Massachusetts, to identify risk factors for CVD (Anderson and others 1991). Based on the findings of this study, researchers developed a score to predict a person's risk of ischemic heart disease over the next 10 years (referred to as the 10-year absolute risk). While the risk score may be specific to this study, it has been adjusted or modified to account for local and current prevalence of risk factors and cardiovascular mortality in various settings (Bhopal and others 2005; Brindle and others 2003; Conroy and others 2003; Giampaoli and others 2005; Hense and others 2003; Liu and others 2004; Thomsen and others 2002).

In light of increasing knowledge about cardiovascular risk and out of concern for the increasing prevalence of cardiovascular risk factors, discussions about feasible and potentially effective approaches to primary prevention are emerging. In the United Kingdom, an ex ante evaluation assessed various strategies for managing risk factors among men using data from the British Regional Heart Study (Emberson and others 2004). The researchers found that treating 10-year absolute risk of 30 percent and above would reduce cardiovascular events by 11 percent, whereas if the treatment threshold were reduced to 20 percent, cardiovascular events could be reduced by 34 percent. Although the study did not calculate costs, the researchers did analyze the option of avoiding laboratory costs and providing the four first-line drugs (a diuretic, a beta-blocker, aspirin, and a statin) to all men aged 55 and over. In this case, CVD events over the next 10 years would have been reduced by 45 percent, and by 60 percent if the threshold were set at age 50.

Another ex ante analysis using the estimated costs from low-, middle-, and high-income countries showed that treating a 10-year absolute risk of 35 percent or more was a cost-effective primary care intervention measured as unit cost per DALY averted (Murray and others 2003). Estimates of the cost-effectiveness ratio ranged from US\$42 per DALY in Sub-Saharan Africa to US\$423 per DALY in South and East Asia.

A bolder proposition based on indirect data called for the development of a multicomponent oral preparation to be administered as chemoprophylaxis for CVD (Wald and Law 2003). The preparation would contain a low dose of aspirin, a beta-blocker, a statin, and a diuretic. Pilot trials of the use of this kind of drug combination for secondary prevention of CVD are under way. Table A2.5 presents estimated cost-effectiveness ratios and the expected number of DALYs averted along with estimates for other primary care–based CVD interventions. While the cost-effectiveness of treating absolute risk is still high, when compared with secondary prevention, the effect in terms of DALYs averted is considerably higher.

Screening for and Early Detection of Cancer

Cancer is not necessarily a fatal disease any more. For several types of cancer, medical interventions allow patients to return to a disease-free state and the same probability of dying as the rest of their birth cohort (Coleman and others 2003; Gatta and others 2005; Sant and others 2003; Surveillance Epidemiology and End Results 2002). Detecting cancer early in its natural history, with the hope of obtaining better results, is intuitively appealing to many clinicians and public health

Table A2.5. Cost-Effectiveness Ratios for Interventions Aimed at Preventing Cardiovascular Conditions Compared with No Treatment

Condition to be prevented and intervention	Cost-effectiveness ratio (US$/DALY)	DALYs averted (hundreds)
Stroke, ischemic heart disease, and hypertensive heart disease		
Combination treatment based on absolute Risk[a]	2,128	61.65
Combination treatment after diagnosed ischemic heart disease[a]	409	—
Ischemic heart disease		
Aspirin and beta-blocker (optional angiotensin-converting enzyme inhibitor)	688	8.40
Plus statin	2,028	3.54
Acute myocardial infarction		
Aspirin	14	1.04
Plus beta-blocker	15	1.04
Plus streptokinase	671	1.04
Plus tissue plasminogen activator	15,869	0.42
Stroke		
Aspirin within 48 hours of acute stroke	149	1.62
Heparin within 48 hours of onset of acute stroke or thrombolytic therapy using recombinant tissue plasminogen activator within 3 hours of onset of acute stroke	1,977	1.22
Recurrent stroke		
Aspirin or combination of aspirin and extended-release dipyridamole	81	1.77
Carotid endarterectomy to remove harmful plaque from carotid arteries	1,458	4.93

Source: Jamison and others 2006a.
Note: — = not available.
a. Data used for these estimates were not based on empirical trials.

professionals. This perspective implies three basic assumptions: first, that accurate and well-tolerated methods to detect and diagnose cancer at early stages are available; second, that detecting cancer at an earlier stage has an advantage over waiting until it is symptomatic; and third, that effective treatments are available.

The accuracy of a screening method and the efficiency of the health service in which the program takes place determine the potential effectiveness of early detection and of a screening program (Zapka and others 2003). Box A2.2 enumerates the basic inputs for a screening program. The accuracy of the screening method is measured by sensitivity, that is, the test's ability to detect those who have the disease, and by

Box A2.2

Basic Inputs for an Organized Cancer Screening Program

Basic inputs are as follows:

- an explicit policy, with specified age categories, method, and screening interval, as well as clinical practice guidelines
- a defined target population
- a management team responsible for implementing and supporting an information system
- a health care team for evidence-based care
- a quality assurance structure
- method for identifying cancer occurrence in the target population independent of the screening program.

Source: Adapted from International Agency for Research on Cancer 2002a, 2005.

specificity, namely, the test's ability to label as negative those people who do not have the disease. Trade-offs between sensitivity and specificity always exist, as do variations across different providers. In addition, the progression of cancer is not always predictable, and often cancers that occur in the interval between screening rounds and are diagnosed by means other than screening progress more rapidly than cancers detected by screening.

The health profession has undertaken many attempts to screen various cancer sites, but the only sites for which evidence of reduction in mortality from screening exists are cancer of the cervix uteri, breast, and colon. In developing countries, external aid agencies introduced cervical cytology as a component of family planning programs in the 1960s and 1970s, yet no decline in mortality from cervical cancer was observed over the next 30 years (Robles, White, and Peruga 1996; Sankaranarayanan, Budukh, and Rajkuma 2001). In some middle-income countries where the indications were that cytology screening may have been working, no information on outputs or outcomes was available that could account for this, and whether the modest mortality declines observed were due to cervical cancer screening or to overall increased access to health services is not clear. In developing countries with a large primary care infrastructure and high coverage of cytology, the lack of quality assurance and low reliability of cytology, as well as the screening of young populations at low risk, can partly explain why screening is not successful (Aristizabal and others 1984; Fernández Garrote and others 1996; Herrero and others 1992; Sepulveda and Prado 2005; Taucher, Albala, and Icaza 1994). In addition, in low-resourced settings, fewer than 25 percent of women screened positive are followed up for additional diagnosis and treatment (Gage and others 2003). This indicates a dissociation between the provision of primary care services and of secondary support services.

Three other screening tests for cervical cancer offer promising results: using liquid-based cytology, undertaking visual inspection with acetic acid or with iodine solution, and testing for high-risk human papillomavirus (HPV) through hybrid capture. A cost-effectiveness analysis conducted with data from five developing countries, two in Africa, two in Asia, and one in Latin America (table A2.6), showed that screening either with HPV tests or using visual inspection could be much more cost-effective than screening using conventional cytology (Goldie and others 2005). The results suggest that the optimal age for screening would be at 35 to 45 years of age. Studies in Brazil, Madagascar, and Zimbabwe reached similar conclusions (Brown and others 2006). However, the effectiveness of visual inspection has not yet been confirmed.

A vaccine for HPV is now available. As vaccine programs are introduced, screening will still be necessary to prevent cervical cancer in women already infected or infected by high-risk HPV types not contained in the vaccines. The screening strategy would, however, need to

Table A2.6. Cost-Effectiveness Ratios for Different Cervical Cancer Screening Tests, Selected Developing Countries
(2000 US$/year of life saved)

Country	Conventional cytology (3 visits)	HPV testing (2 visits)	Visual inspection with acetic acid [a] (1 visit)
Brazil	589	122	56
India	n.e.	+	10
Kenya	n.e.	+	+
Madagascar	379	167	54
Peru	n.e.	152	124
South Africa	n.e.	467	+
Thailand	n.e.	170	109
Zimbabwe	331	117	43

Source: Brazil, Madagascar, and Zimbabwe: Brown and others 2006; India, Kenya, Peru, Thailand, and South Africa: Goldie and others 2005.
Note: + = incremental cost-effectiveness is significantly higher; n.e. = not estimated (in this analysis cost-effectiveness ratios were not calculated for strategies that had low accuracy).
a. Effectiveness still under evaluation (trial in India), but thus far this test has demonstrated high accuracy.

change to achieve community effectiveness and provide the basis for HPV surveillance. An important question for countries seeking to introduce HPV vaccine is the cost-effectiveness of maintaining their screening program versus reorienting their screening strategy or, if screening is inefficient, whether to maintain the screening program at all. If adequate vaccine coverage can be achieved, then screening could start much later and occur less often, perhaps only once in a lifetime, thereby increasing the cost-effectiveness of the overall strategy to prevent cervical cancer (Goldie and others 2005; Goldie and others 2004).

Multiple factors can constrain the successful introduction of new vaccines, principally costs, acceptability, and capacity of local health services to deliver the vaccines; other limitations are related to the vaccine itself. Analysis of the distribution of HPV types worldwide indicates that current vaccines would prevent approximately 71 percent of cervical cancer, but the impact would be primarily in Asia, Europe, and North America (Munoz and others 2004). The duration of immunity is unknown, but measurements of antibody titers in young, vaccinated women indicate that these fall from peak levels soon after immunization and remain stable for at least 48 months (Mao and others 2006). Future reports from ongoing trials will be able to address the need for booster immunizations in older women. As the optimum vaccination age should be before starting sexual activity, minors will need their parents' consent. Given that HPV is a sexually transmitted disease, consent may prove difficult to obtain in many cultures.

Health Care for Chronic Conditions
Several features specific to NCDs can be construed from the conditions examined earlier. Morbidity builds over time and risk of disease and death is cumulative, yet reversible. At earlier stages of the risk-disease process, the probability of reversal is likely to be higher, which provides various opportunities for intervention. In the case of cardiovascular risk, if hypertension and absolute risk are effectively treated, in the context of a low-risk lifestyle, the probability of having a cardiovascular event decreases significantly (Psaty and others 2003), but the management of absolute risk relies on pharmacological therapy over a lifetime. New technologies, such as vaccines, tests, and ambulatory treatment, have the potential to make NCD prevention and management more accessible. The caveat is that early stages of NCDs are asymptomatic and the perception of risk is likely to be low (Slovic and others 2005), hence the difficulty of achieving high coverage of preventive services.

Even if preventive interventions are widely adopted, a proportion of people will still develop severe conditions because of biological or other unknown causes. The evolution of disease is almost never linear, thus continuity of care is necessary. Morbidity is not restricted to one condition. Indeed, as risks and disease evolve or as the person ages, comorbidity is more frequent, thus the need for comprehensive care. In the process of care, one intervention may lead to another, for example, if a patient screens positive for cancer, additional tests and specialized treatment are required, thus the need for coordination of care. Continuity, comprehensiveness, and coordination of care are three features that health care delivery must achieve to provide effective care for chronic conditions (Rothman and Wagner 2003).

The delivery of care for chronic NCDs is transaction intensive and highly discretionary (this is the terminology used by the World Bank 2003). Providers require support to make informed (evidence-based) recommendations that are acceptable to patients. In addition, the process of care occurs not only through visits or encounters with the health care system, but is permanent, as the person lives with the condition. Thus, it is the client who constantly makes decisions about his or her management. Self-management support is the fourth pillar for effectively addressing chronic conditions.

Ample evidence indicates that mortality from preventable chronic NCDs is lower in areas with strong primary care services (Starfield, Shi, and Macinko 2005). In an extensive and rigorous review, Renders and others (2001) concluded that interventions that improved the outcome of diseases such as diabetes were complex and included several concurrent interventions, such as the presence of a clinical information system that allows follow-up of patients; of decision support in the form of clinical guidelines; and of a team approach that shifts responsibilities to nonphysicians, such as nurses, nutritionists, and social workers. To bring about such changes in primary care, many countries may need considerable new resources or make efforts to shift those that are being used for inefficient services.

The Need for Stewardship
The role of the government is not necessarily that of providing, or even purchasing, health care services, but ensuring that if services are available that they are efficient and that the poor can benefit from them. However, the need for an effective primary care approach calls for strong stewardship and regulatory functions exercised by public institutions.

It entails defining a strategic policy framework; generating information for decision making at all levels; ensuring the availability of tools for implementation; building coalitions and partnerships; ensuring a fit between policy objectives, organizational structure, and culture; and ensuring accountability (Travis and others 2003). While these functions are not exclusive to NCDs, undertaking health technology assessments; ensuring drug availability and affordability; and generating intelligence, in which surveillance or the monitoring of health outcomes is a key feature, are critical for NCDs.

Health technology assessment—The high costs of NCD care are among the main concerns of policy makers. Technological developments, such as those described for cervical cancer, and also pressures by advocacy groups, can drive costs upward. Studies in the United States have shown that high costs are correlated with more visits to physicians, particularly specialists; more hospitalizations; and frequent tests, but no relationship is apparent between higher costs and better health outcomes, even after controlling for case mix (Fisher and others 2003a, 2003b). Even though high-income countries are early adopters of new technologies, differences among countries tend to level out over time (Slade and Anderson 2001). In many countries, health technology assessments may play a role in slowing the diffusion of technology, but are not the only mechanism doing so, and by themselves do not necessarily decrease costs (Packer and others 2006). However, health technology assessments are likely to play a role in regulating practice and in providing a framework for more cost-effective use of technological innovations in health care.

The field of health technology assessment has expanded significantly during the past three decades. Its beginnings can be traced to two different milestones leading to pathways that would eventually converge. In 1972, the U.S. Congress established the Office of Technology Assessment in the interests of integrating the evaluation of new technologies into the policy-making process. Even though this office no longer exists, it was instrumental in initially defining the field (Banta 2003).

The second milestone, also in 1972, was the publication of a book by A. L. Cochrane that emphatically called for the use of randomized trials to evaluate the efficacy of medical interventions (Cochrane 1999). This gave birth to evidence-based medicine, which has had an enormous influence on the practice of medicine in developed countries. Evidence-based medicine's main objective is to link evidence to clinical practice, with the aim of improving the quality and effectiveness of individual patient care (Sackett and others 1996).

While originally the objectives of these two disciplines, health technology assessment and evidence-based medicine, may seem different, their respective methodological developments have led to a convergence and to the expansion of a field that continues to evolve. It is no longer restricted to concerns about safety and the efficacy of health care devices and interventions, but now also focuses on effectiveness and cost-effectiveness (Maynard and McDaid 2003). Health technology assessment is a decision support tool that can span from basic provider and client decision making to public policy development. Most important, it is a tool to improve resource allocation.

In many countries, these disciplines have now been institutionalized through the creation of agencies for health technology assessment that serve both clinical patient care and preventive activities. Several agencies in developed countries maintain permanent reviews of evidence pertaining to the effectiveness of preventive services, for example, the Public Health Agency of Canada; the National Institute of Clinical Evidence in the United Kingdom; the United States Preventive Task Force; and health technology assessment agencies in Australia, New Zealand, and Sweden. Increasingly, several of the agencies are incorporating public health services, either by commissioning a different agency, such as the Community Services Task Force in the United States, or by integrating efforts, as the National Institute of Clinical Evidence does in the United Kingdom. Most of the reviews and recommendations are available online.

The appropriate use of technology and the monitoring of its effectiveness can contribute to improved efficiency, client-provider accountability as well as provider-payer accountability. The challenge for low- and middle-income countries is twofold: first, to ensure the availability of local capacity and institutional support to use evidence in decision making within the health system; and second, to establish links with decision makers so that relevant information is made available on time and in a way that can be used and accessed easily. Producing all assessments locally is unnecessary, but it is important to be critical users of the information and to deliver specific recommendations for a particular setting.

Drug policy—One of the main limitations for the management of NCDs is the availability of drugs. Research in the industrial countries strongly suggests that drug coverage is a major driver of patient outcomes, and also a major driver of health care costs. Survey data indicate that adherence is directly linked to costs and drug coverage (Goldman and others 2004; Tseng and others 2003). A recent study in the United States compared the costs and clinical outcomes of two drug plans, one with a US$1,000 cap and another with no cap, among people aged 65 and older affiliated with the same health care provider (Hsu and others 2006). The study found that people enrolled in the plan with a cap had lower treatment adherence, worse clinical outcomes, and higher death rates than those with no caps. In addition, the group with drug caps had higher rates of nonelective hospitalizations and emergency room visits that offset the savings in the drug plan.

WHO analyzed the availability and affordability of 14 pharmacological treatment schedules for five chronic conditions in 24 countries (Gelders and others 2006). A low availability of drugs in the public sector, where they are usually free of charge, forced patients to pay private sector prices, which were at least 3 to 100 times higher than the international reference price. Taxes and duties levied on medicines and markups often contributed more to the final price than the manufacturer's price. The study developed a methodology for assessing affordability based on the lowest monthly salary of a government employee and for monitoring availability. Although any policy approach needs to be country specific, monitoring tools can help evaluate and identify the optimal drug benefit scheme, particularly to ensure affordability and quality, while avoiding the distribution of counterfeit products.

Monitoring and evaluation: surveillance—The process of implementing planned interventions should ideally rely on a monitoring system, including for inputs, processes, outputs, and outcomes (for a more comprehensive discussion of monitoring and evaluation, see World Bank 2005d). Surveillance is a term originally from the field of infectious diseases that referred to monitoring the occurrence of disease to identify outbreaks. It is now more broadly applied to the process of monitoring health outcomes and is defined as the ongoing (continuous or periodic) collection and analysis of population-based data to measure the magnitude of a problem and of trends over time (Last 2001). In a public health context, surveillance is not limited to data collection and analysis, but also implies the dissemination of information about a health-related event for use in public health action to reduce morbidity and mortality and to improve health (Centers for Disease Control and Prevention 2001). Surveillance serves at least seven public health functions: (a) supporting case detection and public health interventions, (b) estimating the impact of a disease or injury, (c) portraying the natural history of a health condition, (d) determining the distribution and spread of illness, (e) generating hypotheses and stimulating research, (f) evaluating prevention and control measures, and (g) facilitating planning (Teutsch 2000). The strength of surveillance as an instrument is its ability to detect changes in health outcomes over time.

A government must have the capabilities needed to make use of data at the analytic level and to disseminate information to various audiences. The use of existing data sources, such as mortality databases, needs to be maximized. Although the selection of monitoring strategies is of a technical nature, cost-benefit analysis of the use of various information systems is useful when deciding in which systems to invest. The following can be considered: (a) tracking mortality trends to evaluate impact; (b) requiring morbidity registration, such as cancer and stroke registries, to monitor survival as a measure of treatment effectiveness and timely diagnosis; (c) undertaking risk factor surveillance; and (d) monitoring health outcomes and health outputs from health service interventions at the local level.

In 2002 and 2003, the World Bank evaluated the epidemiological surveillance systems in Eastern Europe and Central Asia (Miller and Ryskulova 2004). The review included birth registration, death registration, infectious disease surveillance, NCD risk factor surveillance, and morbidity surveillance. The report concluded that the surveillance systems were overly complex, with duplicate and parallel reporting. A large amount of data is collected, but with no clear purposes, and it is often not used at all. In particular, collection of morbidity data consumes a large amount of human resources. In addition, no quality assurance systems were in operation. Many countries had conducted a census in 2000, but no data were available two to three years later when the evaluation took place. At least 17 countries had conducted a survey of risk factors for NCDs. Although probabilistic sampling methods were used, various problems were detected in the data collection instruments and in the analytical techniques used, such as failure to correct for sampling design effects when reporting prevalence rates.

In Latin America and the Caribbean, a capacity assessment for NCDs conducted in 2000 and repeated in 2005 found that in many countries, health information systems were tailored exclusively for maternal and child health (Pan American Health Organization 2006). The number of surveys of NCD risk factors published has increased fivefold since 1955, and as of 2005, at least five countries had conducted national surveys. An analysis of the quality of the data in those surveys found that nearly 75 percent were well designed and data collection was reliable, but only 26 percent provided prevalence estimates correcting for sample design effects (Corber and others 2003).

Middle-income countries of Central Asia, Eastern Europe, and Latin America and the Caribbean are spending resources on monitoring and evaluation systems, but require additional investment to streamline data collection and build capacity to analyze and use information.

Key Messages

The main findings of the review are as follows:

- Evidence indicates that NCDs can be prevented by managing risk in primary care. The challenges include reaching the poor, making drugs available, ensuring adherence to drug regimens, and introducing support for lifestyle changes within and outside health services.
- Evidence supports the potential effectiveness of a primary care–based cancer screening program, but the availability and quality of treatment need to be ensured in advance.
- Effective primary care for chronic conditions requires continuity, comprehensiveness, and coordination of care as well as self-management support for the patient.
- Effective changes cannot occur without ensuring that public institutions exercise their stewardship function.

Conclusion

According to available evidence, countries that are facing the problem of premature mortality from NCDs have several choices: they can decide to concentrate their efforts on preventing risk factors through public policies that can reach large segments of the population, they may choose to incorporate prevention and management in the delivery of health services, or they may implement a combination of both. Making the distinction is important, however, because actions for the development of public policies take place mostly outside the health sector and encompass different stakeholders from actions that occur within the health system itself.

The evidence for implementing tobacco control policies is strong, and government intervention is not only justified, but is endorsed through an international treaty to which countries have agreed. Excise taxation on alcohol has been proved to reduce consumption, and random testing of blood alcohol levels has been found to be effective in preventing driving under the influence of alcohol. Food and nutrition policies offer various options but require further evaluation, with the goal being to guarantee equal opportunity of access to a balanced diet by way of providing information, introducing regulations, or ensuring affordable products. Subnational governments, particularly municipalities, are key players in improving the urban environment for physical activity. The benefits of physical activity are so large that supporting further research to better understand how to facilitate this behavior in various population groups is important for public health.

Several effective interventions to reduce the risk of and premature mortality from NCDs can be implemented by health services. In practice, however, implementation encompasses sets of interventions to address specific health conditions, sometimes several health conditions concurrently. The challenge is to ensure that those who need them, particularly the poor, receive the interventions that are most likely to deliver optimum outcomes. The government is not necessarily responsible for financing the delivery of the interventions, but on the grounds of equity, the government is accountable for ensuring equal opportunity of access and quality. Instruments such as health technology assessments, surveillance, and monitoring and evaluation are important for the government to exercise its stewardship and bridge the gap between evidence of the efficacy of interventions and community effectiveness.

Notes

1. This is a legal framework used by Gostin (2000). This approach has the potential to facilitate further analysis of stakeholders and of institutional capacity to conduct policy changes.
2. Supply-side interventions include restrictions on youth access to tobacco, crop substitution and diversification, and subsidies and price support to local tobacco farmers, along with restricted imports, which may artificially raise the world price of tobacco. All of these are either too difficult to implement or have not shown any effect on tobacco consumption. However, the critical supply-side intervention that requires strong action is illicit trade or smuggling.
3. U.S. Federal Trade Commission. "Cigarette Report for 2003." U. S. Federal Trade Commission. http://www.ftc.gov/reports/cigarette05/050809cigrpt.pdf. Date consulted: September 20, 2006.

4. The corruption perception or transparency index is estimated by a nonprofit organization, Transparency International. This index ranks countries in terms of the degree to which corruption is perceived to exist among public officials and politicians. It is a composite index, drawing on corruption-related data in expert surveys carried out by a variety of reputable institutions. It reflects the views of businesspeople and analysts from around the world, including experts who are resident in the countries evaluated. The choice of the inverse of the index to present these data is done for ease of interpretation. The higher the inverse index, the higher the perceived level of corruption.

5. For additional information, discussion papers, and tools for economic analyses of tobacco control, see http://www.worldbank.org/hnp.

6. In-middle income countries, DALYs attributable to vitamin A deficiency amount to 0.7 million for males and 0.8 million for females, to zinc deficiency are 5.9 million for males and 5.4 million for females, to obesity are 5.1 million for males and 6.0 million for females, and to low intake of fruits and vegetables are 4.6 million for males and 3.3 million for females (WHO 2002b).

7. This survey measured overweight and obesity using body mass index.

8. For updates on policies affecting obese people, see http://www.obesity.org.

9. European directives on food labeling can be found at http://ec.europa.eu/food/food/labellingnutrition/nutritionlabel/index_en.htm.

APPENDIX 3

Challenges of Design and Implementation: Three Country Cases

This appendix focuses on three case studies from Indonesia, Georgia, and India that offer specific country examples of issues related to noncommunicable diseases (NCDs) as a complement to some of the more conceptual discussions earlier in this report. The issues raised are not intended to be exhaustive, but rather illustrative of some of the challenges that health systems must contend with in the "real world" of preventing and controlling NCDs, particularly with respect to service delivery.

A common theme in the three case studies is insight into the important question of what makes NCDs different. Understanding the special features of NCDs, especially as they pertain to service delivery, can represent a valuable first step toward informed decision making related to NCDs. This will become even more true as the epidemiological transition unfolds in many countries around the world. The appendix also addresses what makes NCDs the same as other health challenges. This is important from the point of view of integrated approaches to health service delivery.

As noted, this set of case studies is not intended to be an exhaustive discussion of service delivery. Such an exercise is beyond the scope of this report and is the subject of an ongoing, multiyear work program at the World Bank. This appendix is intended to raise a number of questions of interest to senior analysts and policy advisers and to provide some ideas for further exploration.

The following summarizes some of the key messages from each country study with an emphasis on what makes NCDs different:

- The Indonesia case study highlights issues related to the volume and composition of NCD services during the epidemiological transition. As chronic diseases, NCDs require sustained contacts with the health system, and they also have a greater bias toward inpatient, hospital care. Thus, a disease burden that is shifting from communicable diseases toward NCDs implies greater pressures on health services in general, and on inpatient services in particular. Preparing for changing patterns in the volume and composition of service delivery should be a policy priority. In this context, early emphasis on primary care can lead to better outcomes.
- The Georgia case study identifies a long list of challenges for the health system's response to diabetes, and in doing so helps highlight several issues of special importance to NCDs:
  - Some NCDs require sustained contact with multiple levels of the health system, implying a lot of back and forth in a manner that is more complex than in the case of the typical acute illness. Simply put, they require continuity of care. This underlines the need for clear divisions of responsibility between different types of providers and levels of the system, as well as strong information flows between the various actors.
  - The long-tem nature of NCDs implies greater responsibilities for the patient, that is, self-management. This calls for more emphasis on patient education and support.
  - Many NCDs involve long-term pharmaceutical use, highlighting the importance of drug availability to a greater degree than for acute illnesses, which may require only a one-time prescription. Access to cheap medicines, physical access to pharmacies, and patient compliance are all important in this regard.
- The India case study highlights the long asymptomatic periods that follow exposure to risk factors and precede the recognition of symptomatic disease, and thus the gains to be won by finding ways to detect and diagnose NCDs as early as possible. Moreover, the India case also suggests that the poor may benefit disproportionately from better outcomes on this front. Long asymptomatic periods distinguish most NCDs from most acute illnesses, although important exceptions exist. This issue also highlights the importance of finding new approaches to promote access to care.

- The India case study also highlights the issue of the quality of care. Of course this is an issue for all health interventions, but the long-term nature of NCDs means that if a patient receives an incorrect diagnosis or inappropriate prescription (or both), the medical and financial implications can be even more severe. Quality of care is a broad topic that extends well beyond correct diagnosis and appropriate prescription as used in this example.

Athough the appendix emphasizes what makes NCDs different, recognizing the parallels with certain communicable diseases is also important. For example, the launch of antiretroviral programs in many countries also implies increased service delivery volumes and the need for multiple contacts with different levels of the system. In addition, the importance of early diagnosis also applies to HIV/AIDS, tuberculosis, and sexually transmitted infections, among others. Indeed, lessons from HIV/AIDS, such as the importance of community engagement for encouraging voluntary counseling and testing, of working with nongovernmental organizations and civil society, and of public information campaigns, may be usefully applied to NCDs. Recognizing these parallels will permit the identification of potential synergies with other health priorities.

Other issues that emerge from the case studies include the following:

- Countries are already spending funds on NCDs. How efficiently and equitably are they doing so?
- To what extent can an emphasis on primary care, whether in the public or private sector, provide better value for money?
- What are the relationships among risk perception, prevention-seeking behavior, and information?

Indonesia: Forecasting and Financing Health Care Demand in a Middle-Income Country—Disease Transitions in East and Central Java

Attempts to forecast population health are fraught with difficulties, such as imperfect data and the need to adopt assumptions that are difficult to verify. However, responsible health system policy and planning require as credible a view of future health care needs as possible. Given this necessity, the task becomes how best to use existing information to orient forward-looking policy. As part of the background work for this report, World Bank researchers attempted such an exercise for two of the largest provinces of Indonesia, East and Central Java, which have a total population of more than 70 million people. The results highlight not only the current importance of NCDs for health care demand, but the larger role NCDs will play in the future (for complete details, see Choi and others forthcoming).

Indonesia, like many developing countries, is currently experiencing the dual transition of demographic and epidemiological change. Fertility rates have been declining for an extended period, the population is beginning to age, and the rate of population aging will increase in the future. This necessarily implies a shift in the disease burden toward one common to older age groups. At the same time, Indonesia's economy is expected to grow at a healthy pace over the next 15 years, thereby creating a substantially larger pool of middle-class and wealthy consumers. As household incomes rise, people will demand more health care in general. Finally, the increasing prevalence of key risk factors, such as obesity and tobacco consumption, combined with an older population, will drive an increase in the relative burden of NCDs.

The increasing importance of NCDs creates a significant burden for health care spending, because costs per treatment, both outpatient and inpatient, are, on average, higher for NCDs than for communicable diseases, and because NCDs, compared with communicable diseases, require relatively more inpatient care, which is drastically more expensive than outpatient care.[1] In Central and East Java in 2005, NCDs already accounted for the majority of treatment cases and of spending: 50 percent of 60.1 million outpatient cases, 62 percent of 1.6 million inpatient cases, 62 percent of total outpatient spending (Rp 2.1 trillion), and 73 percent of total inpatient spending (Rp 5.5 trillion).

To estimate current private health care spending (for 2005) as well as spending in 2020, researchers separately modeled four major inputs into health care demand: (a) the total size of the population as well as the size of specific population categories by gender, age, and wealth; (b) the disease prevalence rates for specific disease categories; (c) the treatment rates and duration for each disease category; and (d) the costs of treatment.

Two scenarios are presented here: the first assumes that disease prevalence will change in the future at the rates suggested in the 1990 global burden of disease study for the Southeast Asia region (Choi and others, forthcoming), while the second scenario assumes no change in disease prevalence between 2005 and 2020. However, the overall disease burden in the second scenario will still shift as a result of changes in the population's age and wealth structure. Any difference in the number of cases by disease between the first and second scenarios comes exclusively from differences in forecasted disease prevalence.

Figure A3.1 looks at the relative mix of disease cases for 2005 and both 2020 scenarios. Currently, 39 percent of all illnesses in the two provinces are due to NCDs, but in just 15 years this is expected to increase to 56 percent of all illnesses as a result of aging, income growth, and changes in disease prevalence. Without changes in disease prevalence, the relative burden of NCDs is still expected to increase to 43 percent of all cases of illness. Given the uncertainty that surrounds forecasts of disease prevalence in the global burden of disease study, the range of outcomes presented here gives likely upper and lower bounds on the increasing presence of NCDs in the overall disease burden.

Table A3.1 translates the disease burdens in 2005 and 2020 into standard utilization measures of outpatient visits and inpatient bed days. NCD-driven utilization already accounts for the majority of contacts with the health system in East and Central Java: 54 percent of all outpatient visits and 67 percent of all inpatient bed days. This proportion will increase in the future to 58 to 71 percent of outpatient visits and 72 to 79 percent of inpatient bed days.

Finally, if we look at private health spending as portrayed in figure A3.2, the increase in spending attributable to NCDs is also substantial. In 2005, 70 percent of private spending was driven by NCDs, and this is expected to increase to 75 to 80 percent of total private spending by 2020. By this measure, up to four-fifths of all health care demand will be

Figure A3.1. Distribution of Total Cases by Disease Group, East and Central Java, 2005 and 2020

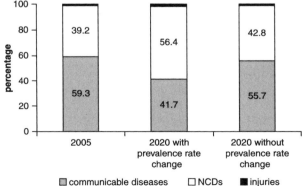

Source: Choi and others, forthcoming.

Table A3.1. Total Number of Outpatient Visits and Inpatient Bed Days by Disease Group, East and Central Java, 2005 and 2020

(thousands)

Category	Disease group	2005		2020 With prevalence rate change		2020 Without prevalence rate change	
		Number	Percentage of total	With prevalence rate change	Percentage of total	Without prevalence rate change	Percentage of total
Outpatient visits	Communicable diseases	71,182	44	50,496	27	95,826	40
	NCDs	87,122	54	130,498	71	138,129	58
	Injuries	2,659	2	3,427	2	3,785	2
	Total	160,963	100	184,421	100	237,740	100
Inpatient bed days	Communicable diseases	2,140	23	2,041	12	3,987	19
	NCD	6,306	67	13,574	79	15,254	72
	Injuries	936	10	1,660	10	1,816	9
	Total	9,382	100	17,275	100	21,057	100

Source: Choi and others forthcoming.

Figure A3.2. Total Private Spending on Outpatient and Inpatient Care by Disease Group East and Central Java, 2005 and 2020

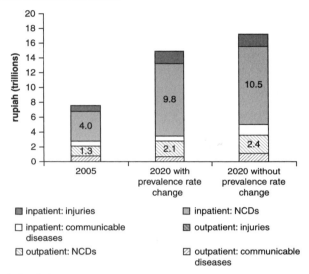

Source: Choi and others forthcoming.

for NCDs. As overall spending, measured in 2005 rupiah, is expected to rise considerably over the 15-year period from Rp 7.5 trillion to between Rp 14.8 trillion and Rp 17.2 trillion, the market for NCD treatment will be at least twice as large just 15 years into the future.

Although the particular forecast of health and health system outcomes depends on the scenario adopted, the general picture that emerges from this exercise is clear: the demand for curative care will increase significantly as the population simultaneously grows, ages, and becomes wealthier. Even though a large number of communicable disease cases will persist, the relative burden of NCDs will increase, perhaps by a substantial margin. The implications of such a change in terms of health care infrastructure and financing needs are significant.

Thus, the Indonesian health system needs to prepare for a future of rising health care demand largely driven by an increasing burden of NCDs. How the health system will meet the future demand for curative care as well as maintain or enhance necessary public health functions is a question that policy makers need to consider now. The forecasts of health care demand in East and Central Java presented earlier enable an analysis of some dimensions of future system costs implied by the rising demand. The focus here is on inpatient care, in particular, the number of required hospital beds, as well as health sector staffing needs more broadly.

To assess available hospital capacity in the future, researchers assumed a 90 percent bed occupancy rate in 2020 among the existing hospital stock, and from this figure inferred the shortfall in beds demanded. For the number of physicians, researchers assumed a goal of tripling the current physician-to-population ratio of 11.3 per 100,000 to bring this ratio closer to international standards. Finally, for the number of nurses and other medical staff, researchers assumed that the current nurse-to-physician ratio of 4.8 will be maintained in 2020. These assumptions allow a calculation of the monetary investments needed to meet the estimated demand in hospital beds, physicians, and nurses.

If hospitals can operate effectively at a 90 percent bed occupancy rate—actual occupancy is substantially lower—currently 12.37 million hospital bed days are available in the two provinces. This meets the estimated demand of 9.4 million bed days for 2005, but the number of extra bed days necessary to meet the increased demand in 2020 is either 4.9 million or 8.7 million depending on the scenario (figure A3.3). Of course, if hospitals operate at their current bed occupancy rates into the future, then the necessary investments under each scenario will be substantially greater.

Switching from bed days to actual hospital beds, researchers calculated the necessary investment for extra hospital beds to meet increasing needs for inpatient care. Currently 38,000 hospital beds are available in the two provinces, but estimated demand for 2020 ranges from 53,000 to

Figure A3.3. Number of Hospital Bed Days in the Context of Current Capacity with an Occupancy Rate of 90 Percent, East and Central Java, 2005 and 2020

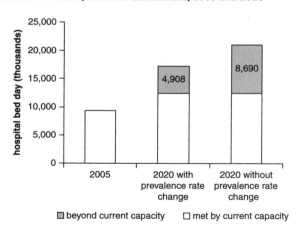

Source: Choi and others forthcoming.
Note: Current capacity is 12.4 million hospital bed days with a 90 percent bed occupancy rate.

64,000, indicating that a shortfall of 15,000 to 26,000 hospital beds will occur. The corresponding investment cost for hospital beds to bridge the gap ranges from Rp 8.7 trillion to Rp 15.4 trillion. These investment estimates are strictly for the cost of providing hospital beds. The costs of providing additional medical equipment could add up to an additional 40 percent of the investment in hospital beds.

Meeting the demand for medical personnel will also present a challenge. In particular, the current capacity of medical schools would not provide enough physicians to meet future demand. Demand in the two provinces will be for about 8,000 physicians, which current medical school capacity cannot meet by 2020. Filling the gap requires another Rp 507 billion. At the same time, assuming that the current nurse-to-doctor ratio will be sufficient in 2020, the current nursing school capacity will produce about 3,000 extra nurses by 2020, implying no shortfall in training capacity for nurses.

To put these estimated investment needs in context, researchers calculated cumulative public sector health spending between 2005 and 2020 and compared it with the estimated cost of investment in infrastructure. As figure A3.4 depicts, estimated total public health spending will come to Rp 49.7 trillion. Currently, Indonesia's public health system not only provides population-based preventive health services, but is also a major provider

Figure A3.4. Cumulative Public Sector Spending and Total Cost of Infrastructure Investment Needed between 2005 and 2020 by Scenario, East and Central Java

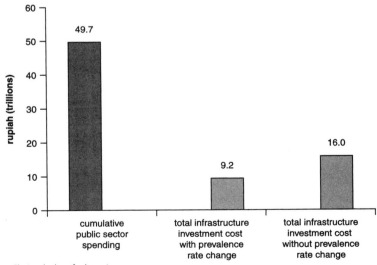

Source: Choi and others forthcoming.

of curative care, handling 42 percent of all outpatient visits and 58 percent of inpatient commitments. Clearly, the need to adjust to the future disease burden is likely to place a severe strain on the public budget.

If the forecast investment needs were to be funded entirely out of the public budget, the total cost of infrastructure investment required would consume 20 to 32 percent of cumulative total future public spending, depending on the scenario. Considering that the infrastructure investment cost estimates do not include such important factors as nonhospital medical equipment, an even higher portion of public spending would be required for comprehensive infrastructure investment. These figures may not be tenable given the essential public health services and salary support for medical practitioners that will also be required over this period.

Of course, the need for core public health services, such as immunization, health promotion, and disease surveillance and prevention, will continue into the future, so the question of how to finance the infrastructure needs becomes crucial. If the future resembles the scenarios presented here, maintaining core public health services while providing for health infrastructure as called for by future needs will present a serious challenge.

Given these forecasts, a medium-term strategy for the health sector would ideally specify the role of the private sector, including the provision of both outpatient and inpatient care. Given limited public budgets, for the public sector to continue to provide almost half of the curative care demanded by the population may not be prudent, unless the public budget can be increased substantially. If private sources of investment are deemed necessary, the policy question becomes one of how to manage the investment climate in the health sector, including such issues as investment guidelines and technology assessments, in order to attract sufficient investment and ensure that investments are efficiently managed and do not shift services onto a high-cost path.

In sum, the shift from relatively more communicable diseases to more NCDs during the epidemiological transition will entail a greater volume of service delivery and higher demand for inpatient care. As the Indonesia case study demonstrates, preparing for these changes should be an important priority for policy makers.

Georgia: Diabetes and Systemic Constraints

Georgia's health system has faced substantial challenges following independence. The system proved to be both unaffordable and poorly suited to the new health challenges of the 1990s, in particular, those posed by complex chronic diseases. Georgia has sought to address these challenges at every level of the health system; however, while the reforms have been bold, they have not yet succeeded in meeting their goals of providing basic health care to all who need it. The aim of this case study is to use diabetes as a lens for identifying health care system constraints that might otherwise be overlooked. The material presented here draws on a background paper that was written as part of the work program underlying this report (Balabanova, McKee, and Koroleva 2006).

In the early 1990s, health care for patients with diabetes essentially collapsed. Until 1995, the Soviet model of health care that had guaranteed free treatment to all patients with diabetes was, in theory, still in place, but in reality, the system of outpatient and inpatient services had broken down and supplies of insulin were no longer guaranteed. Since 1995, the reform process has intensified, especially in relation to primary health care, with the launch of the State Program to provide free insulin to all patients with diabetes. Outpatient services for patients with diabetes were incorporated into the basic benefits package and are currently funded from public sources. Children with diabetes receive particular attention and are entitled to free, high-quality preventive and treatment services.

Using a framework developed in the background paper, the system for diabetes care can be mapped and areas that are underresourced and neglected can be identified. In terms of inputs, Georgia has an extensive network of outpatient health facilities. Despite the overall lack of investment in the health system, people with diabetes are guaranteed a basic minimum of services and drugs. Clearly, however, additional investments, as well as improved allocation of existing resources, are needed to provide all patients with the most basic services, such as consultations with specialists when needed, provision of strips and syringes, and treatment of complications.

However, the problem goes beyond a shortage of funds: no formal clinical guidelines for the management of diabetes are available. Most of the physicians interviewed reported that they treat patients using knowledge received when at university, informal communications with colleagues, or occasional attendance at conferences and seminars that help them learn about modern methods of diabetes management. Few physicians or endocrinologists have access to sources of recognized evidence or formal support.

In Georgia, diabetes is commonly diagnosed by means of a process that involves admitting patients to hospitals. This is inconsistent with international practice, as it is clinically unnecessary and costly. Given that hospital-dominated models of service delivery have changed little, few benefits will result from investing money in training family physicians and endocrinologists in outpatient facilities. Family physicians and endocrinologists in these facilities have lost their skills with the loss of many of their previous responsibilities, for example, prescribing insulin or changing patients' treatment regimens. Polyclinics do not provide specialist care; they serve simply as referral points from which patients with increased blood sugar levels are referred to specialists. In effect, polyclinic physicians act as little more than administrators, authorizing prescriptions obtained at the tertiary level and giving patients forms for obtaining free insulin from pharmacies. Enhanced training without a substantial redefinition of task profiles, the simplification of procedures, and the provision of consistent support will achieve little.

The case study also shows that the presence of appropriate inputs alone will be insufficient to produce an effective model of diabetes care unless the mechanisms to ensure that such inputs achieve their purpose are in place. Even though the government fully finances the supply of insulin (an essential input), an excessively centralized system of insulin distribution and dependency on multiple visits to different levels of the health system mean that, in effect, access to insulin is often obstructed for people who find navigating the system difficult or who live far away from the designated insulin-dispensing pharmacies. In addition, adults with diabetes are not provided with free syringes or related supplies or with hypoglycemic drugs. This creates significant financial barriers to ensuring a continuing supply of insulin, the lack of which increases the risk of complications.

The requirement to admit people suffering from complications of diabetes to hospitals renders such care essentially unaffordable in many cases, leading to catastrophic pressure on family finances (Gotsadze and others 2001). Furthermore, the ubiquitous and extensive out-of-pocket payments to service providers pose a particular threat to those with chronic diseases in need of uninterrupted treatment regimes despite the efforts to provide them with free access to care. In addition, the linkages between primary and secondary care are poor and no effective mechanism for patient follow-up exists. Multiple data collection systems are in place, with every health facility keeping its own records, and mechanisms for providers to exchange information with one another are absent unless informed patients manage the process themselves.

Effective management of diabetes requires empowering patients to take control of their condition, but patients rarely have the necessary self-monitoring equipment because of its high cost. Little effort is made to inform patients and to provide them with the skills for self-care or the knowledge to adhere to an appropriate diet, apart from occasional advice by endocrinologists during visits to facilities. No routine screening of adults for retinopathy or specialized programs to prevent diabetic foot disease are available.

Optimal management of diabetes also requires a system to monitor outcomes from different perspectives (clinical and social). Current data collection systems do not permit reliable assessment of outcomes or routine monitoring. In addition, discrepancies exist between different sources of information. Those indicators that are available suggest that management of diabetes and its complications, for example, coma, is suboptimal. Little information is available about the effects of long-term illness on employment, social inclusion, and families' socioeconomic status.

Even though the government has invested considerably in regulating the system for diabetes care and many of the essential inputs will soon be in place (free insulin, primary care physicians trained to manage diabetes, state-guaranteed package of care), in practice, these inputs fail to translate into more accessible and affordable primary care. This demonstrates the need to look beyond inputs alone by also considering the linkages and interactions between various health system components.

The situation in Georgia resembles what has been observed in other former Soviet Union countries (Hopkinson and others 2004; Rese and others 2005; Telishevska, Chenet, and McKee 2001). Most countries have embarked on ambitious health system reforms, emphasizing primary care, purchasing and contracting for care according to needs, procuring and distributing drugs on a competitive basis, and reforming social protection systems. However, reforms have often involved investing in and transforming particular system components in isolation, with little attention being paid as to how they fit with other system elements and mechanisms. For example, the training of large numbers of primary care physicians has not being accompanied by investments in infrastructure and basic resources or attention to referral patterns to allow the newly trained professionals to provide effective care for diseases such as diabetes and its complications. Problems are also apparent in getting health systems that historically have been hierarchical and organized around vertical models of care to provide the complex care needed to deal with diabetes.

The study shows that the complexity of pathways to care and the uncertainty about the costs involved create a major barrier to continuing care, but those with diabetes, whose expectations of the system were low, did not initially mention fragmentation of the system as a problem. They accepted that they would need to make six or seven visits to different locations to obtain free insulin. The system appears to prioritize control of the insulin supply and prevention of abuse over ease of access by patients. In Georgia, as in other former Soviet Union countries, reforms have rarely taken patients' interests into account, especially those with chronic diseases who require long-term care, and have uniformly involved reliance on out-of-pocket payments at the point of service, thereby creating financial barriers to access (Lewis 2002; Preker, Jakab, and Shneider 2002) and unnecessarily complicated pathways to care. Placing the experience of users and providers at the center of the delivery of diabetes care provides a starting point for exploring the continuum of care and identifying the inputs required at each stage.

The following issues emerge from these findings that are relevant to improving diabetes management in Georgia:

- A model of health care delivery needs to be developed that ensures linkages between primary- and secondary-level health facilities, sharing of information, and patient follow-up. This should facilitate the transfer of responsibility for managing diabetes and other chronic diseases without complications to outpatient facilities and lead to an understanding that hospitalizing all patients with diabetes is unnecessary.
- The delivery systems should be reorganized to simplify pathways to care and medication for people with diabetes.
- A health information system that captures data relevant to diabetes and its complications should be developed.
- A support system that enables people with diabetes to provide self-care, including adherence to effective treatment and to a healthy diet and lifestyle, and to prevent complications should be created.

As noted in the introduction, these priorities reflect some of the characteristics of NCDs that require different approaches from those applied to acute illnesses. These include the complexity of care, including sustained contacts with multiple levels of care; the importance of patient self-care over the long-term; and the frequent need for access to medications along with quality of care considerations. Recognizing the different nature of NCDs can help inform policy priorities.

India: The Value of Information about NCD Status

An important characteristic of most chronic NCDs is that they develop through a continuum, starting (in many cases) with behaviors and going through biological risk factors until disease is established. During this process the patient remains asymptomatic for long periods, but it is precisely at these stages when the process can be reversed and the risk of premature mortality can be decreased. This is true for diabetes; cardiovascular disease; and certain types of cancers, such as cancer of the cervix uteri and of the breast. The focus of this case study is on the value of information about a patient's NCD status and the implications for policy.

When a person has an undiagnosed NCD, he or she may receive no treatment at all, or, alternatively, the chronic illness may be reported and treated as an acute illness, a phenomenon that we will refer to as acute illness displacement. In addition to the medical implications of not receiving the appropriate treatment, there are also financial implications of wasting money on the wrong treatment and potentially spending even more money later on because of the delayed diagnosis. Thus, timely diagnosis of an NCD can be welfare improving in more than one way.[2]

Findings from a Delhi data set help illustrate some of the issues. A longitudinal study of morbidity and health-seeking behavior carried out by a think tank (the Institute of Socioeconomic Research on Development and Democracy) followed 1,600 individuals, asking them about their illnesses during the previous week in 54 visits over two years. The main findings pertain to rich-poor differentials in reporting illness and the response of individuals to information about their chronic illness.

In figure A3.5, the vertical axes plot the percentage of weeks that a person reported a chronic or an acute illness. As illness patterns differ by age, the results are plotted against the age of the individual on the horizontal axes. A particular characteristic of the survey was that individuals were asked about their chronic and acute illnesses separately. Acute illnesses were captured with this screening question: "Were you sick in the last week?" Chronic illnesses were prescreened during the first visit, and in each subsequent visit the person was asked about the chronic condition and what he or she had done about it. Finally, the interviewer also asked whether the person was aware of any new illnesses.

Two main patterns stand out. First, richer people reported chronic illnesses far more frequently at every age than the poor. Second, the poor reported a much greater incidence of acute illnesses than middle-income respondents or the rich. This was true for virtually the entire age cohort. As

Figure A3.5. Reporting of Chronic and Acute Illnesses by Income Group, Delhi

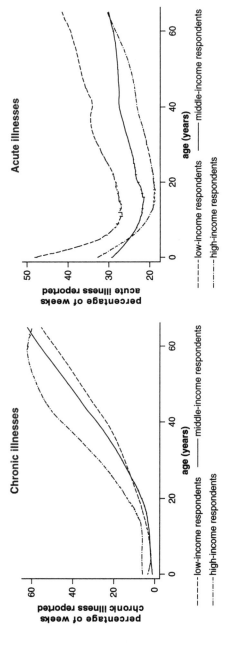

Source: Das and Hammer 2006.

132

would be expected, acute illnesses were higher among infants and young children. In a multivariate regression using age, gender, and per capita expenditure as explanatory variables, a household in the lowest tercile of expenditure was estimated to be 11 percentage points less likely to report a chronic illness, and the effect is equal and opposite for acute illnesses.

Combining acute and chronic illnesses into a single variable referred to as sickness confirmed that rates of self-reported illness were higher among the rich than the poor (with a 6 percentage point, or 15 percent, difference). Reported illness reflects both medical reality and knowledge of illness. Das and Hammer (2006) submit that while part of the difference between the rich and the poor could truly reflect underlying medical conditions, the gap in clinical prevalence studies is too small to account for the full difference, suggesting that information about illnesses plays an important role. For instance, biomedical comparisons of diabetes and hypertension among the rich and the poor suggest that the rich are 7 percent more likely to have one of these illnesses, compared with a more than 33 percent difference in reported chronic conditions in the Institute of Socioeconomic Research on Development and Democracy data. In sum, the results suggest that a better diagnosis can be welfare improving, particularly for the poor.

To address the question of how patients respond to the revelation of information about chronic illness, the longitudinal nature of the data collected in Delhi is critical. In particular, as individuals were followed over a two-year period, some of them were diagnosed with a chronic illness. A comparison of their behavior before and after the diagnosis provides some insights into the potential responses by different population groups.

Das and Hammer (2006) present a detailed econometric analysis in which they examine the effects of the diagnosis, controlling for individual fixed effects, that is, they compare outcomes for the same person before and after diagnosis, and use the fact that the discoveries were at different points in time to control for potential confounding effects due to the timing of illness. Figure A3.6 shows how the diagnosis of a chronic illness changed behavior, in this case, self-medication. The figure looks at the behavior of three groups of individuals: those who never reported chronic illnesses during the two years of the survey (labeled as never chronic), those who reported a chronic illness from the beginning of the survey (labeled as always chronic), and those who were diagnosed at some time during the survey (labeled as discovered individuals).

Individuals who were never chronic did not self-medicate much and the pattern was stable over time. In contrast, the always chronic

Figure A3.6. Self-Medication in the Institute of Socioeconomic Research on Development and Democracy Sample

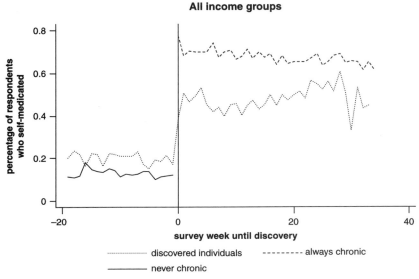

Source: Das and Hammer 2006.

self-medicated almost seven times as much. The behavior of the discovered individuals was remarkable. Before diagnosis, their self-medication patterns were much closer to those of the never chronic, although they clearly medicated more, a characteristic that was almost entirely due to more illnesses among the discovered individuals group. In the week that they were diagnosed, this group demonstrated a large, discontinuous jump in the amount of self-medication. Furthermore, an upward trend in self-medication was apparent, so that by the end of the observation period, the behavior of the always chronic and the discovered individuals was similar. Using multivariate regression techniques, the authors confirmed these results for medication patterns and the reporting of acute illnesses. The basic results are as follows:

- A large increase in all medication (whether self-medicated or received from a doctor) followed the diagnosis of chronic illness. Across all diagnosed individuals, that is, all income groups, self-medication in any given week more than doubled from 20 to 45 percent of individuals.
- A reduction in the reporting of acute illnesses by 23 percentage points occurred across the income groups. The reduction was largest for the

rich, but was also large and significant for the poor and the middle-income group.

- No increase occurred in the health expenditures of the individuals with a newly diagnosed condition. These individuals were already spending on treating the symptomatic manifestations of their chronic illnesses. The diagnosis implied a shifting of expenditures, but not necessarily an increase.

The fact that poor people were able to respond to the new information implies that they were able to finance their own treatments. Of course, that the new treatments did not lead them to incur additional expenditures helped, but this also implies that even for illnesses that require long-term financing, studies need to establish that credit constraints are binding rather than rely on intuition. In relation to the study discussed here, note that drug prices tend to be lower in India than in many other low-income countries, suggesting that the outcome may not be the case in all other countries.

A number of policy implications emerge from these findings. Perhaps the most important is the need for new approaches to access given the potential welfare improvements, particularly for the poor, that can arise from timely diagnosis of an NCD. The first critical contact between a patient and the health system is likely to be more elusive for NCDs than for many acute illnesses because of the potentially long asymptomatic periods. Health worker outreach to engage communities, and possibly conditional cash transfers for screening if warranted, may help in this regard. Lessons learned from cancer screening or from HIV/AIDS case detection may be applicable here. Chapter 2 briefly discussed some of the challenges of reaching the poor.

A second policy implication relates to the quality of care. Access to care is a necessary, but insufficient, condition for welfare improvement, as the diagnosis may be incorrect or the treatment prescribed may be inappropriate. As noted at the outset, there can be long-term medical and financial implications if, for example, NCD symptoms are incorrectly diagnosed as an acute illness and the treatment addresses those symptoms rather than the underlying disease. In the Indian context, where the private health sector predominates over the public sector, this contains an important message for the quality of care provided in the private sector.

In sum, the Indian case study indicates that the poor are less likely to know that they are ill with an NCD, and a timely diagnosis of NCDs can be welfare improving for multiple reasons. Thus, policies aimed at improving the diagnosis of NCDs, particularly for the poor, can be beneficial.

Notes

1. For example, inpatient treatment constitutes only 3 percent of the 61.7 million total disease cases treated in Central and East Java in 2005, but 72 percent of total private spending (Rp 7.6 trillion) is attributable to inpatient care (Choi and others forthcoming).

2. A number of caveats are important in relation to the discussion of the value of timely and accurate diagnosis for NCD patients. For example, an early diagnosis may not be desirable for patients with incurable NCDs. Also some conditions, such as hypertension, may manifest themselves in an episodic manner in some patients, in which case there is a danger of overdiagnosis and overtreatment. Finally, discussions of accuracy should acknowledge the errors of inclusion or exclusion in diagnosis that exist in all health systems. In general terms, however, the basic message of the value of timely and accurate diagnosis still applies.

Selected Noncommunicable Disease Indicators

Country group and country	Annual NCD deaths, 2002* (thousands)	NCD deaths as a percentage of all deaths, 2002*	NCD DALYs as a percentage of all DALYs, 2002*	Age-standardized NCD death rates per 100,000 population, 2002*	Share of excess deaths attributable to NCDs (%) 2002**	Diabetes prevalence, adults aged 20–79, 2003 (%)	Probability of dying between the ages of 15 and 60, all causes 2004 (per 1,000 population) Males	Probability of dying between the ages of 15 and 60, all causes 2004 (per 1,000 population) Females
East Asia and the Pacific								
Cambodia	54.5	34.0	30.8	852.5	23.9	2.0	430	276
China	7,051.1	77.2	66.4	665.0	67.1	2.7	158	99
Fiji	3.9	73.0	66.5	825.2	69.4	8.3	270	169
Indonesia	985.6	60.6	56.0	727.0	44.8	1.9	239	200
Kiribati	0.4	64.2	64.3	773.3	53.6	6.2	297	175
Korea, Rep. of	227.1	82.6	76.1	537.0	79.5	6.4	151	55
Lao PDR	24.1	35.7	27.9	904.0	24.1	1.1	331	300
Malaysia	84.7	71.0	69.6	625.3	56.9	9.4	200	109
Marshall Islands	0.3	70.2	65.2	997.5	65.3	8.6	327	275
Mongolia	12.9	66.1	57.0	967.7	59.7	1.4	303	185
Palau	0.1	73.3	68.1	744.3	67.2	8.7	224	206
Papua New Guinea	18.0	38.4	36.0	814.9	25.5	1.9	322	265

(Continued)

137

Selected Noncommunicable Disease Indicators (continued)

Country group and country	Annual NCD deaths, 2002* (thousands)	NCD deaths as a percentage of all deaths, 2002*	NCD DALYs as a percentage of all DALYs, 2002*	Age-standardized NCD death rates per 100,000 population, 2002*	Share of excess deaths attributable to NCDs (%) 2002**	Diabetes prevalence, adults aged 20–79, 2003 (%)	Probability of dying between the ages of 15 and 60, all causes 2004 (per 1,000 population)	
							Males	Females
Philippines	253.0	56.4	57.6	641.5	36.6	2.4	269	149
Samoa	0.8	70.7	65.7	781.8	64.3	5.9	235	203
Singapore	14.9	82.3	83.5	376.0	90.8	12.3	92	51
Solomon Islands	1.7	55.7	53.7	785.7	46.4	2.1	193	143
Thailand	244.9	58.4	56.9	558.8	28.8	2.1	265	154
Timor-Leste	2.7	40.4	25.5	813.8	27.6	1.4	267	184
Tonga	0.5	73.7	69.9	683.9	64.7	12.4	140	194
Vanuatu	0.8	65.4	60.5	772.4	56.6	2.2	212	170
Vietnam	341.1	66.1	54.9	664.1	47.9	1.0	197	122
Europe and Central Asia								
Albania	18.3	82.9	68.7	813.5	85.0	3.8	171	96
Armenia	23.6	90.4	79.5	800.3	98.6	8.1	248	111
Azerbaijan	51.0	79.5	67.1	891.7	78.3	6.9	205	113
Belarus	122.1	85.0	73.5	839.4	83.7	6.9	377	135
Bosnia and Herzegovina	32.0	91.6	83.4	699.0	105.6	9.6	188	88
Bulgaria	100.0	93.7	87.6	755.7	104.6	10.0	217	92
Croatia	46.1	91.3	87.2	613.2	103.5	5.8	160	66
Czech Republic	93.9	90.9	86.4	567.8	106.5	9.5	161	69
Estonia	15.4	84.4	73.2	673.9	80.4	9.7	301	108
Georgia	57.1	93.2	82.9	745.2	104.1	9.0	161	60

Hungary	111.4	91.2	86.7	694.7	99.8	9.7	249	108
Kazakhstan	144.8	78.7	66.8	1,051.5	76.0	5.5	424	187
Kyrgyz Republic	33.4	73.8	59.5	923.7	68.8	4.3	336	162
Latvia	28.7	85.7	75.6	733.4	83.9	9.9	300	115
Lithuania	34.7	84.6	73.8	639.8	80.9	9.4	304	102
Macedonia, FYR	16.8	88.5	77.2	745.3	94.9	4.9	198	84
Moldova	41.7	86.5	76.7	922.8	88.1	9.3	300	150
Poland	317.0	90.1	83.4	593.3	103.6	9.0	198	79
Romania	232.7	89.9	80.9	727.5	96.2	9.3	232	100
Russian Federation	1,952.7	81.2	68.6	960.2	77.6	9.2	485	180
Serbia and Montenegro	112.9	93.3	87.1	767.4	104.8	5.6	191	98
Slovak Republic	45.0	90.4	83.8	635.9	102.3	8.7	203	76
Slovenia	15.9	87.5	84.6	503.3	92.7	9.6	158	67
Tajikistan	36.4	67.0	52.3	1,035.9	60.4	3.7	166	139
Turkey	346.2	79.2	65.4	757.0	78.1	7.0	180	112
Turkmenistan	30.5	73.1	60.0	1,115.0	70.2	4.0	350	166
Ukraine	679.2	86.7	74.3	891.3	86.7	9.7	386	144
Uzbekistan	136.7	79.7	65.7	898.8	80.5	4.0	223	141
High-income countries								
Australia	113.1	89.4	85.1	362.2	—	6.2	86	50
Austria	64.6	91.7	87.4	405.6	—	9.6	114	55
Belgium	90.2	87.6	86.1	427.1	—	4.2	122	65
Canada	199.0	89.5	86.9	388.4	—	9.0	91	57
Cyprus	6.5	87.3	81.7	529.6	—	5.1	94	47
Denmark	51.8	90.2	88.4	502.8	—	6.9	117	72
Finland	41.7	85.6	82.5	422.4	—	7.2	137	62
France	426.3	85.4	83.8	367.7	—	6.2	132	60

(Continued)

Selected Noncommunicable Disease Indicators (continued)

Country group and country	Annual NCD deaths, 2002* (thousands)	NCD deaths as a percentage of all deaths, 2002*	NCD DALYs as a percentage of all DALYs, 2002*	Age-standardized NCD death rates per 100,000 population, 2002*	Share of excess deaths attributable to NCDs (%) 2002**	Diabetes prevalence, adults aged 20–79, 2003 (%)	Probability of dying between the ages of 15 and 60, all causes 2004 (per 1,000 population) Males	Females
Germany	748.1	91.7	89.5	443.9	—	10.2	112	58
Greece	105.0	92.1	87.3	457.0	—	6.1	110	46
Iceland	1.7	88.4	84.2	384.5	—	2.0	79	52
Ireland	26.6	85.0	84.9	484.2	—	3.4	105	60
Italy	523.0	91.6	88.6	403.2	—	6.6	91	47
Japan	783.6	80.5	84.3	286.7	—	6.9	92	45
Luxembourg	3.0	87.1	83.4	406.0	—	3.8	118	59
Malta	2.6	87.1	87.3	429.3	—	9.2	82	48
Netherlands	123.8	88.8	89.0	442.8	—	3.7	89	63
New Zealand	24.9	91.1	85.5	422.7	—	7.6	95	62
Norway	39.4	87.1	86.5	416.3	—	6.7	93	57
Portugal	81.5	86.4	84.5	460.8	—	7.8	144	61
Spain	321.9	90.5	86.8	395.4	—	9.9	113	45
Sweden	82.4	90.5	88.6	378.8	—	7.3	82	51
Switzerland	54.1	88.9	87.3	357.6	—	9.5	87	49
United Kingdom	507.0	84.6	87.5	434.1	—	3.9	102	63
United States	2,119.7	87.6	83.7	460.4	—	8.0	137	81

Latin America and the Caribbean

Antigua and Barbuda	0.5	82.4	76.6	716.7	81.7	5.8	191	120
Argentina	225.1	80.0	75.9	521.1	61.1	5.4	173	90
Bahamas, The	1.2	64.1	61.8	490.3	24.3	9.0	256	145
Barbados	1.9	82.7	75.9	535.2	73.4	8.5	191	105
Belize	0.9	61.8	56.1	651.5	42.0	5.7	243	135
Bolivia	39.6	54.2	46.5	823.8	40.5	4.8	248	184
Brazil	858.7	70.1	63.3	712.3	57.7	5.2	237	127
Chile	65.9	78.8	76.2	453.2	27.1	5.6	133	66
Colombia	146.3	60.0	52.1	511.5	21.9	4.3	226	93
Costa Rica	14.0	76.6	71.6	457.0	22.3	6.9	124	71
Dominica	0.4	81.5	77.3	589.5	77.7	8.4	204	122
Dominican Republic	32.8	57.8	51.7	687.5	36.2	10.0	280	169
Ecuador	48.2	62.8	57.0	576.1	36.5	4.8	210	128
El Salvador	23.5	57.0	53.4	557.2	27.6	6.2	244	138
Grenada	0.6	78.8	72.4	870.4	74.9	6.8	256	218
Guatemala	32.6	39.8	43.6	562.1	15.7	5.5	276	152
Guyana	4.0	54.5	47.4	821.7	39.4	6.0	291	258
Haiti	33.1	29.4	27.4	786.4	16.6	5.7	417	358
Honduras	24.6	58.9	49.8	758.4	44.2	5.7	258	159
Jamaica	16.6	84.2	76.3	671.7	87.5	7.2	188	120
Mexico	340.1	72.4	66.9	502.8	44.6	7.4	161	94
Nicaragua	15.0	58.3	52.4	655.2	39.4	6.1	214	151
Panama	9.6	69.2	63.1	430.1	—	7.3	139	82
Paraguay	16.7	61.9	55.3	598.2	38.5	3.9	176	127
Peru	99.2	58.3	56.5	583.6	31.3	5.1	184	134
St. Kitts and Nevis	0.3	74.6	72.7	688.5	63.1	6.6	197	145
St. Lucia	0.7	80.1	72.6	646.5	78.3	6.2	209	116

(Continued)

Selected Noncommunicable Disease Indicators (continued)

Country group and country	Annual NCD deaths, 2002* (thousands)	NCD deaths as a percentage of all deaths, 2002*	NCD DALYs as a percentage of all DALYs, 2002*	Age-standardized NCD death rates per 100,000 population, 2002*	Share of excess deaths attributable to NCDs (%) 2002**	Diabetes prevalence, adults aged 20–79, 2003 (%)	Probability of dying between the ages of 15 and 60, all causes 2004 (per 1,000 population) Males	Females
St. Vincent and the Grenadines	0.6	75.8	69.7	684.6	67.4	7.7	301	174
Suriname	2.2	67.1	59.4	780.5	55.4	8.6	261	159
Trinidad and Tobago	8.4	71.2	62.2	729.3	58.0	7.9	257	156
Uruguay	26.2	85.9	78.9	518.2	86.1	6.8	172	87
Venezuela, R. B. de	75.9	66.3	60.2	495.6	26.0	5.2	185	97
Middle East and North Africa								
Algeria	93.9	54.1	45.9	597.6	25.7	4.1	153	124
Bahrain	1.9	81.5	77.8	746.2	119.2	14.9	112	82
Egypt, Arab Rep. of	384.3	77.6	66.9	958.6	77.1	9.8	239	158
Iran, Islamic Rep. of	267.9	69.7	58.9	741.6	58.9	3.6	190	118
Israel	31.1	88.0	83.1	399.5	53.8	7.1	91	48
Jordan	15.2	65.3	57.8	703.1	53.7	7.0	187	119
Kuwait	3.4	72.3	76.1	512.4	58.3	12.8	72	54
Lebanon	18.6	77.5	67.3	741.7	72.9	6.4	198	136
Libya	17.0	73.2	64.9	650.3	64.3	3.7	186	109
Morocco	105.9	68.9	56.5	675.0	54.4	4.2	157	102
Oman	6.3	75.1	66.9	687.6	90.5	11.4	164	92
Saudi Arabia	66.7	68.6	62.3	701.0	62.6	9.4	196	120
Syrian Arab Rep.	51.9	73.2	63.8	728.1	72.5	6.2	186	125
Tunisia	44.5	79.8	70.8	685.0	78.1	4.6	166	110
Yemen, Rep. of	73.1	42.7	34.8	955.7	33.6	7.7	298	225

South Asia

Bangladesh	492.4	44.5	40.7	761.6	28.8	3.9	251	258
Bhutan	9.2	44.0	36.7	770.9	28.3	3.7	255	196
India	5,110.5	49.2	41.4	749.8	31.6	5.9	275	202
Maldives	1.1	55.7	49.4	863.9	42.6	1.8	186	140
Nepal	97.7	41.9	36.8	795.9	27.2	4.1	297	285
Pakistan	546.4	39.4	34.2	743.3	23.0	8.5	222	198
Sri Lanka	110.7	76.1	71.3	711.1	66.9	2.1	232	119

Sub-Saharan Africa

Angola	51.1	16.7	13.9	981.7	10.6	2.7	591	504
Benin	20.4	23.3	19.3	852.2	12.8	2.1	388	350
Botswana	4.2	10.1	11.2	653.0	3.1	3.6	786	770
Burkina Faso	40.0	16.0	12.7	901.3	9.0	2.7	472	410
Burundi	20.7	17.2	14.4	843.4	9.0	1.3	593	457
Cameroon	60.6	25.7	19.4	848.1	14.4	0.8	444	432
Cape Verde	1.6	64.7	50.9	691.8	50.6	2.3	209	139
Central African Republic	15.8	20.8	15.4	862.6	11.7	2.3	667	624
Chad	28.9	19.4	15.1	868.8	10.6	2.7	497	422
Comoros	1.9	35.4	31.2	736.5	18.6	2.5	254	182
Congo, Dem. Rep. of	163.8	16.6	14.3	909.1	9.4	2.5	576	446
Congo, Rep. of	10.4	23.3	20.5	761.6	11.5	2.6	442	390
Côte d'Ivoire	60.3	23.3	19.5	873.1	13.5	2.3	585	500
Djibouti	2.8	32.6	26.7	926.2	21.9	4.9	373	312
Eritrea	9.2	22.3	22.3	762.4	10.6	1.9	345	281

(Continued)

143

Selected Noncommunicable Disease Indicators (continued)

Country group and country	Annual NCD deaths, 2002* (thousands)	NCD deaths as a percentage of all deaths, 2002*	NCD DALYs as a percentage of all DALYs, 2002*	Age-standardized NCD death rates per 100,000 population, 2002*	Share of excess deaths attributable to NCDs (%) 2002**	Diabetes prevalence, adults aged 20–79, 2003 (%)	Probability of dying between the ages of 15 and 60, all causes 2004 (per 1,000 population) Males	Females
Ethiopia	242.8	22.9	20.2	858.5	13.7	1.9	451	389
Gabon	5.8	39.1	28.4	813.2	24.0	2.9	411	344
Gambia, The	5.1	32.3	25.8	805.0	18.3	2.2	344	263
Ghana	68.2	32.6	26.9	785.8	18.1	3.3	349	319
Guinea	27.2	23.7	19.0	853.1	13.3	2.0	364	319
Guinea-Bissau	5.1	19.2	14.9	882.6	10.7	2.0	482	413
Kenya	91.0	22.4	20.5	782.5	12.1	2.5	477	502
Lesotho	7.5	16.2	13.2	784.6	7.9	3.1	845	728
Liberia	10.1	14.6	12.8	955.3	8.6	2.0	596	477
Madagascar	55.2	27.4	21.9	836.7	15.2	2.5	338	270
Malawi	42.7	16.6	12.4	835.0	8.4	1.7	663	638
Mali	39.2	16.2	14.2	909.0	9.6	2.0	490	414
Mauritania	10.7	26.6	20.1	884.2	15.8	3.5	325	246
Mauritius	6.8	86.2	72.0	700.9	94.7	10.7	217	112
Mozambique	55.1	14.3	13.9	720.0	6.1	3.1	627	549

Namibia	6.8	24.0	19.8	754.2	11.5	3.1	548	489
Niger	33.3	13.6	12.5	916.5	7.9	3.1	506	478
Nigeria	438.6	21.9	18.2	889.3	12.7	2.2	513	478
Rwanda	23.6	18.0	16.0	831.4	9.5	1.1	518	435
São Tomé and Principe	0.6	44.8	33.4	764.2	27.4	2.8	301	236
Senegal	26.3	25.6	23.0	831.6	14.5	2.3	358	288
Seychelles	0.4	77.0	68.4	657.2	68.9	12.3	232	83
Sierra Leone	19.1	14.5	11.4	1,016.7	9.0	2.2	579	497
South Africa	189.9	27.9	25.1	808.3	16.1	3.4	667	598
Sudan	142.5	41.2	32.3	902.8	29.0	3.1	390	304
Swaziland	3.3	12.6	11.6	731.5	5.3	3.0	823	741
Tanzania	100.4	16.8	15.6	847.1	9.0	2.3	551	524
Togo	16.2	26.0	20.8	831.2	14.4	2.1	401	327
Uganda	68.5	17.6	15.7	824.1	9.1	1.5	525	446
Zambia	28.9	12.5	12.4	700.1	5.2	3.0	683	656

Sources: Annual NCD deaths: Lopez and others 2006; NCD deaths as a percentage of all deaths: Lopez and others 2006; NCD DALYs as a percentage of all DALYs: Lopez and others 2006; Age-standardized NCD death rates per 100,000 population: Lopez and others 2006; Share of excess deaths attributable to NCDs: Smith 2006b; Diabetes prevalence: IDF 2003; Probability of dying between the ages of 15 and 60: WHO 2006a.

Note: * = Estimates; ** = Estimates. See Appendix 1. Values greater than 100% indicate a greater relative NCD burden than in the world's richest income quintile; — = not available. DALY = disability-adjusted life year. NCD = noncommunicable disease.

Glossary of Selected Health Terms

Blood pressure is a measure of the force that circulating blood exerts on the wall of the main arteries. The pressure wave transmitted along the arteries with each heartbeat is easily heard with a stethoscope. The highest (systolic) pressure is created by the contraction of the heart when it expulses blood and the lowest (diastolic) pressure is measured as the heart receives blood. Blood pressure is measured in millimeters of mercury. Despite being asymptomatic, elevated blood pressure (hypertension) produces structural changes in the arteries, which in turn affect the blood supply to vital organs, the more frequent consequences of which can be seen in the brain (stroke), the heart (myocardial infarction [heart attack]), and the kidneys (renal failure).

Cancers or **malignant neoplasms** originate through the mutation of critical genes in a cell, which leads to progressive loss of differentiation of the cell. Cancer cells lose the ability to balance cell division by cell death (apoptosis) and to interact with one another. Thus, tumors exhibit uncontrolled growth and acquire progressively different characteristics than the cell of origin. They eventually invade neighboring tissues, and via the blood stream or lymphatic nodes also invade other organs (metastasis). This is a multistep process that usually takes several years. It can be initiated by a virus or by environmental damage to an organ, such as that caused by radiation or tobacco smoke, yet only a few of the mutated cells progress to a fully developed cancer. The understanding of how cancer originates has opened the opportunity to improve prevention, including by means of vaccines, detection methods, and therapy for several cancers that if detected at early stages and treated in a timely fashion can lead to disease-free survival for most of those diagnosed.

Cardiovascular disease refers to a group of health conditions that affect the circulatory system and include acute rheumatic fever; chronic rheumatic heart disease; hypertensive diseases; ischemic heart disease; pulmonary heart disease; cerebrovascular disease; diseases of the arteries, arterioles, and capillaries; and diseases of the veins, lymphatic vessels, and lymph nodes. The most frequent diseases are **ischemic heart disease** with and without hypertension and **stroke**.

Ischemic heart disease is characterized by insufficient blood flow to the heart muscle. Its clinical manifestations include myocardial infarction, angina pectoris, and chronic ischemic heart disease. Myocardial infarction (colloquially known as a heart attack) is the death of some portion of the heart muscle when it loses its blood supply. The symptoms, characterized by chest pain, that occur because of a decreased blood supply to the cardiac muscle are known as angina pectoris. The possibility of recovery or death depends on the extent of the affected area.

Stroke occurs when an artery that supplies blood to the brain bursts or is blocked by a blood clot. Within minutes, the nerve cells in that area of the brain are damaged and the part of the body controlled by the damaged section of the brain cannot function properly. The degree of disability and death depend on the extent and location of the damage.

Disability-adjusted life years are a summary measure of health that takes into account the years of life lost because of a particular illness and those years spent living with the resulting disability. The disability life years component is estimated by multiplying the number of incident cases in a given period by the duration of the disease and a weight factor that reflects the severity of the resulting health state on a scale from 0 (perfect health state) to 1 (dead). A 3 percent time discounting is applied. The original estimates of disability-adjusted life years used nonuniform age weights whereby weights were lower for younger and older ages, giving more value to the years lived as a young adult. Currently, some estimates do not use age weights, hence the notation requires a subscript—DALY(r,K)—where r is the time discount rate, K = 1 is the use of weights, and K = 0 is the nonuse of weights.

Demographic transition is a term used to describe the population changes that occur when fertility rates fall, which in turn leads to a fall in crude mortality rates. A woman would have had fewer children at the end of her reproductive years than older cohorts and her children would be more likely to survive to at least one year of age. The consequence is an increased life expectancy and an increase in the median age of the population. Over time, the adult population experiences faster growth than the population as a whole. During the second half of the 20th century, the decrease in fertility was achieved through the direct application of new technology, and hence a faster decline in fertility than historically observed occurred in many countries that had high fertility rates.

Epidemiological transition refers to changes in the relative importance of various diseases in a population's mortality profile. Most of the mortality decline that follows a reduction in fertility rates occurs in infancy and is attributable to a reduction in infectious diseases. In addition, economic, social, and technological changes have permitted an accelerated decrease in mortality from infectious diseases in all age groups, increasing the proportion of deaths attributed to noncommunicable diseases. Other terms used include "**health transition**," which includes changes in exposure to various risk factors, such as those that accompany urbanization; industrialization; lifestyle changes; and risk-averting interventions, such as improved water and sanitation and improved transportation. "**Nutrition transition**" refers to the changing pattern in a population's nutritional status whereby rates of undernutrition decrease and rates of overnutrition increase through stages in which undernutrition and overnutrition can be found in the same household.

Early diagnosis is the recognition of early signs and symptoms of disease that lead to diagnosis.

Human papillomavirus is a common virus that invades the epithelium, which is the protective layer of tissue that includes the skin and mucous membranes of the body, and can also be found in the mouth and elsewhere. It is also associated with the development of warts. The virus is extremely resistant and stable and can be viable outside a cell for up to a week. It is also resistant to organic solvents and moderate heat (56°C). Infection rates are high, with nearly 70 percent of women infected during their lifetime, but nonetheless, the virus is usually cleared by natural immunological mechanisms. Of the more than 100 human papillomavirus types known, 15 have been found to have the capacity to induce cancer. The rest cause asymptomatic infections that last, on average, 5 months, compared with 8 to 13 months for high-risk types of the virus. The persistence of the virus for longer periods of time is indicative of higher potential to develop cervical cancer.

Lipids. There are two lipids of major clinical importance: cholesterol and triglycerides. Cholesterol has three primary functions: it plays a role in the structure of cell membranes, in the synthesis of steroid hormones, and in the formation of bile acids. The major functions of triglycerides are energy storage (in fat) and energy use (by muscles). Because fat cannot readily dissolve in the blood, cholesterol and triglycerides are transported by lipoproteins. Very low-density lipoproteins transport mainly triglycerides, low-density lipoproteins account for the majority of cholesterol circulating in the blood and play a major role in creating fat deposits in blood vessels, and high-density lipoproteins mediate the return of lipoprotein and tissue cholesterol to the liver for excretion in a process referred to as reverse cholesterol transport. Cholesterol levels are determined by measuring these lipoproteins, of which the most critical for cardiovascular risk are low-density lipoproteins.

Metabolic syndrome is a set of signs and symptoms that include elevated triglycerides, reduced high-density lipoproteins, elevated blood pressure, elevated glucose, and abdominal obesity. The International Diabetes Federation and the U.S. National Institutes of Health have developed criteria for diagnosing metabolic syndrome and both require that at least three of the five conditions described be present, the only difference being that the International Diabetes Federation considers abdominal obesity to be a necessary condition whereas the National Institutes of Health does not. The reason for this discrepancy is that abdominal obesity as measured by waist circumference varies across ethnic groups. According to the World Health Organization, for individuals of European origin the level of abdominal obesity at which there is an increased cardiovascular risk is found at

94 centimeters or more in men and 80 centimeters or more in women. For Asian populations, particularly South Asians, who appear to have a higher risk of metabolic syndrome, waist circumference to determine abdominal obesity has been estimated at 78 centimeters and over for men and 73 centimeters and over for women.

Negative predictive value is the probability of not having a disease among those who test negative on the screening test.

Obesity can be defined as body fat accumulated in the abdomen, measured by waist circumference or by body mass index (weight in kilograms/height in centimeters squared). In relation to abdominal obesity, see the definition of **metabolic syndrome**. Overweight is equivalent to a body mass index greater than or equal to 25 to a body mass index under 30 and obesity is equivalent to a body mass index equal to or greater than 30. Although body mass index is a weaker predictor of cardiovascular disease events and deaths than waist circumference, it has been collected in many surveys, and is therefore likely to be available.

Population impact: when an intervention leads to changes in the total population as opposed to changes in individuals. For example, a therapy for a disease may lead to full recovery from that disease in individuals who had therapy; yet that does not mean that the mortality rate from the disease is necessarily expected to change.

Positive predictive value is the probability of having a disease among those that test positive on a screening test.

Primary prevention is aimed at reducing the level of one or more identified risk factors to reduce the probability of the initial occurrence of a disease.

Risk factor is any condition or feature that increases the probability of an adverse health outcome. It is generally accepted that a causality relationship exists between a risk factor and the adverse health outcome or disease if the following conditions are met: (a) temporality, where the cause must precede the effect; (b) strength of the association; (c) consistency over repeated observations; (d) biological gradient, either through a dose response or through a threshold; (e) biological plausibility; and (f) experimental evidence if possible.

Secondary prevention consists of ongoing interventions aimed at decreasing the severity and frequency of recurrent events of chronic or episodic diseases. The rationale for secondary prevention is that if disease can be identified at an early stage, intervention measures will be more effective.

Screening is the presumptive identification of unrecognized disease or defects by means of tests, examinations, or other procedures that can be applied rapidly. Screening does not imply diagnosis, just an increased likelihood of disease.

Sensitivity is the efficacy of a test to detect a disease among those who do have the disease. The counterfactual would be a false negative test.

Specificity is the efficacy of a test to provide a negative result among those who do not have the disease. The counterfactual would be a false positive test.

Years of life lost is a measure calculated by the number of cause-specific deaths multiplied by a loss function specifying the years lost as a function of the age at which death would have occurred. In this report it is estimated using standard life tables, with life expectancy at birth fixed at 82.5 years for females and 80.0 years for males.

References

Adioetomo, S. M., T. Djutaharta, and Hendratno. 2005. "Cigarette Consumption, Taxation, and Household Income: Indonesia Case Study." Health, Nutrition, and Population Discussion Paper, Economics of Tobacco Control, Paper 26, World Bank, Washington, DC.

Alcaraz, V. O. 2005. *Bolivia: Economia del Control del Tabaco en los Paises del Mercosur y Estados Asociados.* Washington, DC: Pan American Health Organization.

Ali, Z., A. Rahman, and T. Rahman. 2003. "Appetite for Nicotine: An Economic Analysis of Tobacco Control in Bangladesh." Health, Nutrition, and Population Discussion Paper, Economics of Tobacco Control, Paper 16, World Bank, Washington, DC.

Aloui, O. 2003. "Analysis of the Economics of Tobacco in Morocco." Health, Nutrition, and Population Discussion Paper, Economics of Tobacco Control, Paper 7, World Bank, Washington, DC.

American Heart Association. 2006. "Heart Disease and Stroke Statistics—2006 Update: A Report from the American Heart Association Statistics Committee and Stroke Statistics Committee." *Journal of the American Heart Association* 113 (6): 85–151.

Ammerman, A. S., C. H. Lindquist, K. N. Lohr, and J. Hersey. 2002. "The Efficacy of Behavioral Interventions to Modify Dietary Fat and Fruit and Vegetable Intake: A Review of the Evidence." *Preventive Medicine* 35 (1): 25–41.

Anderson, K. M., P. W. Wilson, P. M. Odell, and W. B. Kannel. 1991. "An Updated Coronary Risk Profile: A Statement for Health Professionals." *Circulation* 83 (1): 356–62.

Andrieu, E., N. Darmon, and A. Drewnowski. 2006. "Low-Cost Diets: More Energy, Fewer Nutrients." *European Journal of Clinical Nutrition* 60 (3): 434–36.

Aristizabal, N., C. Cuello, P. Correa, T. Collazos, and W. Haenszel. 1984. "The Impact of Vaginal Cytology on Cervical Cancer Risks in Cali, Colombia." *International Journal of Cancer* 34 (1): 5–9.

Arunatilake, N., and M. Opatha. 2003. "The Economics of Tobacco in Sri Lanka." Health, Nutrition, and Population Discussion Paper, Economics of Tobacco Control, Paper 12, World Bank, Washington, DC.

Asia Pacific Cohort Studies Collaboration. 2006. "The Impact of Cardiovascular Risk Factors on the Age-Related Excess Risk of Coronary Heart Disease." *International Journal of Epidemiology* 35 (4): 1025–33.

Babor, T. F., and R. Caetano. 2005. "Evidence-Based Alcohol Policy in the Americas: Strengths, Weaknesses, and Future Challenges." *Revista Pan Americana de Salud Pública* 18 (4–5): 327–37.

Baigent, C., A. Keech, P. M. Kearney, L. Blackwell, G. Buck, C. Pollicino, A. Kirby, and others. 2005. "Efficacy and Safety of Cholesterol-Lowering Treatment: Prospective Meta-Analysis of Data from 90,056 Participants in 14 Randomised Trials of Statins." *Lancet* 366 (9493): 1267–78.

Baines, J., and S. Lata 2004. "Consumer Understanding and Use of Nutrition Information Panels." *Asia Pacific Journal of Clinical Nutrition* 13 (Suppl): S160.

Balabanova, D., M. McKee, and N. Koroleva. 2006. "Systemic Constraints on Service Delivery for Noncommunicable Diseases." Unpublished background report, London School of Hygiene and Tropical Medicine.

Banta, D. 2003. "The Development of Health Technology Assessment." *Health Policy* 63 (2): 121–32.

Barcelo, A., C. Aedo, S. Rajpathak, and S. Robles. 2003. "The Cost of Diabetes in Latin America and the Caribbean." *Bulletin of the World Health Organization* 81 (1): 19–27.

Barro, R. J. 1991. "Economic Growth in a Cross-Section of Countries." *Quarterly Journal of Economics* 106 (2): 407–43.

———. 1996. *Health and Economic Growth*. Washington, DC: Pan American Health Organization.

Barro, R. J., and J. W. Lee. 1994. "Sources of Economic Growth." *Carnegie Rochester Conferences Series on Public Policy* 40 (June): 1–46.

Barro, R. J., and X. Sala-I-Martin. 1995. *Economic Growth*. New York: McGraw-Hill.

Bartosch, W. J., and G. C. Pope. 2002. "Economic Effect of Restaurant Smoking Restrictions on Restaurant Business in Massachusetts, 1992 to 1998." *Tobacco Control* 11 (Suppl 2): ii38–ii42.

Bennett, K., Z. Kabir, B. Unal, E. Shelley, J. Critchley, I. Perry, J. Feely, and S. Capewell. 2006. "Explaining the Recent Decrease in Coronary Heart Disease Mortality Rates in Ireland, 1985–2000." *Journal of Epidemiology and Community Health* 60 (4): 322–27.

Berry, L. L., A. M. Mirabito, and D. M. Berwick. 2004. "A Health Care Agenda for Business." *MIT Sloan Management Review* 45 (4): 56–64.

Bhopal, R., C. Fischbacher, E. Vartianen, N. Unwin, M. White, and G. Alberti. 2005. "Predicted and Observed Cardiovascular Disease in South Asians: Application of FINRISK, Framingham, and SCORE Models to Newcastle Heart Project Data." *Journal of Public Health* 27 (1): 93–100.

Birdsall, N., and E. James. 1993. "Health, Government, and the Poor: The Case for the Private Sector." In *Policy and Planning Implications of the Epidemiological Transition*, ed. James Gribble and Samuel Preston, 229–51. Washington, DC: National Academies Press.

Blakely, T., S. Hales, C. Kieft, N. Wilson, and A. Woodward. 2005. "The Global Distribution of Risk Factors by Poverty Level." *Bulletin of the World Health Organization* 83 (2): 118–26.

Bleil, L. D., J. Kalamas, and R. K. Mathoda. 2004. "How to Control Health Benefit Costs." *McKinsey Quarterly* (1): 104–13.

Bodenheimer, T., E. H. Wagner, and K. Grumbach. 2002a. "Improving Primary Care for Patients with Chronic Illnesses." *Journal of the American Medical Association* 288 (14): 1775–79.

———. 2002b. "Improving Primary Care for Patients with Chronic Illness: The Chronic Care Model, Part 2." *Journal of the American Medical Association* 288 (15): 1909–14.

Bonu, S., M. Rani, P. Jha, D. H. Peters, and S. N. Nguyen. 2004. "Household Tobacco and Alcohol Use and Child Health: An Exploratory Study from India." *Health Policy* 70 (1): 67–83.

Bonu, S., M. Rani, D. Peters, P. Jha, and S. N. Nguyen. 2005. "Does Use of Tobacco or Alcohol Contribute to Impoverishment from Hospitalization Costs in India?" *Health Policy and Planning* 20 (1): 41–49.

Brett, S. E., J. M. Ritter, and P. J. Chowienczyk. 2000. "Diastolic Blood Pressure Changes during Exercise Positively Correlate with Serum Cholesterol and Insulin Resistance." *Circulation* 101 (6): 611–15.

Brindle, P., J. Emberson, F. Lampe, M. Walker, P. Whincup, T. Fahey, and S. Ebrahim. 2003. "Predictive Accuracy of the Framingham Coronary Risk

Score in British Men: Prospective Cohort Study." *British Medical Journal* 327 (7426): 1267–70.

Brown, M. D., G. E. Moore, M. T. Korytkowski, S. D. McCole, and J. M. Hagberg. 1997. "Improvement of Insulin Sensitivity by Short-Term Exercise Training in Hypertensive African American Women." *Hypertension* 30 (6): 1549–53.

Brown, M. L., S. J. Goldie, G. Draisma, J. Harford, and J. Lipscomb. 2006. "Health Services Interventions for Cancer Control in Developing Countries." In *Disease Control Priorities in Developing Countries*, 2nd ed., ed. D. Jamison, J. Breman, A. Measham, G. Alleyne, M. Claeson, D. Evans, P. Jha, A. Mills, and P. Musgrove, 569–89. New York: Oxford University Press.

Cacho, J. 2003. "The Supermarket 'Market' Phenomenon in Developing Countries: Implications for Smallholder Farmers and Investment." *American Journal of Agricultural Economics* 85 (5): 1162–63.

Capewell, S., R. Beaglehole, M. Seddon, and J. McMurray. 2000. "Explanation for the Decline in Coronary Heart Disease Mortality Rates in Auckland, New Zealand, between 1982 and 1993." *Circulation* 102 (13): 1511–16.

Capewell, S., C. E. Morrison, and J. J. McMurray. 1999. "Contribution of Modern Cardiovascular Treatment and Risk Factor Changes to the Decline in Coronary Heart Disease Mortality in Scotland between 1975 and 1994." *Heart* 81 (4): 380–86.

Centers for Disease Control and Prevention. 2001. "Updated Guidelines for Evaluating Public Health Surveillance Systems: Recommendations from the Guidelines Working Group." *MMWR* 50 (RR13): 1–35.

———. 2005. "Annual Smoking-Attributable Mortality, Years of Potential Life Lost, and Productivity Losses: United States, 1997–2001." *MMWR* 54 (25): 625–28.

Chale, S. S., A. B. Swai, P. G. Mujinja, and D. G. McLarty. 1992. "Must Diabetes Be a Fatal Disease in Africa? Study of Cost of Treatment." *British Medical Journal* 304 (6836): 1215–18.

Chaloupka, F., and P. Jha. 2000. *Tobacco Control in Developing Countries*. New York: Oxford University Press.

Chaudhury, N., J. Hammer, M. Kremer, K. Muralidharan, and F. H. Rogers. 2006. "Missing in Action: Teacher and Health Worker Absence in Developing Countries." *Journal of Economic Perspectives* 20 (1): 91–116.

Chinese Academy of Preventive Medicine. 1997. *Smoking and Health in China: 1996 National Prevalence Survey of Smoking Patterns*. Beijing: China Science and Technology Press.

Chisholm, D., J. Rehm, M. Van Ommeren, and M. Monteiro. 2004. "Reducing the Global Burden of Hazardous Alcohol Use: A Comparative Cost-Effectiveness Analysis." *Journal of Studies on Alcohol* 65 (6): 782–93.

Choi, Y., J. Friedman, P. Heywood, and S. Kosen. Forthcoming. "Forecasting Health Care Demand in a Middle-Income Country: Disease Transitions in East and Central Java, Indonesia." Research Working Paper, World Bank, Washington, DC.

Chou, S.-Y., M. Grossman, and H. Saffer. 2004. "An Economic Analysis of Adult Obesity: Results from the Behavioral Risk Factor Surveillance System." *Journal of Health Economics* 23 (3): 565–87.

Clark, D. B., D. S. Wood, C. S. Martin, J. R. Cornelius, K. G. Lynch, and S. Shiffman. 2005. "Multidimensional Assessment of Nicotine Dependence in Adolescents." *Drug and Alcohol Dependence* 77 (3): 235–42.

Cochrane, A. L. 1999. "Effectiveness and Efficiency: Random Reflections on Health Services." Royal Society of Medicine Press, London, U.K.

Coleman, M. P., G. Gatta, A. Verdecchia, J. Esteve, M. Sant, H. Storm, C. Allemani, and others. 2003. "EUROCARE-3 Summary: Cancer Survival in Europe at the End of the 20th Century." *Annals of Oncology* 14 (Suppl 5): v128–v149.

Collins, D. J., and H. M. Lapsley. 1996. *The Social Costs of Drug Abuse in Australia in 1988 and 1992*. National Drug Strategy Monograph Series 30. Prepared for the Commonwealth Department of Human Services and Health. Canberra: Australian Government Printing Service.

Committee on Food Marketing and the Diets of Children and Youth, J. M. McGinnis, J. A. Gootman, and V. I. Kraak, eds. 2006. *Food Marketing to Children and Youth: Threat or Opportunity?* Washington, DC: National Academies Press.

Conroy, R. M., K. Pyörälä, A. P. Fitzgerald, S. Sans, A. Menotti, G. De Backer, D. De Bacquer, and others. 2003. "Estimation of Ten-Year Risk of Fatal Cardiovascular Disease in Europe: The SCORE Project." *European Heart Journal* 24 (11): 987–1003.

Cook, P. J., and M. J. Moore. 2002. "The Economics of Alcohol Abuse and Alcohol-Control Policies." *Health Affairs (Millwood)* 21 (2): 120–33.

Corber, S., S. C. Robles, P. Orduñez, and P. Rodriguez. 2003. "Non-Communicable Disease Surveillance in Latin America and the Caribbean: Advances Supported by the Pan American Health Organization." In *Global Behavioral Risk Factor Surveillance*, ed. P. McQueen and P. Pekka. New York: Kluwer Academic and Plenum Publishers, 227–32.

Cowburn, G., and L. Stockley. 2005. "Consumer Understanding and Use of Nutrition Labelling: A Systematic Review." *Public Health Nutrition* 8 (1): 21–28.

Cowling, D. W., and P. Bond. 2005. "Smoke-Free Laws and Bar Revenues in California: The Last Call." *Health Economics* 14 (12): 1273–81.

Crimmins, E. M., Y. Saito, and S. L. Reynolds. 1997. "Further Evidence on Recent Trends in the Prevalence and Incidence of Disability among Older Americans from Two Sources: The LSOA and the NHIS." *Journal of Gerontology* 52B: S59–S71.

Critchley, J. A., and S. Capewell. 2002. "Why Model Coronary Heart Disease?" *European Heart Journal* 23 (2): 110–16.

Cutler, D. M. 2001. "The Economics of Better Health: The Case of Cardiovascular Disease." Draft, Harvard University and the National Bureau of Economic Research, Cambridge, MA.

Cutler, D. M., E. L. Glaeser, and J. Shapiro. 2003. "Why Have Americans Become More Obese?" *Journal of Economic Perspectives* 17 (3): 93–118.

Cutler, D. M., M. B. Landrum, and K. A. Stewart. 2006. "Intensive Medical Care and Cardiovascular Disease Disability Conditions." Working Paper 12184, National Bureau of Economic Research, Cambridge, MA.

Cutler, D. M., and L. Sheiner. 1998. "Demographics and Medical Care Spending: Standard and Non-Standard Effects." Working Paper 6866, National Bureau of Economic Research, Cambridge, MA.

Das, J., and J. Hammer, 2006. "Chronically Misinformed: Chronic Illnesses, Information, and Income in Delhi, India." Unpublished draft, World Bank, Washington, DC.

———. Forthcoming. "Money for Nothing: The Dire Straits of Medical Practice in Delhi, India." *Journal of Development Economics*.

Daviglus, M. L., K. Liu, P. Greenland, A. R. Dyer, D. B. Garside, L. Manheim, L. P. Lowe, M. Rodin, J. Lubitz, and J. Stamler. 1998. "Benefit of a Favorable Cardiovascular Risk-Factor Profile in Middle Age with Respect to Medicare Costs." *New England Journal of Medicine* 339 (16): 1122–29.

Daviglus, M. L., K. Liu, A. Pirzada, L. L. Yan, D. B. Garside, P. Greenland, L. M. Manheim, A. R. Dyer, R. Wang, J. Lubitz, W. G. Manning, J. F. Fries, and J. Stamler. 2005. "Cardiovascular Risk Profile Earlier in Life and Medicare Costs in the Last Year of Life." *Archives of Internal Medicine* 165 (9): 1028–34.

de Beyer, J., and L. W. Brigden, eds. 2003. *Tobacco Control Policy: Strategies, Successes, and Setbacks*. Washington, DC: World Bank.

Debrott Sanchez, D. 2005. *Chile: Economia del control del tabaco en los paises del Mercosur y estados asociados*. Washington, DC: Pan American Health Organization.

Department of Health and Human Services. 1996. *Physical Activity and Health: A Report of the Surgeon General*. Atlanta: Department of Health and Human Services, Centers for Disease Control and Prevention, National Center for Chronic Disease Prevention and Health Promotion. http://www.cdc.gov/nccdphp/sgr/pdf/sgrfull.pdf.

———. 2001. *The Surgeon General's Call to Action to Prevent and Decrease Overweight and Obesity 2001*. Rockville, MD: Department of Health and Human Services, Office of the Surgeon General.

————. 2006. *The Health Consequences of Involuntary Exposure to Tobacco Smoke: A Report of the Surgeon General*. Atlanta: Department of Health and Human Services, Centers for Disease Control and Prevention, Coordinating Center for Health Promotion, National Center for Chronic Disease Prevention and Health Promotion, Office on Smoking and Health. http://www.surgeongeneral. gov/library/secondhandsmoke.

Department of Health and Human Services; National Institutes of Health; and National Heart, Lung, and Blood Institute. 2003. *The Seventh Report of the Joint National Committee on Prevention, Detection, Evaluation, and Treatment of High Blood Pressure*. Bethesda, MD: National Institutes of Health.

Dishman, R. K., B. Oldenburg, H. O'Neal, and R. J. Shephard. 1998. "Worksite Physical Activity Interventions." *American Journal of Preventive Medicine* 15 (4): 344–61.

Doak, C. M., L. S. Adair, C. Monteiro, and B. M. Popkin. 2000. "Overweight and Underweight Coexist within Households in Brazil, China, and Russia." *Journal of Nutrition* 130 (12): 2965–71.

Doll, R., and A. B. Hill. 1954. "The Mortality of Doctors in Relation to Their Smoking Habits: A Preliminary Report." *British Medical Journal* 4877 (1): 1451–55.

Drewnowski, A., and N. Darmon. 2005. "The Economics of Obesity: Dietary Energy Density and Energy Cost." *American Journal of Clinical Nutrition* 82 (Suppl 1): 265S–273S.

Efroymson, D., S. Ahmed, J. Townsend, S. M. Alam, A. R. Dey, R. Saha, B. Dhar, A. I. Sujon, K. U. Ahmed, and O. Rahman. 2001. "Hungry for Tobacco: An Analysis of the Economic Impact of Tobacco Consumption on the Poor in Bangladesh." *Tobacco Control* 10 (3): 212–17.

Emberson, J., P. Whincup, R. Morris, M. Walker, and S. Ebrahim. 2004. "Evaluating the Impact of Population and High-Risk Strategies for the Primary Prevention of Cardiovascular Disease." *European Heart Journal* 25 (6): 484–91.

Emmons, K. M. 2000. "Behavioral and Social Sciences Contribution to the Health of the Adults in the United States." In *Promoting Health: Intervention Strategies from Social and Behavioral Research*, ed. B. D. Smedley and S. Leonard, 254–320. Washington, DC: National Academy Press.

Esson, K., and S. R. Leeder. 2004. *The Millennium Development Goals and Tobacco Control: An Opportunity for Global Partnership*. Geneva: World Health Organization.

European Diabetes Policy Group. 1999a. "A Desktop Guide to Type 1 (Insulin-Dependent) Diabetes Mellitus." *Diabetes Medicine* 16 (3): 253–66.

————. 1999b. "A Desktop Guide to Type 2 Diabetes Mellitus." *Diabetes Medicine* 16 (9): 716–30.

Ezzati, M., S. Vander Hoorn, A. Rogers, A. D. Lopez, C. D. Mathers, C. J. Murray, and the Comparative Risk Assessment Collaborating Group. 2003. "Estimates of Global and Regional Potential Health Gains from Reducing Multiple Risk Factors." *Lancet* 362 (9380): 271–80.

Farrelly, M. C., W. N. Evans, and A. E. S. Sfekas. 1999. "The Impact of Workplace Smoking Bans: Results from a National Survey." *Tobacco Control* 8 (3): 272–77.

Farrelly, M. C., J. Niederdeppe, and J. Yarsevich. 2003. "Youth Tobacco Prevention Mass Media Campaigns: Past, Present, and Future Directions." *Tobacco Control* 12 (Suppl 1): i35–i47.

Feachem, R., T. Kjellstrom, C. Murray, M. Over, and M. Phillips, eds. 1992. *The Health of Adults in the Developing World*. Oxford, U.K.: Oxford University Press.

Fenoglio, P., V. Parel, and P. Kopp. 2003. "The Social Cost of Alcohol, Tobacco, and Illicit Drugs in France, 1997." *European Addiction Research* 9 (1): 18–28.

Fernández Garrote, L., J. J. Lence Anta, E. Cabezas Cruz, T. Romero, and R. Camacho. 1996. "Evaluation of the Cervical Cancer Control Program in Cuba." *Bulletin of the Pan American Health Organization* 30 (4): 387–91.

Fichtenberg, C. M., and S. A. Glantz. 2002. "Effect of Smoke-Free Workplaces on Smoking Behaviour: Systematic Review." *British Medical Journal* 325 (7357): 188–91.

Filmer, D. 2003. "The Incidence of Public Expenditures on Health and Education." Draft background paper for the *World Development Report 2004: Making Services Work for Poor People*, World Bank, Washington, DC.

Filmer, D., J. Hammer, and L. Pritchett. 2000. "Weak Links in the Chain: A Diagnosis of Health Policy in Poor Countries." *World Bank Research Observer* 15 (2): 199–224.

———. 2002. "Weak Links in the Chain II: A Prescription for Health Policy in Poor Countries." *World Bank Research Observer* 17 (1): 47–66.

Filmer, D., and L. Pritchett. 1999. "The Impact of Public Spending on Health: Does Money Matter?" *Social Science and Medicine* 49 (10): 1309–23.

Fisher, E. S., D. E. Wennberg, T. A. Stukel, D. J. Gottlieb, F. L. Lucas, and E. L. Pinder. 2003a. "The Implications of Regional Variations in Medicare Spending. Part 1: The Content, Quality, and Accessibility of Care." *Annals of Internal Medicine* 138 (4): 273–87.

———. 2003b. "The Implications of Regional Variations in Medicare Spending. Part 2: Health Outcomes and Satisfaction with Care." *Annals of Internal Medicine* 138 (4): 288–98.

Frei, A. 2001. *Kostenanalyse des alkoholkonsums in der Schweiz: teilbericht direkte kosten*. Basel, Switzerland: Healthecon.

French, S. A. 2003. "Pricing Effects on Food Choices." *Journal of Nutrition* 133 (3): 841S–843S.

Fries, J. 1980. "Aging, Natural Death, and the Compression of Morbidity." *New England Journal of Medicine* 303 (3): 130–35.

Gage, J. C., C. Ferreccio, M. Gonzales, R. Arroyo, M. Huivin, and S. C. Robles. 2003. "Follow-Up Care of Women with an Abnormal Cytology in a Low-Resource Setting." *Cancer Detection and Prevention* 27 (6): 466–71.

Gallus, S., A. Schiaffino, C. La Vecchia, J. Townsend, and E. Fernandez. 2006. "Price and Cigarette Consumption in Europe." *Tobacco Control* 15 (2): 114–19.

Garrett, J., and M. T. Ruel. 2005. "The Coexistence of Child Undernutrition and Maternal Overweight: Prevalence, Hypotheses, and Programme and Policy Implications." *Maternal and Child Nutrition* 1 (3): 185–96.

Gatta, G., R. Capocaccia, C. Stiller, P. Kaatsch, F. Berrino, M. Terenziani, and the EUROCARE Working Group. 2005. "Childhood Cancer Survival Trends in Europe: A EUROCARE Working Group Study." *Journal of Clinical Oncology* 23 (16): 3742–51.

Gelders, S., M. Ewen, N. Noguchi, and R. Laing. 2006. *Price, Availability, and Affordability: An International Comparison of Chronic Disease Medicines.* Cairo: World Health Organization and Health Action International.

Gertler, P., and J. Gruber. 2002. "Insuring Consumption against Illness." *American Economic Review* 92 (1): 51–70.

Gertler, P., D. Levine, and M. Ames. 2004. "Schooling and Parental Death." *Review of Economics and Statistics* 6 (1): 211–25.

Ghaffar, A., K. Srinath Reddy, and M. Singhi. 2004. "Burden of Noncommunicable Diseases in South Asia." *British Medical Journal* 328 (April 3): 807–10.

Giampaoli, S., L. Palmieri, A. Mattiello, and S. Panico. 2005. "Definition of High-Risk Individuals to Optimise Strategies for Primary Prevention of Cardiovascular Diseases." *Nutrition Metabolism and Cardiovascular Disease* 15 (1): 79–85.

Giles, T. D., B. C. Berk, H. R. Black, J. N. Cohn, J. B. Kostis, J. L. Izzo Jr., and M. A. Weber. 2005. "Expanding the Definition and Classification of Hypertension." *Journal of Clinical Hypertension* (Greenwich, CT) 7 (9): 505–12.

GKI Economic Research Institute. 2004. *Economic Impact of Smoking and Tobacco Control in Hungary.* Budapest: GKI Economic Research Institute.

Glanz, K., M. Basil, E. Maibach, J. Goldberg, and D. Snyder. 1998. "Why Americans Eat What They Do: Taste, Nutrition, Cost, Convenience, and Weight Control Concerns as Influences on Food Consumption." *Journal of the American Dietetic Association* 98 (10): 1118–26.

Goldie, S. J., L. Gaffikin, J. D. Goldhaber-Fiebert, A. Gordillo-Tobar, C. Levin, C. Mahé, T. C. Wright, for the Alliance for Cervical Cancer Prevention Cost Working Group. 2005. "Cost-Effectiveness of Cervical-Cancer Screening in Five Developing Countries." *New England Journal of Medicine* 353 (20): 2158–68.

Goldie, S. J., M. Kohli, D. Grima, M. C. Weinstein, T. C. Wright, F. X. Bosch, and E. Franco. 2004. "Projected Clinical Benefits and Cost-Effectiveness of a Human Papillomavirus 16/18 Vaccine." *Journal of the National Cancer Institute* 96 (8): 604–15.

Goldman, D. P., G. F. Joyce, J. J. Escarce, J. E. Pace, M. D. Solomon, M. Laouri, P. B. Landsman, and S. M. Teutsch. 2004. "Pharmacy Benefits and the Use of Drugs by the Chronically Ill." *Journal of the American Medical Association* 291 (19): 2344–50.

Goldman, L. 2004. "The Decline in Coronary Heart Disease: Determining the Paternity of Success." *American Journal of Medicine* 117 (4): 274–76.

Gonzales-Rozada, M. 2005. *Argentina: Economia del Control del Tabaco en los Paises del Mercosur y Estados Asociados*. Washington, DC: Pan American Health Organization.

Goodman, C., and A. Anise. 2006. *What Is Known about the Effectiveness of Economic Instruments to Reduce Consumption of Foods High in Saturated Fats and Other Energy-Dense Foods for Preventing and Treating Obesity?* Health Evidence Network report. Copenhagen: World Health Organization Regional Office for Europe. http://www.euro.who.int/document/e88909.pdf.

Gostin, L. O. 2000. "Legal and Public Policy: Interventions to Advance the Population's Health." In *Promoting Health: Intervention Strategies from Social and Behavioral Research*, ed. B. D. Smedley and S. L. Syme, 390–416. Washington, DC: National Academies Press.

Gotsadze, G., D. Gzirishvili, S. Bennett, and K. Ranson. 2001. *Health Service Utilisation and Expenditures in Tbilisi—2000: Report of a Household Survey*. Tbilisi: Curatio International Foundation.

Greenberg, P. E., R. C. Kessler, H. G. Birnbaum, S. A. Leong, S. W. Lowe, P. A. Berglund, and P. K. Corey-Lisle. 2003. "The Economic Burden of Depression in the United States: How Did It Change between 1990 and 2000?" *Journal of Clinical Psychiatry* 64 (12): 1465–75.

Gruber, J., A. Sen, and M. Stabile. 2003. "Estimating Price Elasticities When There Is Smuggling: The Sensitivity of Smoking to Price in Canada." *Journal of Health Economics* 22 (5): 821–42.

Grundy, S. M., J. I. Cleeman, S. R. Daniels, K. A. Donato, R. H. Eckel, B. A. Franklin, D. J. Gordon, and others. 2005. "Diagnosis and Management of the Metabolic Syndrome: An American Heart Association/National Heart, Lung, and Blood Institute Scientific Statement." *Circulation* 112 (17): 2735–52.

Gu, D., K. Reynolds, X. Wu, J. Chen, X. Duan, P. Muntner, G. Huang, and others. 2002. "Prevalence, Awareness, Treatment, and Control of Hypertension in China." *Hypertension* 40 (6): 920–27.

Guindon, G. E., and D. Boisclair. 2003. "Past, Current, and Future Trends in Tobacco Use: The Economics of Tobacco Control." Health, Nutrition, and

Population Discussion Paper, Economics of Tobacco Control, Paper 6. World Bank, Washington, DC.

Guo, X., B. M. Popkin, T. A. Mroz, and F. Zhai. 1999. "Food Price Policy Can Favorably Alter Macronutrient Intake in China." *Journal of Nutrition* 129 (5): 994–1001.

Gwatkin, D. R., and M. Guillot. 2000. *The Burden of Disease among the Global Poor: Current Situation, Future Trends, and Implications for Strategy.* Washington, DC: World Bank.

Gwatkin, D. R., M. Guillot, and P. Heuveline. 1999. "The Burden of Disease among the Global Poor." *Lancet* 354 (9178): 586–89.

Hajjar, I., and T. A. Kotchen. 2003. "Trends in Prevalence, Awareness, Treatment, and Control of Hypertension in the United States, 1988–2000." *Journal of the American Medical Association* 290 (2): 199–206.

Hamilton, V. H., C. Levinton, Y. St.-Pierre, and F. Grimard. 1997. "The Effect of Tobacco Tax Cuts on Cigarette Smoking in Canada." *Canadian Medical Association Journal* 156 (2): 187–91.

Hammond, D., G. T. Fong, P. W. Mcdonald, R. Cameron, and K. S. Brown. 2003. "Impact of the Graphic Canadian Warning Labels on Adult Smoking Behaviour." *Tobacco Control* 12 (4): 391–95.

Hawkes, C. 2004. *Marketing Food to Children: The Global Regulatory Environment.* Geneva: World Health Organization.

———. 2006. "Uneven Dietary Development: Linking the Policies and Processes of Globalization with the Nutrition Transition, Obesity, and Diet-Related Chronic Diseases." Review. *Globalization and Health* 2: 4.

Heller, P. S. 2006. "The Prospects of Creating 'Fiscal Space' for the Health Sector." *Health Policy and Planning* 21 (2): 75–79.

Hense, H. W., H. Schulte, H. Löwel, G. Assmann, and U. Keil. 2003. "Framingham Risk Function Overestimates Risk of Coronary Heart Disease in Men and Women from Germany: Results from the MONICA Augsburg and the PRO-CAM Cohorts." *European Heart Journal* 24 (10): 937–45.

Herrero, R., L. A. Brinton, W. C. Reeves, M. M. Brenes, R. C. de Britton, E. Gaitan, and F. Tenorio. 1992. "Screening for Cervical Cancer in Latin America: A Case-Control Study." *International Journal of Epidemiology* 21 (6): 1050–56.

Hillsdon, M., C. Foster, and M. Thorogood. 2005. "Interventions for Promoting Physical Activity." *Cochrane Database of Systematic Reviews* (1): CD003180.

Hopkins, D. P., P. A. Briss, C. J. Ricard, C. G. Husten, V. G. Carande-Kulis, J. E. Fielding, M. O. Alao, and others. 2001. "Reviews of Evidence Regarding Interventions to Reduce Tobacco Use and Exposure to Environmental Tobacco Smoke." *American Journal of Preventive Medicine* 20 (Suppl 2): 16–66.

Hopkinson, B., D. Balabanova, M. McKee, and J. Kutzin. 2004. "The Human Perspective on Health Care Reform: Coping with Diabetes in Kyrgyzstan." *International Journal of Health Planning and Management* 19 (1): 43–61.

Horch, K., and E. Bergemann. 2003. "Berechnung der Kosten alkoholassozieerter Krankheiten Bundegesundheitsblatt." *Gesundheitsforschung—Gesundheitsschutz* 46 (8): 625–35.

Hsu, J., M. Price, J. Huang, R. Brand, V. Fung, R. Hui, B. Fireman, J. P. Newhouse, and J. V. Selby. 2006. "Unintended Consequences of Caps on Medicare Drug Benefits." *New England Journal of Medicine* 354 (22): 2349–59.

Hu, T.-W., and Z. Mao. 2002. "Economics Analysis of Tobacco and Options for Tobacco Control: China Case Study." Health, Nutrition, and Population Discussion Paper, Economics of Tobacco Control, Paper 3, World Bank, Washington, DC.

Hu, T.-W., Z. Mao, Y. Liu, J. de Beyer, and M. Ong. 2005. "Smoking, Standard of Living, and Poverty in China." *Tobacco Control* 14 (4): 247–50.

Hu, T.-W., Z. Mao, M. Ong, E. Tong, M. Tao, H. Jiang, K. Hammond, K. R. Smith, J. de Beyer, and A. Yureki. 2006. "China at the Crossroads: The Economics of Tobacco and Health." *Tobacco Control* 15 (Suppl 1): i37–i41.

Hughes, J. R., S. Shiffman, P. Callas, and J. Zhang. 2003. "A Meta-Analysis of the Efficacy of Over-the-Counter Nicotine Replacement." *Tobacco Control* 12 (1): 21–27.

Hughes, J. R., L. F. Stead, and T. Lancaster. 2004. "Antidepressants for Smoking Cessation." Cochrane Database of Systematic Reviews (4): CD000031.

Hunink, M. G., L. Goldman, A. N. Tosteson, M. A. Mittleman, P. A. Goldman, L. W. Williams, J. Tsevat, and M. C. Weinstein. 1997. "The Recent Decline in Mortality from Coronary Heart Disease, 1980–1990: The Effect of Secular Trends in Risk Factors and Treatment." *Journal of the American Medical Association* 277 (7): 535–42.

IDF (International Diabetes Federation). 2003. *Diabetes Atlas*. Second Edition. Brussels: International Diabetes Federation.

Iglesias, R., and J. Nicolau. 2005. *Brasil: A economia do controle do tabaco nos paises dol Mercosur e associados*. Washington, DC: Pan American Health Organization.

International Agency for Research on Cancer. 2002a. *Breast Cancer Screening*. Lyon, France. International Agency for Research on Cancer Handbooks of Cancer Prevention, vol. 7. Lyon, France: International Agency for Research on Cancer Press and World Health Organization.

———. 2002b. *Fruits and Vegetables*. International Agency for Research on Cancer Handbooks of Cancer Prevention, vol. 8. Lyon, France: International Agency for Research on Cancer Press and World Health Organization.

———. 2005. *Cervix Cancer Screening.* International Agency for Research on Cancer Handbooks of Cancer Prevention, vol. 10. Lyon, France: International Agency for Research on Cancer Press and World Health Organization.

Jamison, D., J. Breman, A. Measham, G. Alleyne, M. Claeson, D. Evans, P. Jha, A. Mills, and P. Musgrove, eds. 2006a. *Disease Control Priorities in Developing Countries,* 2nd ed. New York: Oxford University Press.

———. eds. 2006b. *Priorities in Health.* Washington, DC: World Bank.

Jernigan, D. H., M. Monteiro, R. Room, and S. Saxena. 2000. "Towards a Global Alcohol Policy: Alcohol, Public Health, and the Role of WHO." *Bulletin of the World Health Organization* 78 (4): 491–99.

Jha, P., and F. Chaloupka, eds. 2000. *Tobacco Control in Developing Countries.* New York: Oxford University Press.

Joossens, L., and M. Raw. 2000. "How Can Cigarette Smuggling Be Reduced?" *British Medical Journal* 321 (7266): 947–50.

Jossens, L. 2005. "The Economic Impact of a Smoking Ban in Bars and Restaurants." In *The Smoke-Free Europe Partnership: Smoke-Free Europe Makes Economic Sense.* A Report on the Economic Aspects of Smoke-Free Policies. Brussels: Smoke-Free Europe Partnership.

Kahn, E. B., L. T. Ramsey, R. C. Brownson, G. W. Heath, E. H. Howze, K. E. Powell, E. J. Stone, M. W. Rajab, and P. Corso. 2002. "The Effectiveness of Interventions to Increase Physical Activity: A Systematic Review." *American Journal of Preventive Medicine* 22 (Suppl 4): 73–107.

Kaiserman, M. J. 1997. "The Cost of Smoking in Canada, 1991." *Chronic Diseases in Canada* 18 (1): 13–19.

Kang, H. Y., H. J. Kim, T. K. Park, S. H. Jee, C. M. Nam, and H. W. Park. 2003. "Economic Burden of Smoking in Korea." *Tobacco Control* 12 (1): 37–44.

Karki, Y. B., K. D. Pant, and B. R. Pande. 2003. "A Study on the Economics of Tobacco in Nepal." Health, Nutrition, and Population Discussion Paper, Economics of Tobacco Control, Paper 13, World Bank, Washington, DC.

Katzmarzyk, P. T., and I. Janssen. 2004. "The Economic Costs Associated with Physical Inactivity and Obesity in Canada: An Update." *Canadian Journal of Applied Physiology* 29 (1): 90–115.

Kenkel, D. S., and W. G. Manning. 1996. "Perspectives on Alcohol Taxation." *Alcohol Health and Research World* 20 (4): 230–39.

Khan, I., V. Dekou, M. Hanson, L. Poston, and P. Taylor. 2004. "Predictive Adaptive Responses to Maternal High-Fat Diet Prevent Endothelial Dysfunction but Not Hypertension in Adult Rat Offspring." *Circulation* 110 (9): 1097–1102.

Kibriya, M. G., L. Ali, N. G. Banik, and A. K. Azad Khan. 1999. "Home Monitoring of Blood Glucose (HMBG) in Type 2 Diabetes Mellitus in a Developing Country." *Diabetes Research and Clinical Practice* 46 (3): 253–57.

Kuchler, F., A. Tegene, and J. M. Harris. 2004. "Taxing Snack Foods: What to Expect for Diet and Tax Revenues." *Current Issues in Economics of Food Markets, Agriculture Information Bulletin* (U.S. Department of Agriculture, Economic Research Service): No. 747–48.

Kuulasmaa, K., H. Tunstall-Pedoe, A. Dobson, S. Fortmann, S. Sans, H. Tolonen, A. Evans, M. Ferrario, and J. Tuomilehto for the WHO MONICA Project. 2000. "Estimation of Contribution of Changes in Classic Risk Factors to Trends in Coronary-Event Rates across the WHO MONICA Project Populations." *Lancet* 355 (9205): 675–87.

Kyaing, N. N. 2003. "Tobacco Economics in Myanmar." Health, Nutrition, and Population Discussion Paper, Economics of Tobacco Control, Paper 14, World Bank, Washington, DC.

Laatikainen, T., J. Critchley, E. Vartiainen, V. Salomaa, M. Ketonen, and S. Capewell. 2005. "Explaining the Decline in Coronary Heart Disease Mortality in Finland between 1982 and 1997." *American Journal of Epidemiology* 162 (8): 764–73.

Lanjouw, P., and M. Ravallion. 1999. "Benefit Incidence, Public Spending Reforms, and the Timing of Program Capture." *World Bank Economic Review* 13 (2): 257–73.

Last, J. M. 2001. *A Dictionary of Epidemiology*. Oxford, U.K.: Oxford University Press.

Laxminarayan, R., J. Chow, and S. A. Shahid-Salles, 2006. "Intervention Cost-Effectiveness: Overview of Main Messages." In *Disease Control Priorities in Developing Countries*, 2nd ed., ed. D. Jamison, J. Breman, A. Measham, G. Alleyne, M. Claeson, D. Evans, P. Jha, A. Mills, and P. Musgrove, 35–86. New York: Oxford University Press.

Laxminarayan, R., A. J. Mills, J. G. Breman, A. R. Measham, G. Alleyne, M. Claeson, P. Jha, and others. 2006. "Advancement of Global Health: Key Messages from the Disease Control Priorities Project." *Lancet* 367 (9517): 1193–1208.

Leeder, S., S. Raymond, H. Greenberg, H. Liu, and K. Esson. 2004. *A Race against Time: The Challenge of Cardiovascular Disease in Developing Economies*. New York: Earth Institute at Columbia University.

Leonard, K., and Masatu, M. C. 2005. "Variation in the Quality of Care Accessible to Rural Communities in Tanzania." University of Maryland.

Lewis, M. 2002. "Informal Health Payments in Central and Eastern Europe and the Former Soviet Union: Issues, Trends, and Policy Implications." In *Funding Health Care: Options for Europe*, ed. E. Mossialos, A. Dixon, J. Figueras, and J. Kutzin, 184–206. Buckingham, PA: Open University Press.

Lewit, E. M., A. Hyland, N. Kerrebrock, and K. M. Cummings. 1997. "Price, Public Policy, and Smoking in Young People." *Tobacco Control* 6 (Suppl 2): S17–S24.

Li, W., X. Jiang, H. Ma, T.-S. I. Yu, L. Ma, J. G. Puente, Y. Tang, and others. 2003. "Awareness, Treatment, and Control of Hypertension in Patients Attending Hospital Clinics in China." *Journal of Hypertension* 21 (6): 1191–97.

Liang, L., and F. J. Chaloupka. 2002. "Differential Effects of Cigarette Price on Youth Smoking Intensity." *Nicotine and Tobacco Research* 4 (1): 109–14.

Liu, J., Y. Hong, R. B. D'Agostino Sr., Z. Wu, W. Wang, J. Sun, P. W. F. Wilson, W. B. Kannel, and D. Zhao. 2004. "Predictive Value for the Chinese Population of the Framingham CHD Risk Assessment Tool Compared with the Chinese Multi-Provincial Cohort Study." *Journal of the American Medical Association* 291 (21): 2591–99.

Liu, J. L. Y., M. Maniadakis, A. Gray, and M. Rayner. 2002. "The Economic Burden of Coronary Heart Disease in the UK." *Heart* 88 (6): 597–603.

Lopez, A. D., C. D. Mathers, M. Ezzati, D. T. Jamison, and C. J. L. Murray, eds. 2006. *Global Burden of Disease and Risk Factors.* New York: Oxford University Press. http://files.dcp2.org/pdf/GBD/GBDFM.pdf. Data also available on World Health Organization. "Burden of Disease Project." World Health Organization. http://www.who.int/healthinfo/bodproject/en/index.html.

Lubitz, J., L. Cai, E. Kramarow, and H. Lentzner. 2003. "Health, Life Expectancy, and Health Care Spending among the Elderly." *New England Journal of Medicine* 349 (11): 1048–55.

Macedo, M. E., M. J. Lima, A. O. Silva, P. Alcantara, V. Ramalhinho, and J. Carmona. 2005. "Prevalence, Awareness, Treatment, and Control of Hypertension in Portugal: The PAP Study." *Journal of Hypertension* 23 (9): 1661–66.

Mackay, J., and M. Eriksen. 2002. *The Tobacco Atlas.* Geneva: World Health Organization.

Mancino, L. 2003. "Americans' Food Choices: The Interaction of Information, Intentions, and Convenience." Ph.D. dissertation, University of Minnesota.

Manning, W. G., E. B. Keeler, J. P. Newhouse, E. M. Sloss, and J. Wasserman. 1989. "The Taxes of Sin: Do Smokers and Drinkers Pay Their Way." *Journal of the American Medical Association* 261 (11): 1604–9.

Manton, K. G., E. Stallard, and L. S. Corder. 1995. "Estimates of Change in Chronic Disability and Institutional Incidence and Prevalence Rates in the U.S. Elderly Population from the 1982, 1984, and 1989 National Long-Term Care Surveys." *Journals of Gerontology* 48 (4): S153–S166.

Mao, C., L. A. Koutsky, K. A. Ault, C. M. Wheeler, D. R. Brown, D. J. Wiley, F. B. Alvarez, O. M. Bautista, K. U. Jansen, and E. Barr. 2006. "Efficacy of Human Papillomavirus-16 Vaccine to Prevent Cervical Intraepithelial Neoplasia: A Randomized Controlled Trial." *Obstetrics and Gynecology* 107 (1): 18–27.

Marks, J. S., and D. V. McQueen. 2002. "Chronic Disease." In *Critical Issues in Global Health,* ed. C. E. Koop, C. E. Pearson, and M. R. Schwarz, 117–26. San Francisco: Jossey-Bass.

Mathers, C. D., and D. Loncar. 2005. "Updated Projections of Global Mortality and Burden of Disease, 2002–2030: Data Sources, Methods, and Results." Working paper, World Health Organization, Geneva.

Mathers, C. D., R. Sadana, J. Salomon, C. J. L. Murray, and A. Lopez. 2001. "Healthy Life Expectancy in 191 Countries, 1999." *Lancet* 357 (9269): 1685–91.

Matson-Koffman, D. M., J. N. Brownstein, J. A. Neiner, and M. L. Greaney. 2005. "A Site-Specific Literature Review of Policy and Environmental Interventions That Promote Physical Activity and Nutrition for Cardiovascular Health: What Works?" *American Journal of Health Promotion* 19 (3): 167–93.

Maynard, A., and D. McDaid. 2003. "Evaluating Health Interventions: Exploiting the Potential." *Health Policy* 63 (2): 215–26.

McMullen, K. M., R. C. Brownson, D. Luke, and J. Chriqui. 2005. "Strength of Clean Indoor Air Laws and Smoking-Related Outcomes in the USA." *Tobacco Control* 14 (1): 43–48.

Merriman, D., A. Yurekli, and F. J. Chaloupka. 2000. "How Big Is the Worldwide Cigarette Smuggling Problem?" In *Tobacco Control in Developing Countries*, ed. P. Jha and F. Chaloupka, 365–92. New York: Oxford University Press.

Michel, J.-P., and J.-M. Robine. 2004. "A 'New' General Theory of Population Ageing." *Geneva Papers on Risk and Insurance* 29 (4): 667–78.

Miller, D. S., and A. Ryskulova. 2004. *Epidemiologic Surveillance Systems in Eastern Europe and Central Asia*. Vol. 1. Washington, DC: World Bank.

Monteiro, C. A., W. L. Conde, and B. M. Popkin. 2004. "The Burden of Disease from Undernutrition and Overnutrition in Countries Undergoing Rapid Nutrition Transition: A View from Brazil." *American Journal of Public Health* 94 (3): 433–34.

Monteiro, C. A., E. C. Moura, W. L. Conde, and B. M. Popkin. 2004. "Socioeconomic Status and Obesity in Adult Populations of Developing Countries: A Review." *Bulletin of the World Health Organization* 82 (12): 940–46.

Morland, K., A. V. Diez Roux, and S. Wing. 2006. "Supermarkets, Other Food Stores, and Obesity: The Atherosclerosis Risk in Communities Study." *American Journal of Preventive Medicine* 30 (4): 333–39.

Mortensen, J. 2005. *Ageing, Health, and Retirement in Europe: The AGIR Project: Final Report on Scientific Achievements*. Research Report 11. Brussels: European Network of Economic Policy Research Institutes.

Muñoz, N., F. X. Bosch, X. Castellsagué, M. Diaz, S. de Sanjose, D. Hammouda, K. V. Shah, and C. J. L. M. Meijer. 2004. "Against Which Human Papillomavirus Types Shall We Vaccinate and Screen? The International Perspective." *International Journal of Cancer* 111 (2): 278–85.

Murray, C. J. L., J. A. Lauer, R. C. W. Hutubessy, L. Niessen, N. Tomijima, A. Rodgers, C. M. Lawes, and D. B. Evans. 2003. "Effectiveness and Costs of

Interventions to Lower Systolic Blood Pressure and Cholesterol: A Global and Regional Analysis on Reduction of Cardiovascular-Disease Risk." *Lancet* 361 (9359): 717–25.

Murray, C. J. L., and A. D. Lopez. 1997. "Alternative Projections of Mortality and Disability by Cause 1990–2020: Global Burden of Disease Study." *Lancet* 349 (9064): 1498–1504.

Musgrove, P. 1996. "Public and Private Roles in Health: Theory and Financing Patterns." Health, Nutrition, and Population Discussion Paper 339, World Bank, Washington, DC.

Narayan, K. M. V., P. Zhang, A. M. Kanaya, D. E. Williams, M. M. Engelgau, G. Imperatore, and A. Ramachandran. 2006. "Diabetes: The Pandemic and Potential Solutions." In *Disease Control Priorities in Developing Countries*, 2nd ed., ed. D. Jamison, J. Breman, A. Measham, G. Alleyne, M. Claeson, D. Evans, P. Jha, A. Mills, and P. Musgrove, 591–604. New York: Oxford University Press.

Nassar, H. 2003. "Economics of Tobacco in Egypt: A New Analysis of Demand." Health, Nutrition, and Population Discussion Paper, Economics of Tobacco Control, Paper 8, World Bank, Washington, DC.

Neal, B., S. MacMahon, N. Chapman, and Blood Pressure Lowering Treatment Trailists' Collaboration. 2000. "Effects of ACE Inhibitors, Calcium Antagonists, and Other Blood-Pressure-Lowering Drugs: Results of Prospectively Designed Overviews of Randomised Trials; Blood Pressure Lowering Treatment Trialists' Collaboration." *Lancet* 356 (9246): 1955–64.

Nestle, M., and M. F. Jacobson. 2000. "Halting the Obesity Epidemic: A Public Health Policy Approach." *Public Health Reports* 115 (1): 12–24.

Neuhann, H. F., C. Warter-Neuhann, I. Lyaruu, and L. Msuya. 2001. "Diabetes Care in Kilimanjaro Region: Clinical Presentation and Problems of Patients of the Diabetes Clinic at the Regional Referral Hospital; an Inventory before Structured Intervention." *Diabetic Medicine* 19 (6): 509–13.

Nicholson, A., M. Bobak, M. Murphy, R. Rose, and M. Marmot. 2005. "Alcohol Consumption and Increased Mortality in Russian Men and Women: A Cohort Study Based on the Mortality of Relatives." *Bulletin of the World Health Organization* 83 (11): 812–19.

Nielsen, S. J., and B. M. Popkin. 2004. "Changes in Beverage Intake between 1977 and 2001." *American Journal of Preventive Medicine* 27 (3): 205–10.

Norstrom, T., and O.-J. Skog. 2005. "Saturday Opening of Alcohol Retail Shops in Sweden: An Experiment in Two Phases." *Addiction* 100 (6): 767–76(10).

Nugent, R., and F. Knaul. 2006. "Fiscal Policies for Health Promotion and Disease Prevention." In *Disease Control Priorities in Developing Countries*, 2nd ed., ed. D. Jamison, J. Breman, A. Measham, G. Alleyne, M. Claeson, D. Evans, P. Jha, A. Mills, and P. Musgrove, 211–23. New York: Oxford University Press.

O'Donnell, O., E. van Doorslaer, R. P. Rannan-Eliya, A. Somanathan, S. R. Adhikari, D. Harbianto, C. C. Garg, and others. 2005. "Who Benefits from Public Spending on Health Care in Asia?" Working Paper 3, Equity in Asia-Pacific Health Systems. http://www.equitap.org/publications/wps/Equitap WP3_2005.09.21.pdf.

Onder, Z. 2002. "The Economics of Tobacco in Turkey: New Evidence and Demand Estimates." Health, Nutrition, and Population Discussion Paper, Economics of Tobacco Control, Paper 2, World Bank, Washington, DC.

Ordúñez, P., L. C. Silva, M. P. Rodriquez, and S. Robles. 2001. "Prevalence Estimates for Hypertension in Latin America and the Caribbean: Are They Useful for Surveillance?" *Rev Panam Salud Pública* 10 (4): 226–31.

Osterberg, E. 2004. *What Are the Most Effective and Cost-Effective Interventions in Alcohol Control?* Health Evidence Network Report. Copenhagen: World Health Organization, Regional Office for Europe. http://www.euro.who.int/document/ E82969.pdf.

Packer, C., S. Simpson, A. Stevens, and EuroScan: the European Information Network on New and Changing Health Technologies. 2006. "International Diffusion of New Health Technologies: A Ten-Country Analysis of Six Health Technologies." *International Journal of Technology Assessment in Health Care* 22 (4): 419–28.

Panagiotakos, D. B., C. H. Pitsavos, C. Chrysohoou, J. Skoumas, L. Papadimitriou, C. Stefanadis, and P. K. Toutouzas. 2003. "Status and Management of Hypertension in Greece: Role of the Adoption of a Mediterranean Diet: The Attica Study." *Journal of Hypertension* 21 (8): 1483–89.

Pan American Health Organization. 2006. "The Preliminary Report of the Global Survey on Assessing the Progress in National Chronic Diseases Prevention and Control." Draft of March 19, Pan American Health Organization, Washington, DC.

Pan American Sanitary Bureau. 1998. *Cost-Benefit Analysis of Smoking.* Caracas: Pan American Health Organization.

Park, H., N. Safdar, and H. Schmidt. 2002. "Decline in Mortality of Coronary Heart Disease among Whites and Blacks in Wisconsin, 1979–1998." *Wisconsin Medical Journal* 101 (3): 23–27.

Parry, I. W. H., R. Laxminarayan, and S. E. West. 2006a. "Fiscal and Externality Rationales for Alcohol Taxes." Working paper, Resources for the Future, Washington, DC. http://www.rff.org/rff/Documents/RFF-DP-06-51.pdf.

———. 2006b. "How Much Should Cigarettes Be Taxed and How Much Should Be Spent on Tobacco Control Programs?" Unpublished report, Resources for the Future, Washington, DC.

Peeters, A., L. Bonneux, J. J. Barendregt, and J. P. Mackenbach. 2003. "Improvements in Treatment of Coronary Heart Disease and Cessation of Stroke Mortality Rate Decline." *Stroke* 34 (7): 1610–14.

Pekurinen, M. 1999. *The Economic Consequences of Smoking in Finland 1987–1995*. Helsinki: Health Services Research.

Piat, G. A., T. J. Orchard, S. Emerson, D. Simmons, T. J. Songer, M. M. Brooks, M. Korytowski, L. Simenerio, U. Ahmad, and J. Zgibor. 2006. "Translating the Chronic Care Model into the Community: Results from a Randomized, Controlled Trial of a Multifaceted Diabetes Care Intervention." *Diabetes Care* 29 (4): 811–17.

Pignone, M. P., A. Ammerman, L. Fernandez, C. T. Orleans, N. Pender, S. Woolf, K. N. Lohr, and S. Sutton. 2003. "Counseling to Promote a Healthy Diet in Adults: A Summary of the Evidence for the U.S. Preventive Services Task Force." *American Journal of Preventive Medicine* 24 (1): 75–92.

Pogue, T. F., and L. G. Sgontz. 1989. "Taxing to Control Social Costs: The Case of Alcohol." *American Economic Review* 79 (1): 235–43.

Pomerleau, J., K. Lock, C. Knai, and M. McKee. 2005. "Interventions Designed to Increase Adult Fruit and Vegetable Intake Can Be Effective: A Systematic Review of the Literature." *Journal of Nutrition* 135 (10): 2486–95.

Popkin, B. M. 2002. "The Shift in Stages of the Nutrition Transition in the Developing World Differs from Past Experiences." *Public Health Nutrition* 5 (1A): 205–14.

Popkin, B. M., and P. Gordon-Larsen. 2004. "The Nutrition Transition: Worldwide Obesity Dynamics and Their Determinants." *International Journal of Obesity and Related Metabolic Disorders* 28 (Suppl 3): S2–S9.

Popkin, B. M., S. Horton, S. Kim, A. Mahal, and J. Shuigao. 2001. "Trends in Diet, Nutritional Status, and Diet-Related Noncommunicable Diseases in China and India: The Economic Costs of the Nutrition Transition." *Nutrition Reviews* 59 (12): 379–90.

Port, S., L. Demer, R. Jennrich, D. Walter, and A. Garfinkel. 2000. "Systolic Blood Pressure and Mortality." *Lancet* 355 (9199): 175–80.

Pratt, M., C. A. Macera, J. F. Sallis, M. O'Donnell, and L. D. Frank. 2004. "Economic Interventions to Promote Physical Activity: Application of the SLOTH Model." *American Journal of Preventive Medicine* 27 (Suppl 3): 136–45.

Preker, A., M. Jakab, and M. Shneider. 2002. "Health Financing Reforms in Central and Eastern Europe and the Former Soviet Union." In *Funding Health Care: Options for Europe*, ed. E. Mossialos, A. Dixon, J. Figueras, and J. Kutzin, 80–109. Buckingham, PA: Open University Press.

Pritchett, L. 2006. "The Quest Continues." *Finance and Development* 43 (1): 18–22.

Psaty, B. M., T. Lumley, C. D. Furberg, G. Schellenbaum, M. Pahor, M. H. Alderman, and N. S. Weiss. 2003. "Health Outcomes Associated with Various Antihypertensive Therapies Used as First-Line Agents: A Network Meta-Analysis." *Journal of the American Medical Association* 289 (19): 2534–44.

Ramos, A., and D. Curti. 2005. *Uruguay: Economia del Control del Tabaco en los Paises del Mercosur y Estados Asociados.* Washington, DC: Pan American Health Organization.

Ranson, K. P., J. Prabhat, F. J. Chaloupka, and S. Nguyen. 2000. "The Effectiveness and Cost-Effectiveness of Price Increases and Other Tobacco-Control Policies." In *Tobacco Control in Developing Countries*, ed. P. Jha and F. J. Chaloupka, 427–47. New York: Oxford University Press.

Rath, G. K., and K. Chaudry. 1995. "Cost of Management of Tobacco-Related Cancers in India." In *Tobacco and Health*, ed. K. Slama, 559–64. New York: Plenum.

Ravnskov, U. 2005. "Europe in Transition: Dietary Fat Is Not the Villain." Letter. *British Medical Journal* 331 (7521): 906–7.

Reardon, T., and J. A. Berdegué. 2002. "The Rapid Rise of Supermarkets in Latin America: Challenges and Opportunities for Development." *Development Policy Review* 20 (4): 371–88.

Reardon, T., C. P. Timmer, C. B. Barrett, and J. Berdegué. 2003. "The Rise of Supermarkets in Africa, Asia, and Latin America." *American Journal of Agricultural Economics* 85 (5): 1140–46.

Renders, C. M., G. D. Valk, S. Griffin, E. H. Wagner, J. Th. M. van Eijk, and W. J. J. Assendelft. 2001. "Interventions to Improve the Management of Diabetes Mellitus in Primary Care, Outpatient, and Community Settings." *Cochrane Database of Systematic Reviews* (1): CD001481.

Rese, A., D. Balabanova, K. Danishevski, M. McKee, and R. Sheaff. 2005. "Implementing General Practice in Russia: Getting beyond the First Steps." *British Medical Journal* 331 (7510): 204–7.

Rex, D., and A. Blair. 2003. "Unjust Des(s)erts: Food Retailing and Neighborhood Health." *International Journal of Retail and Distribution Management* 31 (9): 459–65.

Reynolds, K., D. Gu, P. Muntner, X. Wu, J. Chen, G. Huang, X. Duan, P. K. Whelton, J. He, and InterASIA Collaborative Group. 2003. "Geographic Variations in the Prevalence, Awareness, Treatment, and Control of Hypertension in China." *Journal of Hypertension* 21 (7): 1273–81.

Robles, S. C., F. White, and A. Peruga. 1996. "Trends in Cervical Cancer Mortality in the Americas." *Bulletin of the Pan American Health Organization* 30 (4): 290–301.

Room, R., T. Babor, and J. Rehm. 2005. "Alcohol and Public Health." *Lancet* 365 (9458): 519–30.

Rothman, A. A., and E. H. Wagner. 2003. "Chronic Illness Management: What Is the Role of Primary Care?" *Annals of Internal Medicine* 138 (3): 256–61.

Russell, L. B. 1998. "Prevention and Medicare Costs." Editorial. *New England Journal of Medicine* 339 (16): 1158–60.

Russell, S. 2005. "Illuminating Cases: Understanding the Economic Burden of Illness through Case Study Household Research." *Health Policy and Planning* 20 (5): 277–89.

Sachs, J. D., and A. Warner. 1995. "Economic Reform and the Process of Global Integration." *Brookings Papers on Economic Activity* 1: 1–118. Washington, DC: Brookings Institution.

———. 1997. "Sources of Slow Growth in African Economies." *Journal of African Economies* 6 (3): 335–76.

Sackett, D. L., W. M. Rosenberg, J. A. M. Gray, R. B. Haynes, and W. S. Richardson. 1996. "Evidence-Based Medicine: What It Is and What It Isn't." Editorial. *British Medical Journal* 312 (7023): 71–72.

Saffer, H., and F. Chaloupka. 1994. "Alcohol Tax Equalization and Social Costs." *Eastern Economic Journal* 20 (1): 33–44.

———. 2000. "The Effect of Tobacco Advertising Bans on Tobacco Consumption." *Journal of Health Economics* 19 (6): 1117–37.

Sallis, J. F., A. Bauman, and M. Pratt. 1998. "Environmental and Policy Interventions to Promote Physical Activity." *American Journal of Preventive Medicine* 15 (4): 379–97.

Sander, B., and R. Bergemann. 2003. "Economic Burden of Obesity and Its Complications in Germany." *European Journal of Health Economics* 4 (4): 248–53.

Sandmo, A. 1975. "Optimal Taxation in the Presence of Externalities." *Swedish Journal of Economics* 77 (1): 86–98.

Sayginsoy, O., A. A. Yurekli, and J. de Beyer. 2002. "Cigarette Demand, Taxation, and the Poor: A Case Study of Bulgaria." Health, Nutrition, and Population Discussion Paper, Economics of Tobacco Control, Paper 4, World Bank, Washington, DC.

Sankaranarayanan, R., A. M. Budukh, and R. Rajkuma. 2001. "Effective Screening Programmes for Cervical Cancer in Low- and Middle-Income Developing Countries." *Bulletin of the World Health Organization* 79 (10): 954–62.

Sant, M., T. Aareleid, F. Berrino, M. Bielska Lasota, P. M. Carli, J. Faivre, P. Grosclaude, and others. 2003. "EUROCARE-3: Survival of Cancer Patients Diagnosed 1990–94: Results and Commentary." *Annals of Oncology* 14 (Suppl 5): v61–v118.

Schmid, A., H. Schneider, A. Golay, and U. Keller. 2005. "Economic Burden of Obesity and Its Comorbidities in Switzerland." *Sozial-und Präventivmedizin* 50 (2): 87–94.

Schmidhuber, J. 2004. "The Growing Global Obesity Problem: Some Policy Options to Address It." eJADE: *Electronic Journal of Agricultural and Development Economics* 1 (2): 272–90.

Scollo, M., A. Lal, A. Hyland, and S. Glantz. 2003. "Review of the Quality of Studies on the Economic Effects of Smoke-Free Policies on the Hospitality Industry." *Tobacco Control* 12 (1): 13–20.

Sepulveda, C., and R. Prado. 2005. "Effective Cervical Cytology Screening Programmes in Middle-Income Countries: The Chilean Experience." *Cancer Detection and Prevention* 29 (5): 405–11.

Shenassa, E. D., A. Liebhaber, and A. Ezeamama. 2006. "Perceived Safety of Area of Residence and Exercise: A Pan-European Study." *American Journal of Epidemiology* 163 (11): 1012–17.

Shibuya, K., C. Ciecierski, E. Guindon, D. W. Bettcher, D. B. Evans, and C. J. L. Murray. 2003. "WHO Framework Convention on Tobacco Control: Development of an Evidence-Based Global Public Health Treaty." *British Medical Journal* 327 (7407): 154–57.

Shobhana, R., R. P. Rama, A. Lavanya, R. Williams, V. Vijay, and A. Ramachandran. 2000. "Expenditure on Health Care Incurred by Diabetic Subjects in a Developing Country: A Study from Southern India." *Diabetes Research and Clinical Practice* 48 (1): 37–42.

Shults, R. A., R. W. Elder, D. A. Sleet, J. L. Nichols, M. O. Alao, V. G. Carande-Kulis, S. Zaza, D. M. Sosin, R. S. Thompson, and the Task Force on Community Preventive Services. 2001. "Reviews of Evidence Regarding Interventions to Reduce Alcohol-Impaired Driving." *American Journal of Preventive Medicine* 21 (Suppl 4): 66–88.

Silagy, C., T. Lancaster, L. Stead, D. Mant, and G. Fowler. 2004. "Nicotine Replacement Therapy for Smoking Cessation." *Cochrane Database of Systematic Reviews* (3): CD000146.

Singh, D. 2005. "Transforming Chronic Care: A Systematic Review of the Evidence." *Evidence-Based Cardiovascular Medicine* 9 (2): 91–94.

Singh-Manoux, A., M. Hillsdon, E. Brunner, and M. Marmot. 2005. "Effects of Physical Activity on Cognitive Functioning in Middle Age: Evidence from the Whitehall II Prospective Cohort Study." *American Journal of Public Health* 95 (12): 2252–58.

Slade, E. P., and G. F. Anderson. 2001. "The Relationship between Per Capita Income and Diffusion of Medical Technologies." *Health Policy* 58 (1): 1–14.

Slovic, P., E. Peters, M. L. Finucane, and D. G. MacGregor. 2005. "Affect, Risk, and Decision Making." *Health Psychology* 24 (Suppl 4): S35–S40.

Smith, O. 2006a. "NCDs and Health Financing." Draft, World Bank, Washington, DC.

———. 2006b. "NCDs and the Poor." Draft, World Bank, Washington, DC.

Sowden, A. J., and L. Arblaster. 2000. "Mass Media Interventions for Preventing Smoking in Young People." *Cochrane Database of Systematic Reviews* (2): CD001006.

Starfield, B., and L. Shi. 2002. "Policy Relevant Determinants of Health: An International Perspective." *Health Policy* 60 (3): 201–18.

Starfield, B., L. Shi, and J. Macinko. 2005. "Contribution of Primary Care to Health Systems and Health." *Milbank Q* 83 (3): 457–502.

Strahan, E. J., K. White, G. T. Fong, L. R. Fabrigar, M. P. Zanna, and R. Cameron. 2002. "Enhancing the Effectiveness of Tobacco Package Warning Labels: A Social Psychological Perspective." *Tobacco Control* 11 (3): 183–90.

Strong, K., C. Mathers, S. Leeder, and R. Beaglehole. 2005. "Preventing Chronic Diseases: How Many Lives Can We Save?" *Lancet* 366 (9496): 1578–82.

Suhrcke, M., R. A. Nugent, D. Stuckler, and L. Rocco. 2006. *Chronic Disease: An Economic Perspective*. London: Oxford Health Alliance.

Suhrcke, M., D. Stuckler, S. Leeder, S. Raymond, D. Yach, L. Rocco, and D. Matthews. 2005. "Economic Consequences of Chronic Diseases and the Economic Rationale for Public and Private Intervention." Draft, Oxford Health Alliance Working Group, London.

Suhrcke, M., S. Walters, S. Mazzuco, J. Pomerleau, and M. McKee. Forthcoming. *Socioeconomic Differences in Health, Health Behaviours, and Access to Health Care in 8 CIS Countries*. Copenhagen: World Health Organization Regional Office for Europe.

Surveillance Epidemiology and End Results. 2002. *Cancer Statistics Review 1975–2001*. Bethesda, MD: National Cancer Institute.

Szilagyi, T. 2004. *Tobacco Control in Hungary: Past, Present, Future*. Budapest: Hungarian Foundation. http://www.policy.hu/tszilagyi/BORITO_a.pdf.

Taal, A., R. Kiivet, and T.-W. Hu. 2004. "The Economics of Tobacco in Estonia." Health, Nutrition, and Population Discussion Paper, Economics of Tobacco Control, Paper 19, World Bank, Washington, DC.

Taucher, E., C. Albala, and G. Icaza. 1994. "Adult Mortality from Chronic Diseases in Chile, 1968–1990." *Notas Poblacion* 22 (60): 141–70.

Telishevka, M., L. Chenet, and M. McKee. 2001. "Towards an Understanding of the High Death Rate among Young People with Diabetes in Ukraine." *Diabetes Medicine* 18 (1): 3–9.

Teutsch, S. M., and R. E. Churchill, ed. 2000. *Principles and Practice of Public Health Surveillance*. New York: Oxford University Press. 2nd ed.

Thirumurthy, H., J. Graff-Zivin, and M. Goldstein. 2005. "The Economic Impact of AIDS Treatment: Labor Supply in Western Kenya." Working Paper 11871, National Bureau of Economic Research, Cambridge, MA. http://papers.nber.org/papers/w11871.pdf.

Thomas, D. B., D. L. Gao, R. M. Ray, W. W. Wang, C. J. Allison, F. L. Chen, P. Porter, and others. 2002. "Randomized Trial of Breast Self-Examination in Shanghai: Final Results." *Journal of the National Cancer Institute* 94 (19): 1445–57.

Thomsen, T. F., D. McGee, M. Davidsen, and T. Jørgensen. 2002. "A Cross-Validation of Risk-Scores for Coronary Heart Disease Mortality Based on Data from the Glostrup Population Studies and Framingham Heart Study." *International Journal of Epidemiology* 31 (4): 817–22.

Townsend, J., P. Roderick, and J. Cooper. 1994. "Cigarette Smoking by Socioeconomic Group, Sex, and Age: Effects of Price, Income, and Health Publicity." *British Medical Journal* 309 (6959): 923–27.

Travis, P., D. Egger, P. Davies, and A. Mechbal. 2003. "Towards Better Stewardship: Concepts and Critical Issues." In *Health Systems Performance Assessment: Debates, Methods, and Empiricism*, ed. C. J. L. Murray and D. B. Evans, 289–318. Geneva: World Health Organization.

Tsai, A. C., S. C. Morton, C. M. Mangione, and E. B. Keeler. 2005. "A Meta-Analysis of Interventions to Improve Care for Chronic Illnesses." *American Journal of Managed Care.* 11 (8): 478–88.

Tseng, C. W., R. H. Brook, E. Keeler, and C. M. Mangione. 2003. "Impact of an Annual Dollar Limit or 'Cap' on Prescription Drug Benefits for Medicare Patients." *Journal of the American Medical Association* 290 (2): 222–27.

Tunstall-Pedoe, H., K. Kuulasmaa, M. Mahonen, H. Tolonen, E. Ruokokoski, and P. Amouyel. 1999. "Contribution of Trends in Survival and Coronary-Event Rates to Changes in Coronary Heart Disease Mortality: 10-Year Results from 37 WHO MONICA Project Populations; Monitoring Trends and Determinants in Cardiovascular Disease." *Lancet* 353 (9164): 1547–57.

Tunstall-Pedoe, H., D. Vanuzzo, M. Hobbs, M. Mahonen, Z. Cepaitis, K. Kuulasmaa, and U. Keil. 2000. "Estimation of Contribution of Changes in Coronary Care to Improving Survival, Event Rates, and Coronary Heart Disease Mortality across the WHO MONICA Project Populations." *Lancet* 355 (9205): 688–700.

Urban D., and M. Suhrcke. 2005. "The Role of Cardiovascular Disease in Economic Growth." Draft, World Health Organization European Office for Investment for Health and Development, Venice.

U.S. Surgeon General's Advisory Committee on Smoking and Health. 1964. *Smoking and Health: Report of the Advisory Committee to the Surgeon General of the Public Health Service.* Washington, DC: Public Health Service, Office of the Surgeon General.

Van Walbeek, C. 2005. "Tobacco Control in South Africa." *Promotion and Education* (Suppl 4): 25–28, 57.

Villarreal-Rios, E., A. Mathew-Quiroz, M. E. Garza-Elizondo, G. Nunez-Rocha, A. M. Salinas-Martinez, and M. Gallegos-Handal. 2002. "Costo de la atención de la hipertensión arterial y su impacto en el presupuesto destinado a la salued en Mexico." *Salúd Pública México* 44: 7–13.

Villarreal-Rios, E., A. M. Salinas-Martinez, A. Medina-Jauregui, M. E. Garza-Elizondo, G. Nunez-Rocha, and E. R. Chuy-Diaz. 2000. "The Cost of Diabetes Mellitus and Its Impact on Health Spending in Mexico." *Archives of Medical Research* 31 (5): 511–14.

Viscusi. W. K. 1995. "Cigarette Taxation and the Social Consequences of Smoking." In *Tax Policy and the Economy*, vol. 9, ed. J. Poterba, 51–101. Cambridge, MA: MIT Press.

Vita, A. J., R. B. Terry, H. B. Hubert, and J. F. Fries. 1998. "Aging, Health Risks, and Cumulative Disability." *New England Journal of Medicine* 338 (April 9): 1035–41.

Wagner, E. H. 1998. "Chronic Disease Management: What Will It Take to Improve Care for Chronic Illness?" *Effective Clinical Practice* 1 (1): 2–4.

Wagner, E. H., C. Davis, J. Schaefer, M. Von Korff, and B. Austin. 1999. "A Survey of Leading Chronic Disease Management Programs: Are They Consistent with the Literature?" *Managed Care Quarterly* 7 (3): 56–66.

Wagner, E. H., and T. Groves. 2002. "Care for Chronic Diseases." *British Medical Journal* 325 (7370): 913–14.

Wagstaff, A. 2005. "The Economic Consequences of Health Shocks. Policy Research Working Paper Series 3644, World Bank, Washington, DC.

Wald, N. J., and M. R. Law. 2003. "A Strategy to Reduce Cardiovascular Disease by More Than 80%." *British Medical Journal* 326 (7404): 1419–23.

Warner, K. E. 2000. "The Economics of Tobacco: Myths and Realities." *Tobacco Control* 9 (1): 78–89.

Whelton, S. P., A. Chin, X. Xin, and J. He. 2002. "Effect of Aerobic Exercise on Blood Pressure: A Meta-Analysis of Randomized, Controlled Trials." *Annals of Internal Medicine* 136 (7): 493–503.

WHO (World Health Organization). 2002a. *Innovative Care for Chronic Conditions: Building Blocks for Action.* Geneva: WHO.

———. 2002b. *World Health Report 2002: Reducing Risks, Promoting Healthy Life.* Geneva: WHO.

———. 2004. *World Health Report.* Geneva: WHO.

———. 2005a. *Preventing Chronic Disease: A Vital Investment.* Geneva: WHO.

———. 2005b. *The SuRF Report 2: SUrveillance of Chronic Disease Risk Factors: Country-Level Data and Comparable Estimates.* Geneva: WHO.

———. 2006a. *World Health Statistics 2006.* Geneva: WHO. http://www.who.int./whosis/whostat2006/en/index.html.

———. 2006b. *World Health Report 2006: Working Together for Health. Organization.* Geneva.: WHO.

WHO Expert Consultation. 2004. "Appropriate Body-Mass Index for Asian Populations and Its Implications for Policy and Intervention Strategies." *Lancet* 363 (9403): 157–63.

WHO and World Bank. 2004. *World Report on Road Traffic Injury Prevention.* Geneva: WHO.

Wilkins, N., A. Yurekli, and T.-W. Hu. 2003. *Economic Analysis of Tobacco Demand.* Economics of Tobacco Tool Kit, Tool 3, Demand Analysis. Washington, DC: World Bank. http://web.worldbank.org/WBSITE/EXTERNAL/TOPICS/EXTHEALTHNUTRITIONANDPOPULATION/EXTETC/0,,contentMDK:20365047~menuPK:478898~pagePK:148956~piPK:216618~theSitePK:376601,00.html.

Willett, W. C., J. P. Kaplan, R. Nugent, C. Dusenbury, P. Puska, and T. A. Gaziano. 2006. "Prevention of Chronic Disease by Means of Diet and Lifestyle Changes." In *Disease Control Priorities in Developing Countries*, 2nd ed., ed. D. Jamison, J. Breman, A. Measham, G. Alleyne, M. Claeson, D. Evans, P. Jha, A. Mills, and P. Musgrove, 833–50. New York: Oxford University Press.

Wolf-Maier, K., R. S. Cooper, J. R. Banegas, S. Giampaoli, H.-W. Hense, M. Joffres, M. Kastarinen, and others. 2003. "Hypertension Prevalence and Blood Pressure Levels in 6 European Countries, Canada, and the United States." *Journal of the American Medical Association* 289 (18): 2363–69.

World Bank. 1993. *World Development Report 1993: Investing in Health.* New York: Oxford University Press.

———. 1999. *Curbing the Epidemic: Governments and the Economics of Tobacco Control.* Washington, DC: World Bank.

———. 2003. *World Development Report 2004: Making Services Work for Poor People.* New York: Oxford University Press.

———. 2004. *Rising to the Challenges: The Millennium Development Goals for Health.* Washington, DC: World Bank.

———. 2005a. "Addressing the Challenge of Noncommunicable Diseases in Brazil." Draft Report 32576-BR, World Bank, Latin America and the Caribbean Region, Human Development Sector Unit, Washington, DC.

———. 2005b. *Dying Too Young: Addressing Premature Mortality and Ill-Health Due to Noncommunicable Diseases and Injuries in the Russian Federation.* Washington, DC: World Bank, Europe and Central Asia Region, Human Development Department.

———. 2005c. *Health, Nutrition, and Population Portfolio FY05 Retrospective Review.* Washington, DC: World Bank.

———. 2005d. *Ten Steps to Monitoring and Evaluation.* Washington, DC: World Bank.

———. 2005e. "Tobacco Control and the World Bank Partnership with the Centers for Disease Control and Prevention (CDC/OSH), 1999–2004."

Unpublished report, World Bank, Human Development Network, Health, Nutrition, and Population Department, Washington, DC.

———. 2005f. *World Development Report 2006: Equity and Development*. New York: Oxford University Press.

———. 2006a. *Health Financing Revisited*. Washington, DC: World Bank.

———. 2006b. "Multisectoral Bottlenecks Assessment for Health Outcomes." Annex K of the World Bank Strategy for Health, Nutrition, and Population Results. Unpublished draft, World Bank, Human Development Network, Washington, DC.

———. 2006c. *Repositioning Nutrition as Central to Development: A Strategy for Large-Scale Action*. Washington, DC: World Bank.

———. 2006d. "A Review of Noncommunicable Disease Coverage in Country-Owned Poverty Reduction Strategy Papers and the World Bank's Portfolio." Unpublished background paper, World Bank, Human Development Network, Washington, DC.

———. 2006e. *Social Analysis in Transport Projects: Guidelines for Incorporating Social Dimensions into Bank-Supported Projects*. Social Analysis Sector Guidance Notes. Washington, DC: World Bank.

———. 2006f. *World Development Indicators 2006*. Washington, DC: World Bank. http://web.worldbank.org/WBSITE/EXTERNAL/DATASTATISTICS/0,,con tentMDK:20899413~pagePK:64133150~piPK:64133175~theSitePK:23941 9,00.html.

———. 2007. *Healthy Development: The World Bank Strategy for Health, Nutrition and Population Results*. Washington, D.C.: World Bank. http://siteresources. worldbank.org/HEALTHNUTRITIONANDPOPULATION/Resources/ 281627-1154048816360/HNPStrategyFINALApril302007.pdf. Accessed May 29.

Xie, X., J. Rehm, E. Single, and L. Robson. 1996. *The Economic Costs of Alcohol, Tobacco, and Illicit Drug Abuse in Ontario*: 1992. Toronto: Addiction Research Foundation.

Xu, K., D. B. Evans, K. Kawabata, R. Zeramdini, J. Klavus, and C. J. L. Murray. 2003. "Household Catastrophic Health Expenditure: A Multi-Country Analysis." *Lancet* 362 (9378): 111–17.

Yach, D., C. Hawkes, C. L. Gould, and K. J. Hofman. 2004. "The Global Burden of Chronic Diseases: Overcoming Impediments to Prevention and Control." *Journal of the American Medical Association* 291 (21): 2616–22.

Yach, D., D. Stuckler, and K. D. Brownell. 2006. "Epidemiologic and Economic Consequences of the Global Epidemics of Obesity and Diabetes." Commentary. *Nature Medicine* 12 (1): 62–66.

Yach, D., and H. Wipfli. 2006. "A Century of Smoke." *Annals of Tropical Medicine and Parasitology* 100 (5–6): 465–79.

Yang, M. C., C. Y. Fann, C. P. Wen, and T. Y. Cheng. 2005. "Smoking Attributable Medical Expenditures, Years of Potential Life Lost, and the Cost of Premature Death in Taiwan." *Tobacco Control* 14 (Suppl 1): 2–70.

Zachariah, M. G., K. R. Thankappan, S. C. Alex, P. S. Sarma, and R. S. Vasan. 2003. "Prevalence, Correlates, Awareness, Treatment, and Control of Hypertension in a Middle-Aged Urban Population in Kerala." *Indian Heart Journal* 55 (3): 245–51.

Zapka, J. G., S. H. Taplin, L. I. Solberg, and M. M. Manos. 2003. "A Framework for Improving the Quality of Cancer Care: The Case of Breast and Cervical Cancer Screening." *Cancer Epidemiology, Biomarkers and Prevention* 12 (1): 4–13.

Zatonski, W. A., A. J. McMichael, and J. W. Powles. 1998. "Ecological Study of Reasons for Sharp Decline in Mortality from Ischaemic Heart Disease in Poland since 1991." *British Medical Journal* 316 (7137): 1047–51.

Zatonski, W. A., and W. Willett. 2005. "Changes in Dietary Fat and Declining Coronary Heart Disease in Poland: Population-Based Study." *British Medical Journal* 331 (7510): 187–88.

Zhou, Y., T. D. Baker, K. Rao, and G. Li. 2003. "Productivity Losses from Injury in China." *Injury Prevention* 9 (2): 124–27.

Index

alcohol use and, 86
cancer screening and, 107
DALYs for, 74, 75*f*, 76*f*, 77, 78*f*
Finland, 12, 87
Food and Agriculture Organization
(FAO), 93
food and nutrition, 88–97
cardiovascular disease and, 101
cost-effective programs for, 32
deregulation, 96–97
developing countries and, 77, 99
economic incentives/disincentives,
93–94
food distribution, 92
food labeling, 94, 116*n*
informational environment, 94–95
obesity patterns, 90
optimal public policy approach to, 99
outcome trends related to, 6
regulation, 95–96, 96*t*
vitamin/mineral deficiencies, 88, 90, 116n
Food Standards Program, 95
Framework Convention on
Tobacco Control, 24, 52, 80, 85
Framingham study of CVD, 103
France, 10, 12, 79*b*

G

genetics and CVD, 101
Georgia (country) case study, 126–30
basic health care goal, 127
diabetes treatment, 127–30
clinical guidelines needed, 127–28
improving management of, 130
insulin distribution and, 128, 130
outcome monitoring, 129
patient education/training, 128–29
Greece, 103

H

health care
See also specific disease
for chronic conditions, 108–9, 114
drugs. *See* drug availability
health status relationship, 10–11
private sector role in, 53
screenings, 11
See also specific diseases

spending as percentage of
GDP, 70–71, 71*f*
stewardship. *See* stewardship
health financing, 70–72, 71*f*
health information systems, 52
health insurance
body weight and, 94
cost increases in, 28
public policy and, 25–26
health monitoring systems, 52
health technology
assessment, 35–36, 110–11
cost savings and, 43*n*
demand, 29
World Bank efforts in, 51, 53
heart disease. *See* cardiovascular
disease (CVD)
high blood pressure. *See* hypertension
high cholesterol, 69, 103
high-income countries, 12, 139–40
HIV/AIDS, 39, 55, 119
household monitoring, 56
HPV vaccine, 107–8
human capital computing method, 18
human papillomavirus (HPV),
107–8
hyperlipidemias, 103
hypertension, 69, 101–3

I

implementation of NCD services, 17,
33–39, 38*f*
income
see also poverty; *specific income levels*
country incomes, and NCDs,
5*f*, 5–6, 14*n*
health care and, 11–12
India
cardiovascular disease in, 19, 102
case study, 131–36
asymptomatic patients, 131
detection/diagnosis of NCDs, 118
patient reports of chronic/acute
illness, 131–33, 132*f*, 134–35
quality of care, 119, 135
self-medication after diagnosis,
133–35, 134*f*
causes of death in, 67
health care spending in, 135
obesity in, 19

United States
  cardiovascular disease costs in, 19
  chronic care model development in, 36
  disability and aging in, 10
  drug policy (health care) in, 112
  health technology assessment in, 110
  mortality trends in, 7
  obesity in, 92
unsafe sex, 77

V

vaccine, human papillomavirus, 107–8
value for money, 16–17, 29–33, 33t, 43n
Venezuela, 68

W

warning labels
  on alcohol, 87
  on cigarettes, 83–84
WHO. *See* World Health Organization
World Bank agenda, 45–57

analytical and advisory services, 45–49,
  46–47b, 50, 52–54
document search methodology, 49, 49f
health, nutrition, and population
  sector, 49
knowledge base improvement, 54–56
lending operations, 49f, 49–50, 54,
  56–57
policy advice focus, 50
World Bank reports
  on drunk driving, 88
  on tobacco use, 45–46
World Health Organization (WHO)
  Burden of Disease Project, 6, 9, 59–60
  on drug policies, 112
  on drunk driving, 88
  Food Standards Program, 95
  mental health program, 49
  recommended framework of
    interventions, 54

Z

Zimbabwe and cancer screening, 107